Standards and the LEA
The Accountability of Schools

John Pearce

NFER-NELSON

Published by the NFER-NELSON Publishing Company Ltd.,
Darville House, 2 Oxford Road East,
Windsor, Berkshire SL4 1DF, England

and in the United States of America by

NFER-NELSON, 242 Cherry Street, Philadelphia, PA 19106 – 1906.
Tel: (215) 238 0939. Telex: 244489.

First Published 1986
© *1986 John Pearce*

Library of Congress Cataloging in Publication data

Photoset by David John Services Ltd., Maidenhead
Printed in Great Britain by A. Wheaton & Co. Ltd, Exeter

ISBN 0 7005 1070 2
Code 8248 02 1

Contents

Introduction

We placed almost unattainable expectations on education . . . If you expect education to be the alchemy that is going to transform society, and education doesn't, or society is not transformed, then the putative magicians share part of the blame.

Keith Joseph

Local government is government, not administration.

David Blunkett

This book is about educational standards in the maintained schools of England. It is scarcely a century since regular, full-time school provision was made effective for the great majority of the child population. For large parts of the period since the schooling provided under the 1870 Act became compulsory some years later, the maintained service has been undergoing expansion of one sort or another. Whatever stance we take about the quality of the service in 1985, we have to recognize the massive scale of growth since 1885, and that educational advance of that order cannot be imported like a raw material but must, laboriously, be made to grow. Although there have been periods of intermission in that century of growth, notably during the economic difficulties of the inter-war years, it would seem that a combination of demographic change, renewed economic stringency and shifts in public opinion has brought about quite a new kind of context for maintained education. The service can no longer count on further growth, whether of its resources, its physical size or its unquestioned public acceptance. The process of adjusting to this quite new reality, added to that of accommodating rapidly changing pressures on the curriculum, nevertheless constitutes a scale of change little smaller in degree than any that has gone before. It is this complex interlocking of forces, now a decade or more old but only imperfectly understood and far from universally accepted, that makes the issue of standards problematic.

The dominant feature of the loss of public confidence in the education service is that practitioners in it can see no real evidence to justify such attitudes. It is a fact that more pupils are achieving higher levels of attainment than ever before, in public examinations at 16 and 18, and in primary school attainment tests alike. The teaching profession has been deeply demoralized by its twin difficulty of understanding why the customers are unhappy, and of identifying what it might do to improve matters. The mismatch between public and parental expectations and the ability of the service to meet them proves on closer inquiry to have historical origins which call for explanation, and it is argued later in this book that in one sense the service is becoming the victim of its own success. The generation now forming the parents of middle-secondary pupils was able to take for granted its access to prestige qualifications and in appropriate cases to higher education. At the time this access was more competitive than could be realized, but its beneficiaries, whether they took up the opportunity or not for themselves, now expect it freely for their children. This is one of a number of long-term shifts which the current debate about public education is apt to overlook, and the chapters that follow seek to give them a due place in the picture.

The starting-point of the book's argument is that maintained schools are in some degree accountable to the bodies that maintain them. Because the relationship between maintained schools, which are the overwhelming majority of schools, and their maintaining local education authorities is little understood, the nature and functions of the authority are part of the necessary material for discussion. The history of the local authority is relevant for a deeper reason: relationships between LEAs and schools evolved throughout the period of large-scale expansion that followed World War II, and changed further in the decade since that expansion came to an end. Without apparently intending this, most LEAs have seen one definition of their role *vis-à-vis* the schools almost completely replaced by another. Chapter 1 seeks to show that for much of their history local education authorities saw themselves as administrative agencies and left specifically educational matters entirely to schools and their heads. Very slowly, however, an element of acknowledged responsibility for aspects of curriculum, which had been present in the work of some LEAs from their creation, developed in response to the needs of schools. The gradual emergence of curriculum as a necessary and central concern of the LEA took the form in most cases of the growth of advisory staffs, and for that reason this book is much concerned with advisory and inspection functions.

Chapter 1 offers a brief and selective view of the historical background, laying some emphasis on the distinctiveness of each LEA and the bewildering variation between them. Chapter 2 attempts a definition of accountability, making use of the distinction between utilitarian and professional models. In a context of local education authorities that have done relatively little to hold schools or teachers accountable, and have traditionally left decisions about curriculum entirely to schools, the coming of the curriculum circulars issued by the Department of Education and Science is characterized as marking a radical change in the relation between schools and their maintaining LEA – a change more significant than the more usual suggestion of a change in the balance between local and central government. It is argued that much of the reliance on notions of 'partnership' is rhetoric, and that it would be more realistic to think in terms of a network. There it is natural and proper to accept the teacher's accountability to parents (with an efficiency orientation), to pupils (as primarily moral), and to a sense of profession, none of which precludes, and all of which need, the over-arching accountability to the properly constituted elected authority, which has to interact with all the other participants in the network as not all of the others must.

Standards from the parent's and the teacher's viewpoint alike have to do with habits and assumptions that govern daily practice in schools. The detail of precisely 'how far' a given pupil or class has reached in this or that subject may at times be seriously at issue, but is of minor significance compared with a school's prevailing norms and expectations about behaviour, levels of effort, orderliness and the like. Chapter 3 explores how two main groups of teachers acquire standards in this sense of assumptions and expectations, and discusses the relevance of other possible sources of 'standards' such as tests, examinations, and employment discipline. Chapter 4 goes on to explore how standards in this broader sense operate at levels above that of the individual teacher, particularly at the level of the school. It looks at the distinctive position of the head teacher in the English tradition, as that now much modified role bears on the maintenance of quality in teaching. These four opening chapters thus seek to define the problem of standards in close relation to the practical realities that make for their decline or improvement.

Part Two, comprising Chapters 5, 6 and 7, describes the provision already made in the service for the maintenance and improvement of standards. Chapter 5 portrays what is possibly the least understood aspect of local education authority practice, the functions of advisory and inspection staff. The only existing authoritative account of this work is by Bolam and his team (Bolam *et al.*, 1978), itself based on a sample of LEAs which pre-dated the restructuring of local government in 1974. The case for a new account rests, however, on the great speed and scale of change in LEA practice, the effects of which are accentuated by the way many LEAs rely on their advisory staffs as a principal mechanism for adjusting to change. More widely known are Her Majesty's Inspectors, but the way HMI go about their work has changed a great deal in recent years, so that some readers of Chapter 6 may have a few surprises. There is a deliberate emphasis on the contrast between the coherence and strongly managed deployment of HMI, attributes which in part account for the remarkable preservation of their numbers at less than 500, and the diversity of LEA advisory practice. The latter stems in part from the very wide range of possible functions, in part from the complete absence of any national consensus or guidance about advisory staffing and functions, and in part from the traditional reluctance of LEAs to engage in firm management. What HMI and the LEA inspector have in common is a distribution of time and effort over a large number of schools, a fragmentation that enables any individual teacher or school to perceive only the single fragment that impinges upon them. This creates an inevitable distortion of view that these chapters seek to correct. Chapter 7 sets out the range of procedures open to local authorities to use for the dual purpose of holding schools accountable and being seen to be doing so.

Part Three attempts to resolve the puzzle of how to preserve an adequately professional model of accountability without loss of political legitimation – how to render professionals accountable to laymen without alienating the one group or deluding the other. Chapter 8 takes up the notion of curriculum policy, given prominence in the DES Circular 14/77, and suggests that it needs to be determined at several levels, so that general policies command general support, in some cases political and in others administrative, while other curriculum policies rightly belong at school level. The argument links up at this point with the position taken in Chapter 4, that head teachers are apt to seek and to be given excessive curricular responsibility in the name of autonomy. A number of crucial policy decisions are properly those of the LEA alone, and in demanding of LEAs that they identify their curriculum policies the Department of Education and Science may be viewed as very far from merely seeking more central control. Chapter 9 draws out some of the implications of this pluralistic view of curriculum policy. In particular it points to important changes in the personal experience of education that elected members bring to their consideration of curriculum policy: for the first time many LEAs have members with personal experience of comprehensive schools as pupils or as parents, and with educational careers of their own in the maintained sector extending beyond the age of 14. The readiness of such members to accept a process of being educated about the nature of the service and about curriculum policy is a new and potentially vital element in the future of LEAs. For very similar reasons LEAs cannot continue their neglect of the nature or of the management of the quality arm. The accountability of schools will continue to be a source of proper public concern unless and until accountable schools are maintained by accounting authorities.

The focus of the book is on England alone. It explains why there are widely varying cultures of accountability among the 96 LEAs in England. By extension there are variations in other parts of the United Kingdom even greater and more complex. Thus, in Wales there are proportionately far more HMI than elsewhere and this fact is reflected in their style and presence. In Scotland the education authorities employ advisers but not inspectors and inherit a quite different educational tradition. In Northern Ireland the Education and Library Boards employ few advisers of their own and the position of Department of Education inspectors is significantly different from that elsewhere. I have deliberately avoided expressing or (I hope) implying any view about the future shape of local government, beyond an obvious conviction that a local system is deeply preferable, with all its faults, to the factual ignorance and condescension that characterize executive structures in our central government.

My perspective is largely secondary, but I have sought to remember throughout that half our pupils and half our teachers work in primary schools. I have tried therefore to make my illustrations from either sector or from middle schools fully comprehensible to those acquainted with none of them. My credentials for claiming a wider perspective on local authority practice than that of 15 years working in one of them are given in the Notes on Chapter 5 and some of the papers referred to and listed in the References.

Very few books have been written about maintained education from within the service and below chief officer level. One of the many diversities among LEAs concerns hierarchy: not a few of my readers will blink with astonishment at the candour of what follows, not so much in disbelief as because they are accustomed to writing and speaking only when their chief officer requires it of them, and even then very rarely for publication. Nothing in these pages, however, has been omitted at my superiors' instance or included out of deference to them. On the contrary, they have offered me generous support, ready debate and a freedom much more than academic. Accordingly, the views in this book are mine and it should not be supposed that my Authority or my informants elsewhere share them. In the same way, my illustrative examples are fact but disguised, usually drawn from outside Cambridge-shire, and any resemblance to real situations is quite accidental.

Acknowledgements

This book has grown out of a long period of discussion and thinking in which I have not hesitated to bore colleagues and friends with ideas and arguments. I do not have space to name all those who did me the service of dissenting or trying to re-shape my perceptions. Among those who have been especially helpful, though they might not like the outcome, have been David Alexander, Iain Ball, Charles Barnham, Ann Burridge, David Bridges, Ron Cave, Rex Gibson, Mike Osborne, David Penrose, John Potter, Michael Ridger, Alan Shepley, Brian Stevens and Brian Wilcox.

Developing my thinking in the interstices of a busy life as a working LEA inspector, I have gained more than most from those who have laboured through drafts of this and earlier work: Joan Dean, Ray Dalton, Mary James, Stewart Ranson, Brian Oakley-Smith and Norma Anderson. I am indebted for specific pieces of help to John Ferguson (Cambridgeshire), Pat Melhuish (Haringay), Colin Robinson (SEC), Jo Stephens (Oxfordshire) and Ivor Widdison (CLEA). Several HMI have corrected without necessarily endorsing Chapter 6, but their etiquette forbids me to name them. I am grateful to the staff of the Department of Education Library at Cambridge University and of the Cambridgeshire County Libraries for cheerful help.

Most of all, perhaps, the hundred or so advisers and inspectors up and down the country who gave me their time for interviews about their work during 1984 provided an essential underpinning. However modest each individual's contribution may have felt at the time, the material was always fascinating and has proved cumulatively indispensable. I promised them and their LEAs anonymity and respect that confidence.

None of these colleagues is in any degree accountable for what I have made of their contributions.

PART ONE

The Scope of the Problem

The first four chapters seek to set out the nature and scale of the problem of educational standards. The first outlines the way the English local education authority evolved and suggests the relationship between a vacuum of curriculum policy and the growth of advisory services. The second explores the nature of accountability and outlines the way in which the conventional view of the service as a partnership is under threat. Chapter 3 asks where teachers derive their 'standards', the yardsticks that underpin their day-to-day expectations, and considers the scope for vesting responsibility for educational outcomes in tests, in HMI, and in professional progression. Chapter 4 sets out the very extensive freedom of the head teacher in the English system, and lists a series of ways in which the system shows a serious lack of coherence. The emergence of a number of attempts to remedy this incoherence is noted.

1
The Evolution of the English LEA

The historical background

An organized education service developed in England later than in most countries in Europe. Until 1870 the vast majority of elementary schools had been provided by the churches, most of whose leaders saw the task as part of the enduring competition between the established church and the dissenters. In Germany by contrast the professional basis of a secondary system goes back to the early years of the nineteenth century. Even as late as 1870 there were large gaps in provision, particularly in the rapidly growing cities, and as yet there was no system of local government capable of filling them. The 1870 Education Act created a system of directly elected school boards, and by the end of the century there were 2,000 such boards in England alone. In the same period, however, local government structures evolved, creating predictable tensions between local councils and school boards, not least because they were in effect competitors for public financing by the local populations. The 1902 Education Act resolved the tensions by abolishing the school boards and vesting powers to provide education in a particular set of the local authorities. Of the 315 local education authorities in England and Wales created in this way, the great majority were quite small and were concerned almost exclusively with elementary schools. Secondary schools were very few in number and were the concern of the larger authorities. By the time of the post-war reconstruction based on the 1944 Education Act there were 154 LEAs in England and Wales, all formally speaking providing primary, secondary and further education, many of them in practice delegating much of the school provision to divisional executives and 'excepted districts' which preserved the loyalties of older boards and councils. Of these, 137 were in England, more than half of them serving populations of less than 200,000 and only 21 serving areas of more than half a million people. The long-term trend towards larger authorities was strongly reinforced by the 1974 reorganization of local government, which swept away the divisional and district education bodies and concentrated the service into 98 unitary authorities – 39 counties, 36 metropolitan districts, and the 21 authorities set up by the reorganization of London in 1968.

The formative period in this history was naturally the first 25 years after the 1902 Act. The still new local authorities had far from overcome their initial problems when the First World War broke out. They had hardly caught breath at the end of that war when there descended in 1922 a period of ferocious financial stringency. The overwhelming concern of all English governmental bodies, central and local, became a preoccupation that public money should not be wasted, and in the then still new field of education (new, that is, as an area of governmental activity) this became an enduring resolve to restrict the growth of expenditure. In most other respects LEAs were left to themselves, to conduct their affairs within the regulations as they saw fit, but the regulations were prescriptive both financially and over curriculum. There was nothing untoward in this: a high proportion of LEAs served populations that needed perhaps 20 elementary schools and two, perhaps three secondaries, or a comparable number of all-age schools from which a tiny proportion went on to secondaries run by the larger authority for the area. On an operational base of those proportions it was not possible to maintain an administration of much resource, and even in much larger LEAs the dominant tradition of extreme economy had the same effect. Indeed, the well-known tale of an entrepreneurial Henry Morris drumming up private money to finance the first village college buildings in Cambridgeshire in the 1920s (Ree, 1973) well illustrates the price that had to be paid. A less appreciated part of the tale is that Morris was the only professional officer in the LEA until a professional assistant (as the post would now be called) was provided in 1938.

The English LEA, then, developed as an agency centrally concerned with administrative functions – paying salaries and maintaining buildings, settling accounts and hiring school caretakers, and accounting for every last penny. Only a limited proportion of them were large enough or lucky enough to have in their chief officer an educationist of vision and drive who carried his council with him, and the handful of such officers have gained a legendary status among their successors. Some of them liked to meddle and some to take a close interest in matters that in most LEAs were left to head teachers – we learn of some who interviewed applicants for basic grade teaching posts personally. But in most LEAs any matter defined as 'educational' was regarded as one for the head teacher. Councillors took it for granted that they employed head teachers to be responsible for the good conduct and standards of their schools, and felt quite unqualified to make any judgement on such matters themselves. When anything serious went wrong it was for the education officer to deal with, an officer who had himself qualified and served as a teacher of standing. Where the education officer had doubts, he would refer them to HMI locally rather than dream of consulting his committee until his own line was clear. The standing of education officers and head teachers was such that laymen did not regard it as proper to question their professional judgement, and there would have been no electoral endorsement for doing so. The secondary schools were almost all grammar schools, and were treated with even greater deference. Further education scarcely existed. LEAs did not need to be bureaucracies, and indeed were nothing of the sort.

The established tradition of LEAs managed by very small numbers of professional officers endured in many of them well into the era of expansion that followed the Second World War. As late as 1968 more than a score of LEAs had only two such posts, and dozens of divisional executive and excepted district offices were led by only one. These posts had to be remunerated at levels which recognized their formal seniority to most if not all the head teachers employed in the same LEA, and this made them expensive in relation to other local government posts. Education offices were expert at delegating routine administration to clerical staff, and the reluctance to increase the number of education officers at professional level was marked. In some respects it is still evident: there are some LEAs where annual budgets in excess of £250 million are managed by fewer than 20 officers in the professional grades. Head teachers would argue that this is possible because they exercise no small managerial responsibility themselves, and this is true, but that does not alter the fundamental pattern whereby LEAs have a small and close knit central management in relation to a large number of separate establishments under its formal control. It is quite usual to find LEAs with as many as 20 or even 25 separate establishments for each professional education officer employed. By the span-of-control criteria that operate in business management this is an impossible number for any officer to oversee. The central reality about LEA management is that oversight of any managerial sort is precisely what is not attempted. To explain what happens instead is in one sense the purpose of this book, since without understanding the relationship between LEA and schools it is impossible to appreciate where the accountabilities of teacher, head teacher, and LEA begin and end, and how the functions of governing bodies, Her Majesty's Inspectorate and the LEA inspectorates fit into the picture.

The 1944 Education Act vested the powers of the LEA in its education committee, with co-option to it of 'persons knowledgeable in education' and representatives of the teaching profession, symbolizing the overlapping nature of the interests and accountabilities involved. Co-options also protect lay councillors from being bamboozled by jargon, and help to ensure that policy proposals bear some realistic relationship to the schools where they are to apply. In many LEAs the teacher representatives were appointed by the teaching associations as a matter of course, and the unions were able to exercise still greater influence through the mechanism of Teachers' Consultative Committees, where a group of influential members meets regularly with a substantial group of teachers from all kinds of school to discuss whatever policy issues are of current concern. It was in this machinery that many schemes were hammered out for reorganizing secondary schools as comprehensives between 1960 and 1974. In that period few policy proposals would have had much prospect of adoption without having first gained acceptance in the local Teachers' Consultative. The same kind of squaring of the interests between individuals meeting in private took place at a national level in the same period, where such figures as Gould of the National Union of Teachers and Alexander of the Association of Education Committees would negotiate in confident command of their supporting legions. (For this and a number of other points in this chapter I am indebted to Ranson, 1980.) That era may be distant for the influence of trade unions, but one of its realities still holds good: teachers act as they do by conviction and sense of profession, not by instruction. Leading a teaching staff is not, therefore, a simple matter of wielding managerial authority – for the head teacher or for the LEA.

The era of expansion was naturally one of rising expectations of education. It gradually dawned on public opinion that these hopes were doomed to disappointment. Few understood that the magic qualification of five O level passes at 16 was structured in such a way as to restrict its attainment to less than 15 per cent of the population. The education service was largely insulated from the cold fury of industry that its rapid move up the labour market was not matched by the output of the education service (and still less by industry's readiness to train for industry's needs). The right-wing lobby against maintained education began with the Black Papers of 1969 and gradually took control of right-of-centre political opinion, with the service itself shrugging it off as an irrelevance. While this was happening, local government itself was reorganizing, and destroying its national coherence in the process; education officers fell largely silent and defensive; head teachers appeared increasingly in the guise of an interested party and in any case knew in their bones that the old days of public esteem were over. The old interlocking network of accountability was falling apart: the partnership everybody referred to was breaking down under the onslaught of a much harder discipline. The partners were so used to talking in mutually understood terms to one another that they had little notion how their language sounded to others. The educational world sounded like nothing so much as a cosy club and the suspicion that its cosiness concealed a damaging complacency was all too easily aroused. Shipman (1984) has shown how the collapse of confidence stemmed from sources outside the control of the service. We need, however, to show how the structural habits of thought and practice in the maintained schools govern the accountabilities they acknowledge.

The nature of maintained schools

The development of a generic system of maintained education in England naturally had to wait upon the emergence of an organizational structure that could sustain it. The school board system had existed to provide elementary education only: any provision beyond this was a jealously guarded preserve of a combination of private interests, the churches and an academic tradition focused on the ancient universities and permeating the political and administrative centres of power. The foray of the larger school boards into providing 'higher grade schools' in the mid-1890s provoked a backlash which took a judicial form in the Cockerton Judgement of 1899, a legal form in the 1902 Education Act, and administrative shape in the subsequent regulations of the Board of Education – which attached maintained secondary education firmly to an academic tradition with no trace of vocationalism about it. It is hard to dispute the judgement that in all these steps can be seen the united intention of judiciary, Parliament and civil service to restrict secondary education to the middle classes. In the event the arrangements ensured that there was no consistent national pattern of secondary provision for a long time. Outside the larger cities the dominant pattern of all-age elementary schools and selective secondaries was little challenged until the Hadow Report of 1926, and economic conditions hampered its implementation right through to the end of the Second World War. 'Secondary education for all' was a meaningful slogan in the post-war years precisely because so many children still lacked access to it. The main thrust of development in the secondary sphere, before and long after the 1902 Act, lay with independent schools.

Historically there have been three significant changes in the physical design of school buildings in the past century and a half: the invention of the classroom school, the introduction of specialization in the use of particular spaces, and the use of open planning. The first two of these happened before LEAs were invented, and their impact on educational practice was profound. So was their effect on the psychology of LEA managements.

Schools resemble hospitals, asylums and prisons in being basically custodial establishments. All four emerged in most advanced countries of Europe and America between 1800 and 1870, albeit with a few forerunners, and in that period all four combined two utilitarian principles of design. They inherited the building technology of the multi-storey mills of the industrial revolution, which had shown how to enclose large spaces and superimpose them upon one another, and they recognized architecturally the central need of a custodial institution for surveillance, the ability of those in charge to see all the inmates. So it is that we find Florence Nightingale readily accepting the use of an empty warehouse at Scutari. Indeed, the notion of the hospital as ward, what one Victorian doctor called disease-barn, exercised a grip on later hospital design that long survived the evidence that open wards encouraged cross-infection and exacerbated the problems of managing the difficult patient. In prison building, Bentham himself devised a semi-circular layout he labelled the 'panopticon', with the cells ranged on the edge of the semi-circle round a central control point (Foucault, 1979). It stands to this day in several American penitentiaries, underpins the layout of Manchester's Strangeways, and in its narrowly custodial intention has governed the attitudes of generations of prison officers.

Schools, one might argue, are hardly custodial in the same sense as prisons, but the high window-sills and closely fenced grounds of Victorian schools have uneasy echoes; and press accounts of recently designed open prisons have likened them explicitly to 'the more attactive kind of school'.

More telling, perhaps, is the evidence that monitorial school discipline for much of the nineteenth century was fearsome, while the long struggle to enforce compulsory school attendance has always been and still is explicitly custodial in its intention. The long survival of monitorial schools, with pupils drilled in rows (literally 'forms') to have their lessons 'heard' by the monitor under the overseeing eye of the Master at the end of the vast room, owed much to the cheapness of the system, but it enjoyed the ostensible sanction of adoption by prestigious schools. What went on in the 'Big School' space of the large independent and voluntary schools may have been very different from the events of a monitorial elementary school, but the expansion of the latter in Birmingham was advocated in 1839 on the basis that the local prestige academy, King Edward's, had just built itself such spaces, citing the ease of supervision as one of their many virtues.

However, the single-room school, of whatever size, was to be undermined by the slow emergence of sub-division. The earliest known use of the word *classroom* occurs in 1823, and it retains its earliest connotation, that of what we would now call a group or withdrawal room, in Board of Education model school plans until the late 1870s (Seaborne, 1971). However, it was in the sub-dividing of spaces into classrooms in voluntary secondary schools that the change took place most clearly. Most of these schools were urban, and the classroom school can be found fully developed in examples built in central London before the end of the century. The development had taken place at least 50 years earlier in Germany and the USA, but in England its completion still antedated the creation of local education authorities. Indeed, in not a few LEAs it was argued at the time of the Hadow Report (1926) that public authorities had no business to be competing with private or church bodies by building secondary schools.

The steady development of social demand for post-primary education was not to be stopped by such argument, but the change from *one-room* to *class-room* schools has far-reaching effects on everyone involved. Inside the classroom it sets up a quite new relationship between teacher and class, where mutual assessment, scrutiny and understanding exist all the time, willy nilly. The negotiation of order and the management of conflict become central, enduring tests of the teacher's quality whether supported by the school's disciplinary structure or not. Teachers can begin to mark out and define territory and impose rules of behaviour upon those who visit or presume upon 'their' ground. The change enforces a wholly new route into teaching, by destroying the basis of 'pupil teaching' and generating a new corps of teacher-trainers who in England, fatally and unlike some other European systems, were part of the higher education system rather than serving teachers released from their schools for the work. Classroom schools also cause the movement of classes from room to room, permit the flowering of subject specialization among teachers, encourage comparison between teachers by pupils, and sharply reduce the exposure of children to any one teacher. Until the post-Plowden revival of child-centred primary teaching many junior schools followed the same path, and independent primary (or 'prep') schools found it commercially wise to do so.

For the head teacher the implications of the change were dramatic, and clearly not always welcome. Unfettered daily contact with children and clear, direct oversight of teachers come to an end, unless the head circumvents the problem by giving himself the dual burden of teaching a class as well as running the school. Most schools were small enough until the 1950s, and the demands on management limited enough, for this solution to be very common, so that even today many teachers and parents have ambivalent feelings about the idea of a non-teaching head (and many local political figures, who are a generation older, cannot accept it at all). One of the most influential parts of the ideology of headship, that sustained many who felt deeply guilty about not being full-time teachers as well as heads, was the notion of the head as missionary. The collapse of religion has removed this sublimation, and numerous head teachers have replaced it with the notion of the head as manager.

Logically one might have expected the development of the classroom school to have encouraged unionization among teachers, and in the primary sector this is largely what happened. In secondary schools the dominant tone derived from teachers who were graduates, and therefore belonged to a minority of perhaps 2 per cent of the population which regarded itself as having genuine social status, corresponding rights to respect, and no need whatever to assert those rights or status. They would no more have thought of joining a trade union than would clergy, with whom they felt much in common. The changes in the relative numbers of graduates in the 1950s and especially after the Robbins expansion of higher education make the position prior to World War II a lost era in this respect. Moreover, in most secondary schools, whether maintained or voluntary, teachers tended to see themselves primarily as specialists in subjects.

It was a short step from the building of classroom schools to the designation of each of the spaces for a specific subject or activity. With spaces already specially built for physical education, craft subjects, science and school assembly, it was not a very radical innovation to suggest that other subjects might benefit from such designation. In practice this took quite a long time: we do not find geography rooms or biology laboratories as normal features of new school buildings in the maintained sector until the early 1950s. The reason may well surprise anyone who entered secondary school after 1945 or so: the fact is that geography did not establish itself as a full curriculum subject until the 1930s, and biology took until the 1950s (Goodson, 1983). The earliest well-known buildings to provide earmarked specialist spaces for both subjects were, once more, for independent schools, notably Merchant Taylors Northwood and (again) King Edward's Birmingham, designed in the late 1930s and much regarded in school circles at the time for their provision of separate laboratories for sixth-form sciences. For pupils who went to those schools, however, biology would appear as a normal part of the curriculum: the pupil's ignorance that innovations are new is the means by which schools build new 'traditions'.

Maintained secondary provision developed slowly between the wars, and much of it was partially fee-paying in any case. It drew its practice, perhaps inevitably, not from LEA decision but by adoption from the independent and voluntary sector. The Board dropped the issue of secondary regulations in the mid-1920s and the maintained secondaries eagerly took up the team games, uniforms, modes of discipline, subject-segmented curriculum, preference for abstract academic study, and reliance on public examinations to be found in the high-status independent schools and the voluntary ones that kept up a careful pretence of independence. It was their example that really determined the nature of the 1944 Act's provisions for religious instruction and daily worship.

In curriculum this influence not only encouraged maintained schools to seek a progressive segmentation into ever more specialized 'subjects' but also set a competitive example in early specialization. It was the independent sector that responded pliably to the universities' tendency to impose on them separate sciences, and thereby shackled the maintained sector with its single most intractable curriculum problem. The extraordinary lengths to which early specialization could go, and can still go, are little appreciated: there are many schools where pupils so disposed can evade a science subject entirely after the age of 13, and the dropping of all foreign language work at that age by over 70 per cent of the school population stems directly from its association with specialized study and the related 'standards' set by GCE at 16. The stimulus and lead that were valuable in building, and in fostering a pastoral view of curriculum, were thus a burdensome and illiberal example to schools which could not emulate the early pacing and should not have allowed the specialization.

In this setting, LEA officers and members took it for granted that head teachers would run their schools without interference, and must be expected to view the local education staff, and by extension their maintaining local authority, as a distant and rather low form of life. Officers ventured into such schools rather rarely:

teachers in post-war 'state' grammar schools would expect to set eyes on an HMI more often than on an education officer, and to feel they had more in common. Heads of secondary schools of any size were quite likely to be salaried above the level of any area or divisional officer, and councillors and officers alike treated secondary heads with a certain deference. The idea of seeking to check up on or exercise influence or control over the internal affairs of such schools simply did not occur to officers in the LEAs of the 1950s, and they would have run out of time, manpower and expertise if they had tried. Couple these attitudes with the other features of the LEA tradition already outlined, and with the control of elementary education by regulations in which the LEA had no say, and we can understand why the school in the English maintained system did not develop with any clear sense of accountability to the LEA that maintained it. Reciprocally we can see why LEA officers felt unwilling or unable to make any claims in that respect, and why, when circumstances altered radically, they had so difficult a struggle for legitimacy in doing so. The demand that LEAs now hold their schools accountable in detail for curriculum and its quality is not only very recent: it is fundamentally at variance with the structural development of the service. That is not to reject the demand, which arguably is reasonable: an LEA with a budget in excess of a hundred millions of public money can properly be expected to account for the value for money it obtains as well as for every last penny of spending in the books. The process of adjusting to this new role is bound to be difficult.

The era of expansion

The years between 1945 and 1975 witnessed a continuous and very great expansion in English education. They saw the absorption of rises in the minimum school-leaving age, to 15 in 1947 and to 16 in 1972, as well as a massive growth in the numbers opting to stay at school beyond the leaving age. In England the number of separate schools grew from about 26,000 to more than 33,000. The number of pupils, however, grew from about 5 million to nearly 9½ million: on average each school grew by more than half. The expansion of higher education in the later part of the period is well known, but this was largely outside the LEA sphere, unlike the very much larger expansion of further education. There some 400 colleges, catering for a mere 41,000 full-time students in 1947 and mainly working with part-time and evening classes, developed into a network of about 600 well-founded and often very large colleges with a student population of over half a million full-time students alone. The LEA provision was thus both for new colleges, each very large, and for greatly expanded older ones, some of which developed quite rapidly into full universities.

There were three main effects of these expansions on local authorities. Those LEAs large enough to undertake building and provision in further education had to develop appropriate staffs for the purpose, often in the form of expanded Sites and Buildings branches and sections devoted to manning the system of student grants, many of them discretionary and all entailing a thrice-yearly issuing of cheques to students. Analogous changes took place *vis-à-vis* schools and the LEA branches that serviced them. Secondly, the expansion created a sharper set of divisions between the larger LEAs which could afford the major development and the smaller ones which could not, even though many of the new buildings were placed cheek by jowl with the district education office of the small LEA. Indeed, there were reported instances of large county LEAs obtaining compulsory purchase orders on sites, wanted for new colleges of further education, where existing tenants included local divisional executives' offices. Thirdly, the traditional solitary position of the education officer broke down, and a career structure developed within the professional staffs of the LEA service. This reduced the influence of the small group of very large LEAs whose offices had generated dozens of chief officers for smaller LEAs, such as Manchester and the West Riding, but it also created a national market which gave to LEAs of all kinds an enriching cross-fertilization.

Those large and influential LEAs, however, had set an important example about how education offices should be organized. Most LEAs still follow it: there are branches for schools, further education (subsuming the youth service and student awards), sites and buildings, finance and administration, and often but not invariably a section or branch concerned with planning and development. These branches vary in their internal form (*cf.* Brooksbank, 1980), but are usually led by professional education officers recruited after graduate training and teaching experience, rather than administrative officers who have come up through the local government ranks. Such structures will doubtless change further, and indeed are changing all the time. One respect in which change can be observed is the way in which they incorporate the most recent of LEA branches, advisory and inspection services.

The expansion was not without its price. Between the wars education officers prided themselves on knowing 'their' schools. Many reminiscences and researches (e.g. Wilson, 1984) confirm this paternalist image, which some actually expressed as having an episcopal function in the schools. Many, perhaps most, set themselves the aim of being seen in every school in the course of a year, and at divisional and district level this was realistic, as well as in many of the borough LEAs. In the larger authorities chief officers had recourse to more dramatic and charismatic ways of being known to their teaching force, notably Arthur Clegg in the West Riding and others of the generation that came to retirement in 1974 or thereabouts. The tradition of regular visiting became attenuated by the scale of the expansion, except where the chief officer set himself free by ruthless delegation, and the officers to whom they passed out the work developed neither the taste nor the skills for such visiting. In any case, the expansion was imposing an inevitable degree of bureaucratization on the relationship between schools and their LEA. This had never been a simple line-management one, and the strains of the process were the more difficult and damaging for that very reason. Thus, head teachers had no tradition of reporting at intervals to 'the office', and the LEA had no direct means of ensuring the quality or curriculum of a school. HMI were a latent presence, Board of Education regulations long abandoned formally remained a potent influence, and teacher training was a deeply conventionalizing force. Such cracks as there were could be papered over by 'the Chief' going walkabout.

The era of expansion was well under way, however, when a major change took place in the relationships between the central and local arms of government. The Department of Education and Science had been accustomed to exercising a close scrutiny of recurrent expenditures by LEAs, and to directing LEAs collectively along the paths of fiscal and administrative virtue by circulars and memoranda, many of them making demands of exacting detail.

The growth of the local service made this supervision increasingly difficult to manage. The growing political strength of local government, the rising power of the teaching unions, and the wider climate of opinion about central–local relations led this supervision to be somewhat discredited as well. In a series of changes barely perceptible to the schools or their staffs at the time, power swung steadily towards the local authorities and the formal arrangements were adjusted accordingly. The most signal event was the introduction of General Grant in 1958, but local control of capital expenditure followed, and the stage was set for the dramatic exercise of local freedoms that ushered in comprehensive reorganization. It was no accident that Circular 10/65 offered LEAs a range of alternatives for this reform but did not attempt to dictate the choice of one of them. Indeed, the under–management found in the LEA tradition was as painfully evident in the Department of Education and Science itself, where straightforward local schemes could wait many months for approval.

This sharp swing away from central direction between the late 1950s and the late 1970s was to become the formative experience of most of the professional and political leadership that had to face the dire financial circumstances to come in the 1980s. It also provides a context against which to appreciate both the rhetoric and the realities attaching on the one hand to head teachers' claims about 'autonomy' and to the development of LEA advisory services on the other. This is not to suggest that head teachers did not put their considerable freedoms to excellent use. Still less should advisers in the 1960s and after be dismissed as superfluous functionaries with no effect on the achievement of large-scale and often traumatic reorganizations.

The growth of an advisory service

Before they were abolished in 1902 the larger school boards had emulated Board of Education practice and appointed some inspectors of their own. Where they existed, such bodies were taken over little changed by the successor LEA, and so it comes about that the title of Inspector survived – in Middlesex until the London restructuring in 1965, in Kent, Surrey, Essex, Birmingham, Manchester and elsewhere to this day. (HMI viewed them with disdain, but when this private opinion became accidentally public the mistake nearly cost the great Morant his career.) Other LEAs acquired some advisory teachers in 1902, and later some advisers, who under the boards had been called Organizing Teachers. Their title evolved into that of Organizers, covering a group of teachers brought into LEA offices to direct useful work they had often developed from a school base (such as area orchestras or drama festivals). Such posts were also used in many LEAs to provide the practical and local skills that teachers' training was too academic to allow for. The London authority had had Laundry Mistress posts from the late 1880s, and many LEAs had Organizing Teachers of cookery and dressmaking from the mid-1890s. We find posts in bee-keeping, dairying, leatherworking and many traditional and regional crafts. They were paid craftsman wages, of necessity, which put them very much on a par with the elementary school teachers they assisted.

The existence of this group provided the Board of Education with an opening to exploit: in 1917 it took a unilateral decision to offer 50 per cent grants to LEAs for the appointment of advisers in physical education (on condition they were not used to teach pupils!). The decision arose from the discoveries made by recruiting offices about the physical condition of the masses, and very similar problems and solutions arose in the field of nutrition. Within a year more than 40 LEAs had appointed advisers in PE, and from the mid-1920s for fully 50 years the number of LEA advisers in PE and in Home Economics, taken together, exceeded those in all other subjects combined.

The Secretary for Education in Cornwall has illustrated the position in his own LEA in the 1930s (Barr, 1984). He quotes from the Cornwall Education Committee Handbook for 1934–7, which lists 'administrative and executive officers' and 'shows that S.P. Heath was Secretary for Education and was assisted by three chief clerks and eight district clerks. The medical and dental officers are listed, followed by the advisory staff: county agricultural organizer, county horticultural superintendent, chief dairy instructress, county poultry instructor, three agricultural assistants, county organizer of physical instruction, county housecraft organizer, instructress in dressmaking and county librarian.' As late as 1950 there were still a dozen advisers in bee-keeping employed among the LEAs. The close match between the perceived needs of a service overwhelmingly concerned with all-age schools and the Cornwall list seems obvious, however much we may smile at it today.

Such advisory staff, outside the big cities, were modestly paid. Indeed, the advisers collectively formed an association chiefly to ensure that as former teachers they secured access to the Teachers Superannuation Scheme set up in 1918. The Board of Education and the LEAs classed them as local government officers and resisted the advisers' demand for over ten years. Many, perhaps most, were designated Organizers in the inter-war period, and the diversity of function as well as designation found among advisory staffs in LEAs doubtless contributed to their enduringly modest status in the office. Their utilitarian functions and modest salaries meant that in almost all LEAs organizers and advisers were recruited from schools within the authority. There was a striking contrast between them and the few big-city inspectorates, but even these did not aspire to the independence and status of the LCC Inspectorate, which was consciously, at various times, both modelled on and a model for Her Majesty's own Inspectorate.

If the school board inspectorates, the war-inspired advisers, and the inter-war organizers form three phases in the growth of advisory services, the era of expansion brought a fourth. It reflects the diversity and independence of LEAs in that period that they developed their advisory teams in many different ways and for widely varying ostensible reasons. Some were recruited formally speaking to advise the LEA on the design and equipment of new schools. Some were brought in as a thinly disguised stratagem for taking the workload off overburdened (but then more expensive) education officers. Some were appointed to oversee the reorganization of schools as comprehensives, assessing teaching staffs for their suitability to the new system's senior posts and guiding them when appointed. In many authorities in this period there were some immediately obvious financial benefits: in one case an adviser demonstrated the irrelevance of full-size language laboratories to schools and saved his LEA a quarter of a million pounds in eight years, while another standardized his authority's purchasing of audio-visual equipment and used its buying power to achieve even greater saving. The era of expansion was much more, however, than the time of going comprehensive. It was in particular a time when the teaching profession underwent a marked change in its professional calibre, and began to make the insistent demand for updating of knowledge and enhancement of skills that continues today. It was not the done thing to admit it too loudly in staffrooms, but teachers began to find advisers very useful.

Through the 1950s and 1960s there was a steady, if little perceived expansion in the number of advisory posts and in their salary and status. The clearest marker of the rise in status was the steady discarding of the title of Organizer, which had fallen into virtual disuse by 1970, but the change to the term Adviser also signified the adoption of a broader role – one thrust upon advisory staff by the schools quite as much as one they sought. This gradual shift followed a more specific change that the LEAs had already recognized when they inserted into the Soulbury salary agreement for 1956 a new category of 'general' adviser, paid on a higher scale attractive to promoted teachers and in some cases heads of schools. 'General' in this context signifies an adviser not confined to the field of the specific subject he supports, which in practice means an adviser to heads as well as, and in some cases rather than, to subject teachers.

Throughout this period the total strength of HM Inspectorate varied between somewhat over 300 to close to 400. The sharp rise in the number of advisers in LEA service as a result of the 1916 grant policy seems to have caused some questioning about possible duplication. At any rate the Board of Education felt constrained to attach to its Annual Report for 1922–3 a substantial bound volume giving a history of HMI, the drift of which was to show their superior background, intellect and influence, and to imply that the 500 officers of LEAs 'engaged in inspection for any part of their time' did not duplicate the functions of HMI because they lacked the necessary qualities. There are indications (NAIEO, 1947, 1959) that local advisers still numbered over 500 in the early 1930s and over 600 at the end of the following decade. Their numbers had increased by 1967, however, to the point where the selfsame doubts arose again, and this time the House of Commons Select Committee on Education held an inquiry. Alexander (House of Commons 1968) gave evidence for the LEAs and provided a detailed census which (unlike the CIPFA Statistics) kept advisers and inspectors separate from educational psychologists and set aside careers officers altogether. The 1968 figure for England was 1,260. The Committee was left feeling satisfied that LEA staffs and

HMI did not duplicate each other's work, but in spite of the outstanding quality of the local advisers' witnesses they did not deliver a clear picture of their work and significance, chiefly because neither the LEAs nor the advisers themselves had any way of achieving an adequate overview that was both sensitive to variations and coherent about the common threads.

The fourth phase in the growth of advisory services was to continue to the end of the era of expansion. Reorganization of local government saw numerous areas where counties and boroughs well accustomed to advisers were merged with divisions and districts quite unused to them. In most cases the new LEAs sought to fill the obvious gaps that such mergers would leave, while the teachers and heads in the previously unadvised schools had adjustments to make which many found painful. A significant if numerically fairly minor strand in advisory recruitment from the mid-1960s onwards had been to cater for curriculum development and innovation. So it was easy for head teachers to allow their suspicion of the new-fangled to enhance their pain at being newly visited by advisers. If a large new county found itself with five advisers for PE and four for home economics, but none for English or mathematics or science, that too was easy meat for the critics. It was thus hardly surprising that the 1975 conference of the National Association of Head Teachers passed a strongly worded resolution criticizing these appointments. Relationships have improved out of all recognition in the succeeding years in almost every LEA – indeed, in many LEAs the teaching associations are the most vociferous defenders of advisory staffs that members bent on economies want to reduce or dismantle.

By the mid-1970s advisory staffs in many LEAs were beginning to develop a coherent pattern. Until the 1974 reorganization of local government too many LEAs were too small to be able to afford a balanced team and very few had even thought about such balance. (It was the leadership of the Council of LEAs under Alexander and the executive of the National Association of Educational Advisers and Inspectors (NAIEA) that put this aspiration to the Commons Select Committee.) The wide gap between the gentleman inspector and the workaday organizer was being filled in the era of expansion by advisers recruited mainly as subject specialists. But they were all paid on a local government type of salary scale which created unfavourable relativities with the teachers and (especially) the heads with whom they chiefly worked. The 1975 salary agreement made a fundamental change, by linking advisory salaries to those of head teachers of medium-sized schools. This was expensive for the authorities, but it gave them two assets of great value: they could recruit nationally instead of being limited to local applicants, and they could expect a general–adviser role of all their appointees. There were some 1,650 advisers in post at the time.

Advisers in the eighties

The period between 1975 and 1985 has combined an increasing financial stringency with a marked interventionism on the part of successive Secretaries of State. LEAs have generally sought to consolidate their advisory teams by adjusting the deployment. As numerous advisers in PE and home economics, and smaller numbers in drama and music, have come to retire, their posts have been redirected. The chief beneficiary has undoubtedly been primary education, hitherto a seriously under-provided sector. Some of this redirection has been in response to external forces such as the 1981 Education Act's measures about children with special educational needs and the Cockcroft Report on mathematics teaching the following year. The emphasis on subject posts, however, has fallen: Cockcroft inspired many fewer advisory posts in mathematics than the Bullock Report of 1975 did in English. All LEAs faced the climate of criticism of the service that grew up in the late 1970s, and most of them faced it in the form of individual local councillors who genuinely believed that the maintained system was giving poor value for money. The majority of LEAs at that date had no means of rebutting the charge – few of them even collected and analysed public examination results. The effects of this change in climate were numerous and diverse: it would be quite wrong to think that LEAs and their staffs were not deeply affected by it.

An early response was to lead numerous LEAs to redesignate their advisers as inspectors, recruit one or two more to fill gaps (in a subject range determined, of course, by the schools), and ask them to mount some inspections. Another was to discuss formal schemes of self-evaluation with schools and teaching unions. Perhaps surprisingly, very little remains of the latter: Oxfordshire and ILEA require school self-evaluation over a cycle every few years, but LEA-based self-evaluation has gone the way of most other passing educational fancies. Inspection, not always by that name, is more common. LEAs as diverse as Essex, Nottinghamshire and Hillingdon practise regular formal inspection or review of whole schools on an organized programme in accordance with procedures and criteria agreed with the local teaching associations. The precise number of LEAs doing this is hard to establish, and indeed varies from year to year, but in 1982–3 there were at least 20 that inspected ten or more schools a year and possibly two or three times as many that inspected often enough for its inspectorial machinery to be said to be in working order. In view of the nature of advisory recruitment, which from the 1950s until well after 1970 was firmly geared to a supportive, non-threatening model, and the natural dislike of the unions for inspection, this is a substantial change – and a surprisingly unknown one. The absence of serious teacher opposition will be readily understood from the discussion in the next chapter.

The change in climate brought many other consequences for LEAs. The least noticed, perhaps, is the change in the way many or most of them treat major educational documents. In the past, publications such as the Cockcroft Report (1982) or the recent DES Policy Statement on Science 5–16 would have been treated as business for officers and schools. They are now widely treated as matters for information of members, and some parts of them as 'Matters for Determination'. More overtly, central government initiatives dictate responses from LEAs which each LEA has to manage – the administration of substantial funding from TVEI, appointing support staff under Education Support Grants, distributing hardware and organizing in-service training under the Microelectronics Programme, re-training teachers for GCSE and much else. The bulk of the managerial work involved has fallen on advisers and inspectors. These changes have had to be accounted for to members, who have also demanded, in my view quite properly, that the officers employed by the LEA to ensure the maintenance of standards respond to the climate of concern about quality. Advisers and inspectors have traditionally been given little or no contact with committee, but in a growing number of LEAs are 'on the agenda' regularly and increasingly.

These pressures mean that the work of advisory staff in classrooms and teachers' centres, working directly with teachers on quality, is fragmented to the point where everyone is unhappy. Most LEAs staff their advisory services on the basis that an adviser can support or oversee between 350 and 450 teachers in a school year of 190 working days. Under the new demands of recent years this never very realistic practice has broken down, and the management of falling rolls has greatly added to the burden. In consequence many schools, perhaps most, now expect to see an adviser when they ask or when things go wrong – and the mix of saviour and hatchet man may accentuate the dualism inherent in the adviser's functions to the point of incoherence. There are other modulations in the work of LEA officers and advisers, some of them traced more fully in Chapter 5, which strain the relations between them too. If the LEA is so slenderly manned and managed at the top as to afford no chief adviser, the group most in need of the protection of clear priorities is deprived of it and the threat of fragmentation goes unchecked. With the production of curriculum guidelines, statements of curriculum policy, teacher appraisal and growth on a massive scale in in-service training all on the horizon, there is cause for anxiety about the capacity of LEA managements and advisory services to handle the level of demand.

Corporatism and centralism

While education authorities generally have been developing and adjusting their relationship with schools through the medium of more adequately manned advisory staffs, they have also been accommodating a very sharp financial discipline. If some LEAs have reacted to the stringencies by closing down their school meals services and others by shutting their school library support, none has ventured to disband its advisory staff. Some, it is true, have sought a severe restriction of their numbers, but in a remarkably high proportion of such cases the establishments have recovered within two or three years. Meanwhile LEAs have had other problems. It has taken a decade for the local government changes of 1974 to exert their full impact on some education departments, but one of that reform's underlying drives was a desire, on the part of almost all other departmental interests, to tame the power and independence of education. In many areas, education was viewed as local government's over-mighty subject, and over the past ten years the common thrust of members and chief executives alike in most local authorities has imposed a marked difference of style (and in many cases attitude). There is not space here to discuss the merits of corporate management, which education departments have experienced with every kind of frustration and benefit. It would merely be incomplete to omit it as a significant factor in the ways that LEA managements have had to work. If corporatism has had any common effects on LEAs they are the absorption of the personal time of chief education officers, the heightened consciousness of financial constraint among education officers at all levels, and a greater need to educate colleagues in other local government departments which provide services that in the past education departments would secure for themselves.

The pressure of central government on local education has been more obvious, and has certainly received more attention in educational literature. There is a danger of conflating several quite distinct elements into what is then represented as a grand centralist conspiracy, which may be attractive in theory but is hard to substantiate. The climate of opinion about maintained education is one part of this, and it can be viewed as a genuine, widespread change in public opinion. It can also be viewed as little more than a carefully orchestrated campaign on the part of a right-wing lobby or pressure group, drawing equally right-wing political support in influential positions, and skilfully manipulating the correspondents of a largely right-wing, private-school-educated press. As we shall see in a later chapter, there are good social and historical reasons for taking it seriously and accepting that anxiety about the quality of maintained education is a preoccupation of large numbers of parents – an anxiety not difficult to set at rest in most cases, but one requiring a serious response.

The financial stringencies imposed on local government by the Treasury through the Department of the Environment and its grant mechanisms are likewise widely viewed as part of a centralist conspiracy to draw all power into the centre. There is plenty of evidence of right on both sides of the argument: the physical condition of school buildings almost everywhere is a clear indication of trouble now and greater trouble ahead, abundantly vouched for by HMI, but there is equally clear evidence in some local authorities of spending which in most rational minds would be questionable in a time of stringency. The difficulty in which central policy places education authorities is the mirror-image of their position when things were expanding: as the largest single spender, education had the main benefit of each year's increases in grant and rate income, and now incurs the main penalty of each year's crunch between rising costs and fixed budgets. This position may or may not be part of a centralist conspiracy, but it is unavoidably a dominant preoccupation for education departments and their senior officers.

The other element often cited as centralism at its most threatening is specifically educational, the alleged intention of government to 'control' the curriculum. For a time such conspiracy theorists based their claim on the setting up of the Assessment of Performance Unit (e.g. Lawton, 1980), but broader perspectives (e.g. Salter and Tapper, 1981) and the inability of the APU to express its findings in mass-daily headlines have shown reality to be more complex and the curriculum less susceptible of 'control'. Moreover, the Department of Education and Science is not reverting to the pre-1944 style of regulation: Circulars 14/77, 6/81 and 8/83 are at one level doing no more than asking LEAs to testify to their conduct of a stewardship vested in them by the 1944 Act. If the LEAs have discharged that duty by vesting it in the schools, society is entitled to challenge their conduct. As the only available agent of society for this purpose, the Department has to steer between its duty in that capacity and allegations of centralist hunger for power. The basic relationship that is being changed by the DES curriculum circulars is less between DES and the LEAs than that between the LEAs and their schools. The first, Circular 14/77, sought information and established that most LEAs knew little of their schools' curricular arrangements (and by implication cared less, as their more experienced advisory staff knew). Very few LEAs read the signs well enough to set their curricular house in order, and the warning shots of Circular 6/81 did not stir many more from their lethargy. As we shall see, the inquiry in Circular 8/83 was a challenge to both parties: the LEAs are proving more reluctant to adopt any explicit curricular role than might have been expected.

A working partnership?

From 1974 virtually all local education authorities followed the politicizing of local government and fell under party political control. LEA staffs on the whole have lived with this, but the possible mix of party power and curriculum responsibility could be uneasy. Most elected members accept the political impartiality of administrators. The political or social preconceptions of members are always liable to be upset by some aspect of school life, be it covert racism, sex education with mixed classes, or assemblies using the forms of worship of a variety of religions, or sexist language in reading schemes – the list of such complaints, justifiable and otherwise, is lengthy, and teachers and advisers have to educate their masters about what is proper and accept the correction of what is not. The genteel aspiration of keeping education 'out of politics' rests on a fallacy, since all education is inherently political, and nowhere more so than among those who claim to have no politics.

The days have now gone when LEAs could hardly move in matters of policy without first squaring the teachers, but no LEA can hope for the successful implementation of policies that the teachers' representatives have not discussed and endorsed or, at worst, reluctantly conceded to be necessary. In many authorities, however, the consultations involved are no longer with the teaching unions alone. There is an increasing will to regard head teachers as themselves part of management and as requiring to be consulted for their advice as managers of their schools. This situation enables the LEA in some cases to circumvent anomalies created by trade union legislation: a union which represents its members in salary negotiations has rights to be consulted on policy issues, but such a union may have its negotiating position nationally without having any large membership in a given local authority. Consulting secondary head teachers, for example, in their capacity as local managers is thus differentiated from having to consult one or both of their national bodies through the local TCC. Even so, a wise LEA ensures that good relations are preserved and opinion fully sounded, which takes officer time.

The position of governing bodies varies very widely between LEAs and almost as widely within an LEA (Kogan *et al.*, 1984). There are a very few authorities where governors are expected to undertake some training and where their service includes sub-committees, and in such cases the necessary commitment of time and thought has the effect of winnowing out those appointed as local worthies without much thought for the needs of the work. There are a few heads of schools in most LEAs who have succeeded in developing their governing bodies in the same way. The great majority, however, exercise only the most formal of functions as governors, attending one or two meetings each year and seeing their task in the narrowest of terms as being 'to support the head'. In spite of the Taylor Report (Taylor, 1977) and sustained efforts by a handful of LEAs, the service has yet to find a way to make governing bodies a self-reliant partner. By extension, the same has to be said for parents: schools have not yet found generally satisfactory ways of articulating their interest and concern where it exists, or of arousing it where it does not.

Structurally most local education authorities reflect their history. Officers are answerable to committees which meet to make policy decisions at intervals from three weeks to four or five months – the norm appears to be four cycles in each year. The interest of members in matters below the policy level has increased in recent years. The relationship between officers and schools is on the whole rather distant and bureaucratic, with the exception of a minority of local or area officers who have no more schools than they can hope to visit each year if necessary. The main weight of contact between authority and schools rests on the advisory staff, whose contact is often greatly enriched and deepened by participation in local short courses of in-service training. Sometimes these courses are mounted in and for the individual school, often arising out of a formal appraisal, but the scale of in-service provision away from the school provides a basis for very considerable interchange between heads and between assistant staff. It will clarify the realities involved if the numbers of officers, advisory staff and schools are set out for a representative group of LEAs (Table 1). The figures fully bear out the proposition made earlier that no LEA can aspire to manage its schools in the way a business manager expects to manage his departments. Can it then aspire to do as a retail chain expects to manage its separate stores? What exactly are the educational equivalents of turnover and profit? This issue and other less questionable versions of it will be the concern of the rest of this book.

The nature of an authority's management of its schools is a critical issue since the appearance of the DES curriculum circulars and the evidence that there is no significant political or popular dissent from their propriety, even on the part of the teaching unions. It is critical because the circulars drive the LEA into the position of having to determine curriculum policy for their schools, a position fundamentally different from that served by the development we have described. The 'partnership' between LEAs, teachers, governing bodies and schools which has prevailed hitherto is certainly threatened by the requirements of the DES curriculum circulars. The position of each of the partners *vis-à-vis* each of the others is bound to change, and those LEA officers who have the most contact with schools will be affected the most. If the circulars mean what they say, schools will become accountable as never before, and the means by which LEAs will hold them accountable will be their advisory staffs. We must now turn to the nature of the circulars and their implications, and to the accountability of teachers, heads and schools in the light of what they signify.

Table 1   Population, numbers of schools and professional manning levels in a sample of LEAs

LEA and type	Population ('000s)	No of schools Prim.	No of schools Sec.	No of schools Other[1]	Total schools	Professional staff[2] Educ'n Offrs	Professional staff[2] Advisers	No of schools per officer Advisers only	No of schools per officer Advrs and Educ Offrs
Counties									
Cambridgeshire	598	286	49	18	353	18	25	14.1	8.2
East Sussex	657	224	39	15	278	17	24	11.5	6.7
Wiltshire	530	300	38	18	356	15	19	18.7	10.4
Metropolitan Districts									
Rotherham	252	118	21	6	145	13	14	10.4	5.4
Sheffield	537	271	38	23	332	14	17	19.5	10.7
Stockport	291	127	20	7	154	14	11	14.0	6.2
Outer London Boroughs									
Bexley	218	73	19	4	96	8[3]	10	9.6	5.3
Haringey	203	84	10	6	100	12	14	7.1	3.8
Hillingdon	226	75	20	8	103	7	14	7.4	4.9

[1]   covers special and middle schools and sixth form colleges.
[2]   Nursery schools classified as Primary, isolated classes omitted.
   i.e. officers with teaching qualifications and experience.
[3]   Here, as possibly in other LEAs shown, some functions carried by education officers in many LEAs are carried by corporate services providing for all departments.

Source: *Education Year Book 1985* (Councils and Education Press) and further inquiries of individual LEAs where necessary

2
What Does Accountability Mean?

The purpose of this chapter is to suggest a working definition of accountability, and to show how the accountability relationships that have characterized the last three or four decades have developed into a network rather than a hierarchy. In this network, which has conventionally been labelled a partnership but has always been far too competitive to deserve such a label, teachers have dominated: parents, pupils and governing bodies have received some degree of recognition as participants in the accountability of teachers and heads, but the LEA has been at best peripheral. As we have seen, the response of the LEA to this has been to adopt a minimalist stance in its management. In this context, the curriculum circulars issued by the Department of Education and Science between 1977 and 1984 signal a marked change, to some extent in the relationship between centre and local, but above all in the relationship between LEA and school.

Towards a definition

It is hard to better Sockett's definition (in Finch and Scrimshaw, 1980):

> The purpose of a system of accountability is to maintain and improve the quality of educational provision and, where possible, to provide information to show that this is being done.

That said, however, there are scores of attempts to go beyond a definition and say what accountability means in practice. These attempts fall into three main categories, the historical/legalistic, the analytic, and the realistic/descriptive. The problem with the first of these is a necessary detachment from recognizable experience, and with the third that any one such account will be governed by an individual and hence partial perspective. A brief example of each will bear this out.

The standard work on educational administration (Brooksbank, 1980) refers to the absence of any explicit reference to curriculum and responsibility for it from the 1944 Education Act, and cites the point that it is the Ministry's regulations that vest the general direction and conduct of the curriculum in the secondary school's governing body. This endorses the technical position that arose when the Board of Education under Bryce abandoned the publication of Secondary Regulations in the 1920s, thereby diffusing power over curriculum to heads, teachers and LEAs. Brooksbank goes on to show that for the most part the LEAs neither wanted nor accepted such power: a handful of chief education officers over the years evinced strong personal interest in the curriculum, but when one of them sought to enlist his fellow chief officers in collective study of it they gave the proposal a very cool reception. In more recent times the education officer who achieved a public alignment of his LEA in support of a curriculum change or issue was identifiable not only as verging on the charismatic but also as very far from the main stream of his kind.

At the other extreme, a realistic study of accountability will select one or more of the partner interests in the service and try to identify how a representative sample of them view their own accountability. There is a considerable literature of this kind of inquiry, and the theoretical issues involved are still unresolved, as the best review of it suggests (McCormick and James, 1984). For example, accountability is widely identified with evaluation, which in turn has become too closely associated with the assessment of specific curriculum projects to bear on our present topic easily. The only recent study that seeks to engage acountability of schools with the practical realities facing LEAs is that by Becher and his colleagues (1981). More typical of the genre is Elliott *et al.*'s *School Accountability* (1981), which elicited the attitudes of teachers in six schools.

The teachers are described as seeing themselves accountable to their clients (i.e. to children and their parents) and to others within the school where they work, from the head down to equals and junior colleagues. The width of the latter range suggests a strong sense of within-the-profession accountability. The more hierarchical the school organization, the less accountability teachers felt to each other, the more their accountability to clients was felt as personal. Teachers do not feel accountable to clients in any collective way if they do not share responsibility for the school's work as a whole. Nor do most teachers in this study sense any accountability to governors or LEA officials. In elaborating the findings, Elliott goes on to argue, in effect, that the accountability debate can really be reduced to a need for improved communication: what is needed, it is suggested, is not greater public control over curriculum decisions but more information about them provided for the client groups. The need for better communicative understanding is clear and urgent, but on a much more two-way basis than Elliott admits, and in any case is not sufficient to meet a profound general anxiety. This is somewhat to misread the issue: political and parental concern about the quality of the service has certainly been manipulated by the media since 1976, but it has a bedrock of substance which mere improved communication will not meet. The anxiety is very complex, compounded of fears of failure, unrealistic family aspirations, ignorance about how children learn and at what ages, mismatches between parents' experience of school (or mis-rememberings of it) and what they see their children encountering, and much else. Meeting such a complex of feelings requires more than skilled publicity on the part of schools.

However, the Cambridge Accountability Project on which Elliott's work rests also brings home a central issue for our present discussion. The schools studied are described in detail, and supporting papers make clear that they did not form a representative group. The teachers' responses may well have shown the usual convergence with the assumptions and values of the researchers, but when all allowance is made for these elements, we cannot escape the lesson that in many schools the maintaining LEA is most hazily perceived. The councillors and officers of an LEA may take it for granted that a key part of the school's accountability is to the LEA that maintains it, but teachers do not see it in that way. Teachers feel accountable, Elliott's findings are saying very clearly, to people they see and know. If they are to feel any accountability to the LEA that pays their salaries, it needs to be much more visible than pay-cheques alone can make it.

Utilitarian and professional models

It is necessary both to go behind the legalism of treatments which rest on the law and the regulations stemming from it, and to be more general than a specific research project allows. A satisfactory analysis also has to take account of the fact that teachers and educationists generally are very uneasy about the notion of accountability that appears to inform much parental and political comment on the service, while parental, political and (especially) journalistic views are suspicious or even cynical about the reluctance of the professionals to say plainly what they doing about quality. This conflict is dramatized in some now quite common situations: a report on an inspection by HMI is published, the severe criticisms it contains are known by the LEA officers to be well justified, but there is no case for dismissing any teachers and the preservation of local confidence is a proper objective – so how does the local education officer answer local press questions? Why is it that in such cases the lay public in its anxiety and the professionals appear to be at cross purposes, appear to have different languages about accountability? Why are views so divided about the way to use, in Sockett's words, 'a system of account-ability . . . to maintain and improve the quality . . . and . . . to provide information to show that this is being done'?

Sockett's own paper goes on to propose one of the most useful explanations. He draws a distinction between two models of accountability, respectively the utilitarian model and the professional. In the utilitarian model (and what follows is a crude compression of a subtle philosophical argument) the teacher is accountable to a single agent or body, usually one claiming a representative status or authority, which will exercise the accountability by a process of measurement. The outputs that are measured are of course pupil performances, which are measured by means of tests of attainments and teaching objectives fulfilled. In the professional model the teacher is accountable to a diversity of interests, reflecting the teacher's 'clients' (pupils and parents) as well as representing them and other interests; this diverse constituency exercises its accountability on the teacher and the school by means of a process of mutually informing evaluation, sometimes formalized and often informal. The outcomes that are evaluated are not so much pupil performances as educational practices adhered to in the classroom and in the school as a totality, practices which are themselves principled (e.g. informed by a concern for truth, reason, respect for persons, open-mindedness, etc.). In the utilitarian model the teacher as an individual is accountable for results attained by his pupils and if the results are not what his contract stipulates the penalty is dismissal. In the professional model the teacher is one of a group which is held accountable for standards of professional practice observed in creating the conditions and incentives that lead pupils to learn. If the outcomes are less good than the client body finds acceptable, the penalty is professional inquiry which may lead to remediative action – and in extreme cases the action in question might also be dismissal. In crude language, under the utilitarian model a teacher whose pupils do not reach the stipulated test scores at the end of the year will be sacked, whether or not the stipulations are themselves reasonable in relation to the ability and history of the class. Under the professional model the teacher is not treated as a social technician claiming an expertise confined to means, but as an autonomous professional whose interests extend properly and necessarily to ends as well as means.

It greatly oversimplifies Sockett's distinction to label it as the difference between being accountable for results and being accountable for standards, since that would imply that the latter exclude the former, which is not the case. The pressure from public opinion and the media that the education service has felt in the past decade has often been understood as a concern exclusively about results, and the media certainly tend to represent it in that light. Committed as they are to a professional model of accountability, teachers and LEAs have responded, with understandable frustration, by pointing out that by all available criteria the service has never done better: examination performance has been better, among a larger part of the school population, than ever before, levels of literacy among less able leavers have never been better, and so on. Yet these claims seem to fall on deaf ears, which nevertheless remain open to tendentious media reports of research, reports designed to tell readers the bad things about schools they are believed to want to hear. The reality of the matter is that the service itself and its clients have both been undergoing profound changes, little understood on either side.

Before turning to those changes, it is necessary to deal with a common confusion. There are some who would claim that results, in the test-score or exam grade sense, are the only standards worth consideration. This is a tenable view, but it is not one which appears to be shared by HMI, the Department of Education and Science, or any recent Secretary of State. Employers' organizations call for school leavers with a social competence, inquiring minds, a developed critical sense, a feeling for the expressive arts, racial and religious tolerance, and so on. A school process which restricts itself to the ruthless pursuit of test scores or examination grades not only fails to develop these attributes: it develops attitudes that run directly against them. More seriously still, a results-centred type of schooling alienates young people in relation to training, and this hostility carries a terrible cost in industrial and social inefficiency. The belief that the instrumentalist option is a real choice open to schools can stem only from a complete ignorance of the parental and socio-economic realities from which a vast majority of today's pupils come and to which they are destined after school.

Structural change

It would be understandable if the attitudes to the education service held by different social groups varied widely. The county councillor who started school in 1934 and left school when secondary education was still competitive and partly fee-paying may well not see secondary education in the same light as a parent of children aged 11 and 13 who was himself in the twentieth intake after secondary education was made free and universal. It was not until 1981 that a teacher appointed to be the head of a comprehensive school claimed to be the first such head to have been himself a pupil at a comprehensive. There is no chief education officer who attended a comprehensive as a pupil, and only a handful of chief and senior education officers as yet have been teachers in comprehensives. Even fewer have experienced teaching in primary schools or special education. This discontinuity between previous experience and the nature of the service such officers now have to administer has always characterized LEAs. It does not appear to have much impeded adaptability, chiefly because the LEA tradition had deputed so large a curricular freedom to individual schools. At the same time, the scale and pace of structural change in the service is very easy to overlook. The immense changes in primary education associated with and widely disseminated by the Plowden Report are less than 30 years old. Comprehensive secondary education did not become the dominant pattern across the country until 10 or 12 years ago.

The scale of growth in the higher and further education system outlined in Chapter 1 is part of this structural upheaval. Looked at in terms of the proportion of the parent population who can expect their children to have access to training or education beyond school, the change is dramatic, and the school sector has underpinned it very successfully. The related growth in teacher training, now sharply reduced, is a further factor influencing the school sector's potential for quality over the past three or four decades. But one consequence for the teaching profession at school level is inescapable: the sheer numbers of its clients, relatively and absolutely, grew out of all recognition – and grew for longer durations of school life for their children. The parent population also grew dramatically in the level and range of its own education and qualification. It would be surprising, in a sense, if the accountability of schools had not become a major public issue as a result. Equally predictably, schools on the whole failed to register these changes, failed to enlist the support of their increasingly educated parent populations, and failed to adjust their notions of what parents generally should be expected to know and to understand about schools. There have been some striking changes in these respects in the last ten years, largely in response to the changed climate of opinion, and the growth of the community education movement shares a similar motivation. These responsive adjustments, however, have left many other schools behind, and many of their maintaining LEAs with them.

The long processes of structural change operate within the schools as well as outside them. We are witnessing in the 1980s an extraordinary growth of interest among teachers in what we might call the meta-curriculum, that area embracing the personal and social education of pupils for which the academic subjects of the formal curriculum do not provide. The activities involved include proper constructive use of the 'form' or 'tutor' period in secondary schools, serious health education, records of achievement, guidance with career choices or social and domestic problems and much else. This trend is not a reassertion of old secondary–modern values hitherto submerged in the bright new comprehensives: it is a response to a vividly sensed need, among teachers of all kinds. The most helpful explanation of it points to the way in which subject setting and option schemes in comprehensives have a fragmenting effect on the social cohesion of pupil groups, not unlike the effect of moving the population of an urban street of old terrace houses to isolating flats on the edge of the town. The development is a signal that our so-called monolithic comprehensives are more responsive than myth would have us believe. The process of discovering their best nature is still going on, and is in part a search for legitimacy. The problems of managing the unsocial, containing the disruptive, running what has been called the 'dirty' end of teaching, are ever-present in teaching – not mainly because unemployment removes incentive, but because the system is constantly extending its reach in line with the massive growth in the service sector. The minority who can be allowed to reject school learning has to be made smaller and smaller all the time, and even very minor losses of momentum in keeping up with changes in the labour market can transform the standing of the system, as we have seen since 1976[1].

Whose accountability?

Sockett's distinction between utilitarian and professional models of accountability lodges the focus of accountability on the individual teacher in the one case and on the school in the other. One of the hindrances to the professional model, therefore, is autocratic management by the head teacher, which many researches modelled on Hoyle's (1975) contrast between types of school have shown to be inimical to the development of initiative and responsible planning by rank and file teachers. There may be no connection between the rise of LEA advisory services and the decline of autocratic styles of headship, but the two are inherently likely to come into conflict, and advisory and officer influence on promotions has reduced the scope for potential autocrats. At the same time, very few LEAs have pondered the kind of organizational cultures they seek in their schools (Handy, 1984), still less worked out the machinery of selection that will appoint head teachers in the light of such preferences (Morgan *et al.*, 1983).

Even autocratic head teachers, however, delegate a great deal in matters of curriculum practice. The head may seek to allocate funds for books and equipment, but increasingly consults first. Decisions on teaching methods or materials lie with individual teachers. Many issues are settled not by any decision process but by accepting without examination the customs of colleagues or one's own teachers. Teachers will be called to account for such matters as their marking habits or homework-setting if things go wrong, and sometimes not even then. This is in striking contrast to some European practice, where initial training pays assiduous attention to these 'taken for granted' features, but in a tradition where pupil failure to learn is viewed primarily as failure by the teacher. The corresponding English tendency to place the blame for such failure on the pupil is deep-seated, and bears closely on the intractable nature of sex bias and racial bias in the curriculum.

The belief that many curriculum decisions are taken at classroom level is also hard to reconcile with the consistency and uniformity that characterize English primary as well as English secondary schools, where curriculum and outcomes vary relatively little in spite of perceptible variations in school climate and teaching strategies. In reality, a great many of the so-called classroom decisions taken by teachers should properly be recognized as habits. These are habits of thought, derived in large part from the segmentation of knowledge into 'subjects' (*cf.* Bernstein, 1971) which in turn structure how educational knowledge is broken down for transmission. They are also habits of action, in relation to how that transmission is assumed to need managing – how the work is to be paced, or ordered over time, how it is to be pitched, or ordered over difficulty, how it is to be assessed, or ordered over performance. The habits are not only those of teachers, but also those of the pupils and their parents, but where the latter conflict with the habits of teachers it is the parental ones that may be set aside. The distribution of reward and incentive within teaching reinforces these habits of thought and action, and the research community has been very slow to regard them as sufficiently problematic to warrant academic investigation. Curriculum then needs to be understood in terms of habits as much as of decisions. These factors also consolidate the teacher's 'sense of profession' and enhance his acceptance of a professional accountability. They harmonize the system and reduce its actual degree of variation. In theory such variation should be greater in primary than in secondary schools, but in practice the reverse seems to be the case. Marked abnormalities like William Tyndale Junior would seem to be either much rarer or much less cause for concern than such well-publicized cases as Madeley Court or Sutton Centre or Countesthorpe, all of them secondary schools which provoked some local outrage and a partially engineered massive attention from national media. In almost all these cases what was at issue was not (as at William Tyndale) a judgement about the competence of the regime but a dispute about its acceptability to client groups. As with William Tyndale, the professionals involved were deeply divided, and it was this division that caused the cases to 'go public'. Many LEAs have had similar unconventional schools with similar parental or political concern, but professional solidarity has kept the disputes out of the media – and most experience of those cases that reached the media suggests that such publicity does damage to most pupils, chiefly by the ill repute it brings the school.

It may signify that most such instances have been new schools, and green field sites naturally attract innovative heads. The employing authority, having failed to be explicit about the kind of school it wanted, sometimes having failed to understand the educational messages embodied in the buildings it has put up, finds itself dragged into a whirlpool it does not admit to having caused, and the earnest head teacher becomes the sacrificial victim of a lack of system that few participants understand. The LEA has its own accountability.

Accountability as network

Teachers recognize, in varying degree, four main elements in their accountability: pupils, parents, profession and superiors. For most teachers the superiors will be heads of department and heads. For head teachers the superiors will be governors for some purposes and LEA officers for others, but like their assistants many heads share a sense of accountability to their peer-group. This has until recently meant other head teachers, but the perception is growing that deputy heads, education officers and even inspectors may belong in it (*cf.* Lambert, 1984). But what a head teacher is accountable for and to whom will depend in part on how we use the term. Thus, it is argued that a head is accountable to his staff for providing a workable timetable. This is plausible nonsense: the head is accountable for managing, motivating and deploying the staff, and his accountability therein is to the employer that pays him for that responsibility. (The employer may use a mechanism such as a governing body in the process, but if the head teacher failed the governing body would perhaps ask the employer to take action, not the other way round.) Any other view of accountability must fail on the point that subordinates cannot dismiss their superior unaided. A teaching staff can, if it is unusually skilful and resolute, precipitate action against a head by the LEA, but that only underlines the point. The difficulty with Elliott's use of the notion of accountability, that is to say, is that it sidesteps the issue of enforcement: the only real accountability, even in the educational world, is that which is enforcible on its holder.

'Enforcible' does not of course have to imply coercion: most of our ordinary accountabilities in life are matters of values and training and habit. Our formal accountabilities relate to what we are paid to do, and we have to face the fact that until recent years very few accountabilities in education were enforcible on anyone, short of criminal conviction or admitted moral turpitude. This position reflects a combination of reliance on social forms of control, convention and propriety with the reality that teaching was a profession to aspire to and take pride in belonging to. That combination is only now breaking down, and its resilience could be seen both in the reluctance of many teachers to take strike action over pay, and in the way loss of public and political esteem provided as strong a motivation for such action as did actual pay levels in the period since the 'Houghton' award. We must expect the breakdown of the former values to continue, partly because of the sheer size of the education industry, and their replacement by more formal mechanisms to be a slow and difficult process.

There are many examples of the way accountabilities in the educational world can be enforced or enacted without being seen or felt as coercive. The teacher's accountability for working in ways which engage the interest and activity of pupils becomes vividly enforced by their choice or rejection of that teacher's subject when they select their options. Many of the details of how a school runs are communicated to new members of staff not as formal rules or bureaucratic requirements but as local peculiarities better accepted than challenged. The generic absence of a coercive approach to accountability created problems for the management of the service which had to be solved by devising mechanisms to deploy and canalize its requirements. The classic instance is the governing body. In the independent sector, which provided the formal model in this as in so many other ways, the governors of a school provide managerial counsel and share in important long-term decisions with real power. In the maintained system the formal powers of governors are very modest, their personal abilities are frequently ill-suited to providing counsel, and their operation often becomes an empty formality. Their existence is necessary as a fail-safe to legitimize action that would otherwise appear, and would often be, coercive. As we have seen, the Teachers' Consultative Committee operates in many authorities quite as much as a sounding-board for new policy as an assertion of union power. These and other mechanisms operate with a widely celebrated quality of mutual courtesy, and the absence of public controversy surrounding them has given rise to the notion of partnership as the central characteristic of the English service.

Unfortunately the notion is almost entirely a rhetorical one. Real partners, whether in business or in domestic life, form their relationships because they find them enjoyable as well as mutually beneficial. Real partners do not customarily seek to criticize one another in public or to gain influence within the partnership at the expense of other partners. The pecuniary benefits of a partnership are in real life divided on a basis of agreement in which the coercive powers of the partners are not exercised. And real partners are able to accept comparable obligations and duties because they bring to the partnership comparable contributions and assets. The educational enterprise is not like this, for reasons that are obvious to everyone. Why then do so many of the participants in it refer to it as a partnership? In terms of the foregoing discussion, the rhetoric is a cover for a set of interlocking accountabilities which lack enforcement. The reality beneath the rhetoric is better described as a network rather than a partnership, since that description does not imply that the accountabilities involved are similar or equally enforcible.

The notion of a network of accountability enables us to accept the claim of many teachers to be accountable to their own sense of profession, but the acceptance cannot be wholly unselective. There are many staffrooms where the charge of unprofessional conduct is the harshest available – but the conduct that merits such a description in many schools will pass as unremarkable or unexceptionable in many others. The concentration of teaching unions on their trade union functions has limited their attention to defining such matters in ways that command assent from all of them. It has also led many teachers to perceive their employing LEA as enemy in the salaries battle so that they have rarely perceived the LEA as participant in the accountability network. A similar qualification has to apply to the teacher's sense of profession as a function of initial training. Where a long socialization into professional assumptions and practices is possible, with several protracted initiatory phases of 'teaching practice', a deep-seated set of loyalties and values develops. Where the initiating process lasts for less than 36 weeks and involves a single period in a school, that outcome is at best fortuitous and at worst improbable. That a growing majority of new teachers enter by the latter route may seriously undermine the prevailing claims of teachers to a highly developed sense of profession.

The network idea also makes it easier to recognize the participation of the employing LEA in it. This is not merely an accountant's argument based on the bone-headed logic that it is the LEA that pays the bills as the statutory agent of the central government. Merely paying the bills and salaries is no basis for any rights or duties in the curriculum. But the bills do include the provision of specialized spaces, as we have seen, and the salaries go to often highly specialist teaching staff whose only employers are local authorities (aside from a very small independent sector). Historically the responsibility for curriculum was lodged with the LEAs in the 1944 Education Act, and a large part of it was in turn vested in head teachers and governing bodies through the medium of articles of government that almost always rested on a model provided by the Department. This delegation was believed by all authorities and their chief officers to absolve the LEA from specific duties in the curriculum field, and the 'partners' in the service were only too happy to endorse their view.

As we have seen, this convenient arrangement came under pressure. Indeed, it may never have escaped some degree of difficulty, whether in the case of laggard LEAs being chased to complete the reorganization of all-age schools in the 1950s or in the medium-term problems arising from the raising of the leaving age in 1947 (which led to the Newsom Report some 15 years later). By the late 1950s the expansion of numbers and the demands of parental opinion were driving many secondary modern schools into emulating the conventional subject curriculum of the grammar schools, but instead of resorting to the kind of curriculum development proposed by Newsom the system was hooked on formal examinations and the outcome was the CSE examination system. Meanwhile many schools and authorities were becoming desperate for expert help on how to cope with new kinds of pupil groups, new levels of parental expectation, and often new levels of teaching requirement at a time when there were many unqualified teachers still working. In appointing organizers and advisers to meet these needs, albeit in a rather haphazard way in relation to subject coverage, an LEA was implicitly acknowledging the curricular accountability vested in it by both the 1944 Act and the needs of the service. Many schools also sought help with curriculum areas that could only be managed above the level of the individual school, such as county orchestras, borough drama festivals, LEA-wide sports tournaments. The advisory staff appointed to co-ordinate these activities provided what seemed at the time a logical extension of an existing practice and a model for the rapid development of full subject coverage that became the object of many LEAs for their advisory staffs by the mid-1970s.

Grasping the nettle of a previously rather ramshackle approach to curriculum advice leads an authority logically into working out what advisers are employed to do. For some LEAs this logic led inexorably to recognizing the accountability for curriculum hitherto lying dormant in decades of custom and practice. Only a minority of LEAs followed the logic through to developing codified curriculum policy or guidance to the schools in documentary form – Cleveland's was an early and notable instance covering the whole curriculum. The issue of curriculum guideline documents is now quite common, but few LEAs have recognized the need to put this material together in a coherent framework, so that there are some authorities where the science document conspicuously emphasizes discovery learning and problem solving while most of the others make little reference to classroom process and focus on content. Perhaps more seriously, few curriculum documents of this sort enjoy support from parental or political sources of legitimation, and very few teachers or inspectors would admit any need for it. I shall argue in a later chapter that this omission continues at a high price, but here the absence of parents and elected members from the functioning of the accountability network exposes the emptiness of much of the rhetoric about partnership. The network seeks to paper over the cracks by many adaptive devices in the meantime, but the collapse of confidence in the service after 1976 suggests that those outside it are not fooled.

The adaptive devices designed to sustain the accountability network without significantly changing it have come and gone with the appearance of mere fashions. Self-evaluation was one of the most widespread, and while it was never as common a practice as some of its enthusiasts have claimed, it remains attractive, especially where it is institutionalized. (I give an account of the Oxfordshire practice in Chapter 7.) There was an upsurge of interest in inspection among LEAs in the late 1970s, which frightened the teaching unions until they found that what looked likely to be utilitarian was going to be professional accountability. Even so the vogue for inspection died when elected members realized what its demands would do to the other work they relied on advisory staff to carry out. In the meantime the employment legislation of the early 1970s gave rise to agreed codes of disciplinary procedures which, while primarily protecting the employee from improper practice on the part of the employer, also provided a machinery for the dismissal of incompetent teachers. These codes now exist in all county LEAs and in a majority of others, and have been used far more widely than lay comment in the media has recognized. The most significant adaptation, however, has been a change in the system's consciousness of quality and the priority that attaches to it. Examination results are only a limited index of quality, as we shall see, but their publication is a good illustration of Sockett's principle of visibility. In theory any good journalist with a calculator could assemble the exam results for a group of schools and publish a league table, but no editor has judged such a project sufficiently newsworthy. What matters for accountability purposes is not the information but the knowledge that it is available. In principle the same now holds for all other aspects of the service: the knowledge that any part of it may be subject to lay inquiry by properly entitled people is a governing reality of much local authority work and is one which maintained schools universally share. In the curriculum field this process of rendering the mysterious accessible is still only beginning, but at secondary level is very significant. It takes the technical form of the development of grade criteria for the new GCSE examination. As a symbol of the wider process it would be hard to better. The other main central government step may question the nature and functioning of the accountability network itself, as well as implying a profound change in the role of LEAs.

The DES curriculum circulars

The so-called Ruskin College speech by the then prime minister, James Callaghan, in 1976 was not intended as an attack on the education service: rather it sought to define its problems. Its effects, however, were far wider than its intentions, and only partly because a right-wing dominated press made the most of the invitation to maximize the deficiencies, real and merely alleged, of the school system. There is not space here to rehearse the charade of the so-called 'Great Debate', which was intended to relieve tension by bringing problems into the open and to alert the education service itself to the real state of opinion, but largely had the effect of driving the service into a thoroughly defensive posture. The event which was to signal the beginning of a radical change in central–local relations in education was the issue, in the summer of the following year, of Circular 14/77.

In itself this Circular seemed a curious mixture of the innocuous and the naive. It took the form of a series of questions, some of them very pointed, collectively a very thorough examination of the position and practice of the LEA in the curriculum field. Many of them were difficult to answer, because they imputed to the LEA a role it had never claimed or exercised in the past and did not relish for the future. Here are some examples:

A7   What steps have the authority taken to help schools comply, so far as curriculum is concerned, with the provisions and intentions of the Sex Discrimination Act, 1975?

B5   How do the authority help secondary schools provide for (*i*) moral education, (*ii*) health education, (*iii*) careers education, (*iv*)   social education through community links etc, whilst giving adequate attention to the basic educational skills? What part is played by the idea of a core or protected part of the curriculum?

C14   What is the authority's policy for the provision of science courses for pupils up to the age of 16 in secondary schools? To what extent is the present position in the authority's area in accord with that policy?

At that date very few LEAs could give the factual answers to the last part of C14: most neither knew the detail of curricular practice nor had any machinery for collecting it. If the 60–odd LEAs that (at that date) had an adviser for science were fortunate, that adviser might have a very close approximation to the facts, but most LEAs had to make an informed guess or had to circulate the schools to find out. But the first part of C14 posed a question that appeared many times in the Circular, that assumed something that was simply not there: most LEAs did not have curricular policies as such at all. A great many fell back on one of two strategies: they described as best they could what their schools actually did and underwrote that as constituting the LEA's policy; or they set out what the relevant adviser/inspector recommended to schools, in most cases with firm moral support from senior officers or members or both, and characterized that as LEA policy. Neither style of answer can be said to constitute 'policy' in any meaningful sense.

That degree of fudging the issue was an understandable reaction to the curiously unreal content of the Circular. The authorities were reinforced in it, however, by a generic resistance to the role the Circular ascribed to them by its repeated use of the formula found in A7 and B5: asking how the authority seeks to 'help' schools do this or that was regarded as implying an intrusiveness on the authority's part nicely calculated to alienate schools and teachers. Many authorities took the word at its most literal and minimal reading, suggesting or implying that they offered the schools abundant help but it was up to the schools to accept it. Indeed, a large majority of the topics where Circular 14/77 asks about the authority's 'help' to schools were topics on which most authorities had not hitherto regarded themselves as having a duty. Such questions raised many issues which constituted quite novel aspects of the relationship between schools and LEAs. For example, why social education necessarily entails community links was obscure, even in LEAs committed to community education. Again, many authorities had to answer some questions by reference to the curricular assumptions underlying their school building practices (e.g. in science) – and since those practices were in turn closely controlled by DES approval procedures the circularity of the questioning was evident.

Nevertheless the Department attempted a collation of the answers and published it (DES, 1979a). The picture that emerged was strikingly bare of formal policy statements and guidelines. Under almost every topic the great bulk of reliance was on LEA advisory staff. This pattern of response was unquestionably in accord with the facts, but was so far from the picture implied by and expected in the formulation of the original questions as to make analytical summaries of the responses impossible. For example, we learn that over 60 per cent of LEAs advised schools to include careers education at third year level of the secondary school and maintain it through the fifth year, but we do not learn how many find this advice is acted on. The emphasis on advisory staffs suggests that for most LEAs their very existence was held by the LEA to discharge its curriculum responsibilities. By extension such staff were held to discharge the LEA's responsibility for standards, whether the advisers provided adequate curriculum coverage and were appropriately managed or not. The adviser had become the typical LEA's substitute for curriculum policy.

The formal reaction of the Department of Education and Science was delayed by a change of government, but in Circular 6/81 the authorities were informed that a further inquiry would seek information on the nature and scope of their 'policy for the curriculum'. This should have been a strong signal, but many LEAs were at the time absorbing a marked hardening of the financial climate. The oft-repeated government message that financial stringency need not mean poorer performance found few listeners in the LEA world. When the promised Circular appeared as 8/83 it asked many questions which LEAs of foresight had anticipated by setting up working parties of teachers to develop curriculum guideline and policy papers, but such LEAs were still relatively few. The questions were very differently framed, too. The unwelcome presumptions of Circular 14/77 had been abandoned, but what took their place was a penetrating simplicity that rested on the obvious fact that the authorities had at least been warned. For example:

5 The Secretary of State now asks each local education authority to provide:

(a)   a report on the progress which has been made in drawing up a policy for the curriculum in its primary and secondary schools . . . (relevant documents requested)
(b)   a description of the roles played in the processes of drawing up the policy by heads and other teachers, governors, parents and other interested parties in the local community.

It seems that in their responses the LEAs have exploited the uncertainty provided by the Circular's omission to define 'policy'. Some, as before, rested on the endorsed practice of their schools. Some have referred to curriculum guides and advisory documents. Some have sent in guideline papers of varying degrees of prescriptiveness. Others, taking a deliberately more dynamic or process-oriented stance have cited provision for systematic curriculum review by teachers, the resourcing of innovation, and similar initiatives. The Department has yet to publish any analysis or commentary.

What does seem clear, nevertheless, is that the Department is gradually bringing about a significant modification of the curricular autonomy that only a few years ago schools took wholly for granted. There have been several factors at work to bring about this far from predictable development. Financial stringency would seem to have had less influence than the diminished local influence of the teaching unions. The spread of the realization among teachers that LEA review and inspection was not the blight they anticipated has been helpful to the new relationships. But the exercise of trying to draw up curriculum documents is itself a healthy corrective to the more ambitious claims of teachers, many of whom learn the hard way that genuine curriculum specification is a very difficult art. In the end, however, teachers have a very proper scepticism about the influence of curriculum paper. They have realized that the less they make loud public proclamations of their academic freedoms the more they are likely to retain them undisturbed.

The series of DES circulars was thus an opportunity for LEAs, had they wished to take it, to grasp an altogether more positive role in curriculum policy. The definitions of the locus of curriculum responsibility have always been crucially obscure, so that LEAs have never felt confident that a given initiative would find endorsement in the courts or at the DES, and this uncertainty explains most of their reluctance. But a second factor arises from confusion over the way the term 'curriculum' itself embraces decisions and policies which are in reality proper to a number of levels but have been treated in the past as entirely matters for the individual school. This ideological commitment to the school as the locus of curriculum policy has so far resisted analysis which would have shown that in a number of important respects the schools need to be rescued from such atomistic practice.

Whether a secondary school should offer German or Chinese or Urdu as its first foreign language is a question that all professionals would lodge at school level. But some questions relate to more than one level of establishment: should a junior school undertake algebra, for example, or should an 11–16 school attempt RSA Stage III in typewriting, are issues affecting not just pairs but whole sets of establishments. Whether to fund graded test development or a leaving certificate in a key subject, however, is a question for the LEA which it can settle without overmuch discussion. Some issues are of wider significance and the consultations will lead to decisions that need to be binding on everyone. The adoption of two-subject science in place of three-subject science is a good example of such an issue, on which consistency is necessary but unanimity unlikely. LEAs are at present persuaded that the autonomy of the school in these matters is proof against any attempt to exercise control. The DES, through its curriculum circulars, has made clear its firm belief that this persuasion is groundless. It is hard to disagree with the

DES position, since the price that many pupils and parents have to pay for the present confusion and incoherence is often high.

The financial stringency now gripping many schools and all LEAs makes it likely that heads and governors will refuse responsibility for curriculum decisions forced on them by lack of resources. The schools will present this in the form of cuts that have been forced on them, but any secondary school curriculum is a product of choices. Few schools will ask the authority to make for them the choice between, e.g., A level in Economics and the pre-vocational course in business studies. They will delete one and wait for complaint. Similarly, fourth-year option choices will be reduced, not by asking the LEA to select two from classical studies, computer studies, needlework and Spanish, but by calculating the parental clout behind each and taking the line of least predicted resistance. This is why option schemes have come to operate so heavily in favour of the already privileged. The same mechanism is at work in the admission of pupils with special needs to mainstream classes. In most such challenges the local inspector is likely to be called on to adjudicate. It is easy to read such curriculum deletions as an evasion of responsibility, but in declaring that lack of resources are affecting standards (as they assuredly are) teachers are asserting their central accountability – for what happens to pupils in school. It is all very well for parents and teaching lobbies to claim that children have curricular rights – what dietary rights had Old Mother Hubbard? – but in less strident form the argument is real: the conflict between public expectation, limited resourcing, and the teachers' obligation to their accountability as professional is different in kind from any tension that LEAs have had to deal with.

The difference stems from all three elements in the tension. Parental expectations are rising exponentially, reflecting the arrival into parenthood of the pupils of the era of expansion. The LEAs face acute fiscal pressure of a new degree of severity. The teachers collectively are the product of a strikingly longer and deeper professional preparation, initial and in-service, than ever before. There can be no easy answers in so complex and unprecedented a situation.

To the question posed by this chapter's title there are easy answers in plenty. At one extreme is the view that teachers, because they are 'professionals', can identify and correct their own deficiencies. At the other extreme are those who see themselves as having 'common sense', and maintain that any professional can be held accountable by some basic yardstick – the doctor by his cure rate, the prosecuting lawyer by his conviction rate, the teacher by her pupil's test scores. Realistically, we have to recognize that the professional can only be held accountable by another professional: evaluating a doctor's performance is for other doctors to do, and so for other groups. We have also suggested that accountability entails a process of enforcement, whether through the training and culture of the professional or through overt penalty of some kind. Far more significant in the educational context than the accountability of the individual teacher, however, is the accountability of the school. In the maintained system that must sooner or later lie with the education authority. Because maintained schools are within their broad kinds very similar, it is reasonable for the LEA in turn to be held accountable for its schools collectively.

Note

1   There is now a considerable literature of ethnographic research into life in comprehensive schools as the pupil sees and feels it. Ball (1984), Delamont (1984), Goodson and Ball (1984), Hammersley and Hargreaves (1983) belong to it, and such material is revealing, especially for teachers and those in related occupations who have little experience of the schools in their more overtly custodial and coercive functions. Many of these illuminating fragments, however, give the reader far too little contextual information about the structural features that characterize the school and in many ways generate the patterns being observed. It is interesting that there should be so little apparent contact or commonality between this material, with its 'micro' focus given calculated 'macro' implications, and the thinking in Shipman (1984), which offers a persuasive explanation of the 'macro' social and economic context surrounding the service as a whole.

3
The Freedoms of the Teacher

Teachers claim insistently that the quality of their work and standards stems from their 'academic freedom'. This chapter sets out to examine that claim by exploring how and where teachers acquire their 'standards'. The link between the acquisition of standards and the quality of teaching differs as between primary and secondary schools, and middle school teachers find themselves on one side or the other of this divide, which is deeper than it may at first seem.

Standards

I am using the term 'standards' in its commonsense meaning, to cover both the scholastic expectations the teacher has, and the norms of behaviour that are exacted of pupils. The layman shares this notion, but teachers have to go further, to deal with pacing and the nature of learning experiences. The lay notion of standards usually contains an unconscious association with 'being tough' and setting difficult work, as though low marks raised every child's morale. This mirrors the dim memory that educational success in the layman's childhood went to those who could do the 'hard' sums and so on, and forgets the teacher's obligation to the whole class and its need for success and motivation and pride in attainment. The dogma that for children to work at their own pace is always permissive (and hence negligent) of the teacher is relevant only to ineffective teachers. Effective teachers design the learning that children do in ways they can handle: teachers know, as who better, that there are no Brownie points for having pupils fail to learn.

Moreover, standards are more than merely behavioural and scholastic. How we are taught is usually more memorable than what. The climate of a school is educationally potent, as HMI reports constantly reiterate, albeit obliquely. We have to consider schools as organizations, their susceptibility to outside example and influence, and the system's response when teachers fall short of its collective standards as well as when they surpass them. For the freedoms of teachers make them accountable for their use of them.

Where does the teacher get standards from?

The central folk-belief that children hear from their parents about school is its need for order. When a child is told 'Now be a good boy at school' he is being instructed, as he and his parents both know, to accept the school's requirement for orderly behaviour. Children do not always act upon the instruction – far from it. But one of the reasons why they are in school is to learn its real meaning, for the school to act as a surrogate for adult society in its rejection of disorder. This function of the school is explicit in the ideology of schools all the way from the Ragged School onwards. The media know this well and exploit it regularly with scare stories about 'thugs' of nursery age, often given them by teachers hoping to show that their job is harder than it used to be. In reality matters were otherwise: teachers in urban schools in the latter part of the last century faced vast classes of such uncivilized little terrors (Lowndes, 1969). But teachers who make such complaints are voicing an expectation about orderly behaviour that the pupils share: the most recent fieldwork (e.g. Delamont, 1983, 1984) shows clearly the respect of adolescents for teachers who can gain and retain control. At the classroom level the expectation of orderliness as the foundation of the teacher's standards is acquired as a pupil and is reinforced by the climate of the pupils' demand.

At the school level the requirements and symbols of orderliness are both more complex and more public. A well-ordered class can exist in a disorderly school, it is true, but no individual can restore order to a school – not even the head teacher if the rest of the teaching staff fail to support him. Parental and public judgement is disproportionately influenced by what teachers usually regard as superficial symbols at best – uniform, behaviour on the way to and from school, rejection of hairstyles and other forms of teenage assertion–dress. But it is in the less immediately obvious signals that the quality of a school's real orderliness appears – the manner of conversation between pupils and teachers, the body-language with which pupils enter or leave or sit in classrooms, and much else. The necessary or expected attributes are like public examination results in that their absence is more problematic for outsiders than for the teachers. The staff of a school that lacks both the shows and the substance of order acclimatize to the deficiency: in a sense they cease to notice it, in part because if they did notice it they might not survive. Parents and outside observers are much more likely to be concerned, but the nature of the problem renders it very intractable to their complaint, precisely because the teaching staff have ceased to regard it as they do.

If social expectations are one source of a teacher's standards, her own experience of being a school pupil is another. In the English system this experience takes a distinctive form, that of successive achievement in academic examinations. These socially applauded successes carry the strong endorsement of the school, and build up in the future teacher the assumption that since educational success is the passing of examinations, the good teacher is one who prepares successful candidates for them. The many young people who combine a vision of themselves as enjoying contact with children with dislike or fear of examinations almost inevitably gravitate to primary school teaching. For the rest, examination–passing is a very limited conception of standards, and initial training establishments usually try to dismantle its more constricting features, but the association between standards and examinations is very deep–seated throughout the secondary sector. The fixity with which most universities demand success in written examinations from students seeking to qualify for teaching only reinforces a nexus that some of the training has sought to undermine.

The purposes of initial training usually include the fostering of other notions of attainment and the broadening of the student's awareness of curriculum and its modes of delivery. The scale of modernization in the teaching and learning methods in contemporary comprehensive schools suggests that much of this training has been successful. The process of change cannot everywhere have been smooth: there is a necessary tension between the established practices of teachers and the innovations that newcomers among them might wish to set going. The pace and scale of the changes in methods and materials in recent years is also evidence, however, that the academic freedom claimed by teachers is a reality. The verdict of this chapter on initial training of teachers is a very mixed one, but the amount of time available in its courses for serious attention to method is usually quite modest, and very good use often seems to be made of it.

At the same time there are other aspects of teaching, vital to the future teacher's actual and perceived standards, for which room does not appear to be found in three- and four-year courses, still less in the 30-week post-graduate certificate courses now to be lengthened to 36 weeks. Teachers in training have to acquire some clear notions of the levels of attainment to expect of pupils in a given year group, the levels to expect of sets of particular levels of ability in the year, and the range above and below the norm to be expected and accepted within each class. In subjects which have some element of linear progression this kind of bench-mark is easier to acquire than in others, but even in mathematics and foreign languages, which look to the layman entirely linear, there are important aspects of attainment lying outside the linear thread – spatial awareness in the one, insight into the culture where the language is native in the other, to cite only obvious examples. The evidence of HMI surveys and of research like that conducted for the Cockcroft Committee suggested convincingly that there are no nationally current criteria of attainment in the main subject areas that apply with any uniformity. It is this discovery that has inspired the resolve of the Department of Education and Science to make sure that attainment bench-marks or criteria be available for the whole period from the age of five to the school leaving age (e.g. DES, 1984c). This DES intervention is viewed by some teachers as an unprofessional intrusion, but it is likely to acquire the status, influence and durability of its predecessor, the Board of Education's Handbook of Suggestions to Teachers which first appeared early in the century and was still used in initial training in the early 1950s.

The new primary teacher

The teacher who enters the primary sector begins with a class of her own. If she has been primary trained she will have been exposed to sole charge of a class for a total ranging between eight and fourteen weeks, although not usually for more than five or six weeks at a stretch. In most schools she will have found some kind of curriculum document about the content to be attempted in each year-group and about the aims the school has set itself. Unless she has been unusually badly trained she will expect to consult experienced colleagues all the time, and she will be very unlucky to find them slow to offer help. Her problem is not of course one of having too little freedom: rather it is one of needing guidance and concrete definitions of what parts of the children's regime to take on board unchanged, so as to reduce the uncertainty that seems so forbidding. But the new primary teacher will meet in her first term in the job two experiences for which no training can prepare her in advance, at least within our existing course structures.

The first is likely to be a profound uncertainty about how fast to expect to move her class along, how much to expect of them not merely at a given moment but over a period of time like a term or a year. Her training will have prepared her to resist the temptation this anxiety brings: she will know enough to avoid trying to do the job by intensive teacher-centred instruction, because she knows that what has to happen in her class is pupil learning rather than teacher talking. But her training can never hope to protect her from the full impact of the expectations problem in her second and third terms in the job. The second problem she will meet is the discomfiting discovery that children forget what they have learned and have to learn it again. Most primary teachers remember these experiences so vividly that they are strongly predisposed to help their novice colleagues through them. The daily commerce of their staffrooms is full of the hundreds of fragments of information that add up to important parts of the new teacher's standards. Thus, 'Did you have trouble with Darren Kirby's handwriting too?' is seeking his previous teacher's 'standards' and a confirmation of his present teacher's own. A wise novice will ask many such questions, and an unhurried visit to a similar class in a different school will answer hundreds more unasked ones.

The induction of a new teacher to primary work, however, is

one thing when her colleagues are individualists operating by private criteria, another when they have thrashed out a shared set of curricular values and can answer such questions on the basis of a coherent curriculum scheme. The need to provide this is especially marked in the school where each age-group has only one class, and even more so where a solitary teacher caters for all three infant years and two others share the junior work: for the new teacher such schools present distinct problems of learning the trade. In the larger primary schools the formal device of the probationary year (or the training grade if that comes to pass) can never take the place of the detailed, daily transmission of values between novice and experienced colleagues. In small primaries the probationary year becomes the formal machinery for putting novice colleagues in necessary contact with other schools, other teachers of the same age-group, and indeed other novices.

Until very recent years the freedoms of the primary school teacher to decide the content, style and expectations of the curriculum were formally speaking almost absolute. Removal of selection tests at the age of 11 took away one of the most destructive influences on the junior curriculum, and most schools were disposed to see their curricular freedom as a duty for the head teacher. The characteristic style of the post-war years was for lists of curricular content to be drawn up by the head and issued to teachers as directives. Nothing was prescribed about classroom method or teaching style, and in many cases the curriculum plan derived some of its parts from the contents pages of textbooks. Schemes of work like this left a great deal to the teacher, giving rise to a diversity of practice which the head then had to control, if he so desired, by day-to-day supervision, direct correction, and careful selection of teaching staff – though until 1974 very many LEAs, perhaps most, recruited primary teachers centrally and assigned them to schools without giving the head teacher much say in the matter. (This practice is now regarded in most LEAs as thoroughly unprofessional, but it survives in a few places.)

The liberation of primary teaching that teachers associate with the Plowden Report was well under way before it appeared in 1967, but the movement towards a child-centred teaching style which Plowden so strongly encouraged also brought some important side-effects. In most schools it changed the relationship between teachers and head. Assistant teachers became an integral part of the school's evolution of its curriculum scheme, and their interpretation of it acquired a new coherence and professionalism. The experience of developing a curriculum document is much more common among primary teachers today than among secondary staffs. There are numerous LEAs where every primary school has been asked to develop its own agreed policy for reading and language, a detailed work scheme for mathematics, a policy for science, a statement about project or topic work, and much else. The status of these documents is descriptive; their value lies in the effect on the teaching of the process of writing them. Newcomers to the staff have a framework to fit into, parents can be immediately reassured that the school knows its business, and governors can discuss the papers at regular intervals. But heads and inspectors alike know that there is no benefit in trying to use such documents prescriptively: a teacher who strikes out on her own will not be brought into harmony with her colleagues by mere directives. This view places a heavy responsibility on the head to ensure that things do not go wrong, a point to which we return.

The only other source of a primary school teacher's standards is experience. Its value varies with its nature. Thus, to teach three successive classes in the same age-group will be more instructive than taking the same class through three successive years, because the different classes provoke comparisons and set up provisional norms in the teacher's mind which are enriched and modified over time. Similarly, the cultural and social characteristics of a single school may be disproportionately instructive to a teacher experienced in other schools, and moving to another school every three or four years is a recognized part of the pattern of promotion for this reason. At the other extreme, a decade or more in a single school whose pupils are of low aspirations and attainment can have thoroughly undesirable effects on the expectations of a teacher, and LEAs regularly encourage such teachers to transfer to more stimulating experience. It is for the same reason that LEAs are often reluctant to promote to headship from within the same school, in sharp contrast to the habits of some of the smallest pre-1974 LEAs.

The secondary sector

The new teacher in a secondary school has a quite different experience. Teaching practice will usually have taken the form of a whole term on the staff of a school, or of quite long periods entirely out of contact with the training base. The student will often have been left much more to his own resources and devices, while being expected to minimize the intrusive effect of his teaching on the courses the pupils are pursuing. The habitual, taken–for–granted insistence of the primary school on sound lesson–planning is apt to be missing in the secondary school: many heads of department feel inhibited about asking to see preparation notes, though discussion and assessment of them are just as necessary. The student may find that nobody in the practice school has any interest at all in his lesson notes, while the principal kind of interest that does come his way is more concerned to limit any harm to the pupils than to enhance the benefit to the student. There are exceptions, and some training institutions now select for teaching practice only those schools willing to take their proper share in the work, but many trainees go through teaching practice in conditions of real neglect: the tutors cannot supervise closely and often and the teachers do not understand that they need to.

The absence of proper formal guidance on teaching practice naturally increases the influence of informal 'guidance', whether it be banter about getting the tough classes or the traditional solemnities about starting tough and letting up slowly. This mild and often well–meant hazing consolidates the novice's anxieties about control without actually giving him any help with it. Strangely, it was not until 1978 that a basic manual of technique on this topic was published for the young teacher (Marland, 1978), but a large majority of new entrants encountered by a group of inspectors working with them in six LEAs were found to have no knowledge of it in 1983–5. Marland's little book is practical, direct and in places properly dogmatic, but it does not attempt to address the question of expectations. Nor, it would appear, do initial training establishments address that question as directly as they should with secondary trainees. The reason may be that on teaching practice and in their first posts the trainees will usually teach classes in several age–groups, and comparisons between them will quickly give them a picture of what should be expected at each level. Since above the second year such classes tend to be in sets ranked by ability the comparisons to be made are seen as an immediate source of 'standards'.

In reality, however, novices in secondary teaching experience

face just as serious a first-year crisis as their colleagues in the
primary schools, and in some respects it is more severe. The central
requirement, they believe, is to be effective in the classroom – and
to be seen as effective by pupils and by the rest of the staff. There
are very few obvious or accessible criteria of effectiveness, and in
very many secondary schools the novice teacher feels his teaching
staff colleagues to be watching for every sign of his ineffectiveness
rather than eager to support and strengthen such skills as he has.
This perception may not match realities, but it can be a potent
source of anxiety. At the same time the novice is expected to be
able to manage a growing diversity of learning resources and set up
learning experiences for pupils whose attainments in them may be
neither readily apparent nor easily measured. He has often learned
from his training that to use a provided textbook is an admission of
defeat, although many secondary schools will expect him to issue a
textbook and will be surprised at his refusal to use it. Great stress is
laid by training institutions on the weighty messages of HMI, in
the so-called Secondary Survey (DES, 1979b) and other
publications, about the need to foster oral competence and the skills
of open-ended thinking – but both oral work and open-ended
questioning pose an implicit threat to the control which is the
novice's central aspiration. All these pressures operate, moreover,
in a school climate where the old certainties about naughtiness and
punishment have departed, where confrontation is to be avoided,
where class-control is often a slow, wearing abrasion between the
pupil's easily distracted obstinacy and the teacher's quiet relentless
insistence on the work of the class.

In these circumstances it is expecting too much of a single
probationary year to expect that the new secondary teacher will
develop his 'standards' to an adequate level of breadth and delicacy.
There is nothing casual about the proposal that the entry grade into
teaching should last for three years. In reality the secondary teacher
cannot hope to achieve a fully developed set of standards until he
has observed a class or year-group go right through the age-span
covered by the school, at least from 11 to 16. There is wisdom in
the adage that it takes five years to make a good teacher of English
or mathematics. The adage would hold good in any school system
that had 16 as its leaving age, but it applies with particular force in a
system locked into a terminal examination at 16. Teachers have to
come to terms with the criteria built into GCE and CSE

examinations for 16-year-olds, and to achieve their own understanding of the pre-requisite or 'knock-back' effects they impose on younger classes. These effects vary: in some mathematics syllabuses they reach back into the second or even first year of the secondary school, while in economics, for example, courses can start at 14 or 16 with no more than a required understanding of arithmetical graphs. But such backwash effects are not confined to the very able who take GCE Ordinary level, because the children who meet the pre-requirements for O level courses are marked off from those who do not – and the latter constitute the source of the school's future 'failure corps'. That many schools virtually create their own failure corps by the messages of success they convey to some is one of the most well-attested research findings of all (Jackson and Marsden, 1962, Lacey, 1968, for grammar schools; Hargreaves, 1972, 1974 for comprehensives).

In any case examination syllabuses and the criteria they reflect back to younger classes side-step a number of the aims and objectives which for most adults and teachers are central to any meaningful notion of standards. The narrow focus on written tests, even in modern languages, devalues the oral competence that is both a dominant social need and a clear demand from HMI. In written essay-form answers the examiners in subjects other than English are instructed not to take account of grammar, style or orthography unless they totally obstruct communication. Even in English there are no minimum criteria for handwriting or orthographic competence, so that English teachers have come to regard time spent on handwriting and punctuation as time taken away from more mark-worthy considerations. The effect on expectations is exactly what a great many employers claim, and the insistent demand for minimum competences (*cf* Worswick, 1984) becomes more than ever difficult to resist. The belief that explicit and detailed criteria for examinations at 16+ will remedy this situation, which motivates the current development of grade criteria in the coming GCSE examinations, is understandable. It will prove well-founded, however, only if teachers translate the assumptions built into the criteria to their classrooms. Thus, if a large majority of 16-year-olds omit all apostrophes and practise erroneous spelling, the criteria that demand something better will fail unless and until pupils and their parents, as well as most teachers, endorse the criteria. The bureaucratic process through which the grade criteria have been generated poses a risk that that endorsement may not be forthcoming.

The secondary teacher's standards are still further complicated by the problem of span of attainment. Cockcroft pointed out (para 342) that young people may come to understand place value at any time in a span of as much as seven years. In the mixed-ability classes now common in lower years of comprehensive schools such a span of attainment is quite common. Yet, as HMI have repeatedly pointed out (DES, 1979b, 1984b, 1984d), such classes are very often taught as uniform groups using the same materials, the same undifferentiated tasks and worksheets, and given the same instruments of assessment. The slow or less mature learners in these circumstances do badly on the tests, of course – and teachers then classify them mentally as 'not good at my subject' (DES, 1984a). Teachers are developing in large numbers an understanding of this mechanism, but their pupils are less perceptive: they regard the teacher's attempts to cater appropriately for slower learners as wasting time on pupils who cannot benefit from it – and when their own turn comes to find something difficult to learn or understand they round on the teachers, as the docile slow learner does not, for making it needlessly difficult.

Probation

Mention has been made of the probationary year of service. Teachers undergoing this formal mechanism of induction are becoming rare in many schools. The Department of Education and Science issued an astonishingly belated Administrative Memorandum early in 1983 which overhauled the archaic machinery involved and gave LEAs and schools a clear definition of their duties towards new entrants. For many years most LEAs have taken probation seriously enough to regard it as a prior claim on the time of their advisory staffs to observe probationary teachers at work and ensure support for them. Primary schools have long been supportive, but even today many secondary schools and even a handful of LEAs feel no duty of guidance or support. One purpose of the DES move was to bring such stragglers into line, by reducing the part played by HMI and placing the operation of the probation system firmly with the LEAs, which meant in effect with their advisory staff. This in turn allowed advisers to vest the proper responsibility where it belongs, in the individual school, but a majority of LEAs continued to use advisers to do supervision of probationary teachers in person rather than through heads and heads of department.

It was Marland's tart comment that the conventional practice of letting the new teacher 'find his feet' might often be a case of letting him drown. By the time the supervisor visits after a month, let alone a whole term, habits of contact between teacher and class have become set. Good practice now provides each probationary teacher with a mentor, ideally locating that colleague in a neighbouring classroom, as well as mounting a formal process of induction that shows the novice how the school is organized and run, who manages what, the functions of the LEA adviser, and above all the criteria by which his performance will be judged. It is correspondingly necessary for the LEA to have a well-defined procedure for dealing with those who do not meet those criteria. In primary schools these are likely to relate to classroom organization and levels of expectation. In most secondary cases both these needs are apt to be subsumed by the selection of a textbook, since the first requirement on the probationary teacher is control. Most secondary beginners and many of their immediate superiors have an incomplete grasp of the link between control and the nature and level of the demand made on the pupils' attention and effort, or what HMI call 'match'. Choosing well-tried classroom materials short-circuits the problem, and for some beginners this is sometimes necessary, but their use creates the danger that insufficiently demanding material will keep the class superficially happy and delude the teacher into seeing the choice as successful. Similar effects occur when the culture of a school imposes on new teachers the low levels of expectation that pupils have become used to from others.

Tests and examinations

The uncertainties attending standards in the sense of what attainments to expect of pupils have been attacked in many ways. The French 'programme' of centrally determined content and levels is widely cited by Englishmen who do not know the condition of almost total breakdown into which it has fallen. Much more culpable is our insular ignorance of West Germany's use of detailed curriculum guidelines drawn up by teachers in each of the Länder and approved in due course by political authority. These specify content and criteria for each year in each type of school and course – and do so in far more detail and with much more illustrative example than any public examination syllabus in England. The horror stories about teachers in the USA losing their jobs because their pupils do not reach required scores in annual tests have reverberated in staffrooms in England, but the almost universal American abandonment of merit pay and employment-by-results is hardly thought newsworthy. Meanwhile, the true position about tests and examinations continues to be misunderstood by professionals and laymen alike.

The crisis of confidence in the service that broke through in 1976 brought a clear increase in the incidence of testing. The belief that nationally available tests could establish how well schools were doing led to the creation of the Assessment of Performance Unit (APU), while numerous LEAs investigated and some adopted 'blanket' tests. Research published a few years later (Gipps *et al.*, 1983) found that no more than 71 LEAs were testing a specific aspect of attainment, namely reading; 40 tested for IQ (which is not of course an attainment) and 36 for mathematics. Of the 71 LEAs, moreover, a majority were using a test more than ten years old and taking only 30 minutes each year. This very modest level of testing should not be attributed to teacher reluctance or political cowardice. Test design and development has never been the large-scale industry known in the USA. Lacking investment and expertise, it has produced few tests that meet even the most basic of standards of quality (Levy and Goldstein, 1984). It has been very difficult for LEA officers to advise their LEA or head teachers that any of those they could afford would be worth using. Even the most respected source, the National Foundation for Educational Research, has discovered belatedly that many of its attainment tests in language were defective and needed replacing. Many other commercially marketed tests are out of date or inappropriate, while teachers have gained enormously in their understanding. To remedy all this would require both professional conviction that a test-based regime would benefit pupils and the kind of huge financial investment that the English system, almost uniquely, makes in public examinations. The latter would be hard to find, but teachers are not hostile to testing as such. Indeed, their justifiable anxiety about the crude practice of some American school boards partly reflects their recognition that in England we have virtually no formal criteria of attainment for children before the age of 16, and teachers recognize the political as well as the professional weakness in this situation.

The APU was originally viewed by teachers as a weapon of central control. In the event all the APU teams discovered the poverty of test development and had to devise test procedures from new. Most APU tests need trained testers and are expensive to mount and score on any scale: they do not provide an affordable model for the service as a whole. Nor has APU testing exposed any wholesale need for a test-based regime. It has, however, shown up many current examination practices as amateurish, while the marking and assessment habits of most schools appear in an even less favourable light. Having invested heavily in the APU, the DES is now seeking to disseminate its methods and materials among teachers. In the minds of teachers this must create a battle between APU resources and the requirements of GCSE, and that is bound to be a case of 'no contest'.

For the General Certificate of Education (GCE) and its forebears have 'set the standards' for over a century. Designed for the academic pupil, GCE has always catered for the ablest 20–25 per cent at 16 and the most academic 10–15 per cent at 18. As the system grew and the proportions going through it at the academic end of the spectrum rose, the pupils involved had only GCE to aspire to. But the inherently selective and competitive nature of the examination, which after 1965 was heightened by the availability of the less prestigious CSE alternative, was rarely well understood. Two illusions have thus been all but universal. Among laymen, 'standards' were believed to be 'not what they were', although the objective evidence of old and recent test papers showed a massive growth in the levels of assumed knowledge and in the technical difficulty of the tasks set. Among teachers, few grasped that since pass-rates altered little over time the number of successes to be striven for was not necessarily related to the number or the abilities of those sitting as candidates. Both illusions obscure the truth that examinations only measure standards: it is teachers that set them and teachers and pupils that achieve them.

In some respects, moreover, public examinations preserve standards that are too low or quite inappropriate. The poverty of CSE English is notorious, as is the over-specialized nature of GCE science at both levels, discouraging many pupils at too early an age. These weaknesses stem chiefly from a system that has been less flexible than the schools it has served, without any co-ordination or oversight, and the creation of the Secondary Examinations Council should put that right. The danger of standards becoming too static for the system's good, however, also lies in wait for many other tests, whether they be the competency certificates issued by numerous LEAs in arithmetic or the certificates in basic skills like those now being set up by the major examining boards. The real need is for the criteria and exemplar material approved for use in the examination system to be revised, as in West Germany, at least once every decade.

Why cannot HMI set the standards?

There are fewer than 500 HMI in a system of over 30,000 schools. Their influence is nevertheless considerable, chiefly through their publications (and would be much greater if many of them were not priced for sale). The previously rather mandarin style of HMI was transformed into a firmly managed corps as one response to the changing climate of opinion, and the consequences are traced in more detail in Chapter 6. On the evidence, HM Inspectorate began to exert itself as a collective body in the 1970s. A very important technical advance was made when modern survey techniques were applied to the selection of a range of primary schools for closer study by HMI as a valid sample of the primary sector as a whole. The studies made included conventional full inspections and visitations of other kinds, and the conclusions were assembled in the document universally known as the Primary Survey (DES, 1978). Broadly similar processes lay behind the so-called Secondary Survey of the following year (DES 1979b). The summarized assessment of the sample that appeared in each case had an unavoidable generality: it was very much a matter of a school reacting if it felt that 'the cap fitted'. In the primary sector the Survey provoked a considerable rediscovery of science in the junior curriculum, and more professional LEAs both expected applicants for primary headship to know the Survey and found many who did. The findings of the Secondary Survey were less easy to absorb, and have tended to join several other well-written pamphlets in providing a sustained orchestration of inspectorial disapproval of much that characterizes the secondary sector.

What is clearly missing from this material, and from HMI's own inspection reports, is any evidence of measurement of attainment. HMI would seem to share the wider profession's view of currently available tests, and prefer to rely on their experienced observational technique and their knowledge of the service. The absence of 'objective' measurement does not appear to inhibit HMI (or local inspectors) from roundly characterizing a school's expectations as too low, and teachers accept such judgements as based on a far wider range of observation than they can hope to achieve. As a large-scale, structural element conducing directly to standards, however, HMI lack both the numbers and the acknowledged function that would be necessary for them to be able to 'set the standards'.

The teacher's development

There is some considerable contrast in the English school system between primary and secondary teachers' attitudes to their own professional development. Most LEA advisory teams confirm an eager readiness to grasp in-service opportunities to broaden their professional expertise on the part of a significant minority of all teachers, but find this proportion to be very much greater in the primary sector than in the secondary one. It is difficult to form a fully convincing explanation of the difference. There is no generic difference such as the overall length of the school day when taken in conjunction with preparation and marking. It is possible that the more fragmented school day of the secondary school, coupled with the greater incidence of overtly unco-operative pupils, may engender a more marked immediate fatigue, and the frequency of in-school meetings in the after-school time is very often more marked in the secondary school. The research literature has some suggestions that there are many graduates for whom the process of gaining a degree is a social process that implants a reluctance to believe that one is in need of any further preparation. A more realistic view would be that secondary teachers are more problem-orientated and enter into in-service training willingly when it offers a relatively immediate pay-off – as in starting up a new course or the working out of a new examination syllabus. The same is true of primary teachers, of course, but their broader definition of what consitutes a problem remains.

Perhaps a large part of the difference lies in the nature of the teacher's early experience of the work. We have seen that the secondary teacher's central concern when he starts work is to be and to be seen to be effective. We know too that the heart of his problem is class-control, and that in the vast majority of cases post-graduate trainees receive little or no guidance about it. This fact places a premium on the young teacher's powers of survival and strength of character as an individual. Entry into secondary teaching, that is to say, maximizes that individualism which is already a deeply ingrained disposition derived from the competitive nature of schooling and its reinforcement in the examination system at 16, 18 and 21–22. The primary school teacher has a very different entry into teaching. For one thing her initial trainers are much more disposed to deal with such matters as control without imagining that to touch on them is to infringe the trainee's personal privacy: in my own experience as an inspector it has been quite usual to find probationary teachers in real difficulties of control who admit, in conversation, that their pre-entry training gave no attention whatever to the problems involved even though they had been obvious on teaching practice. As a rule, primary trainees cannot escape such attention.

The professional development of teachers beyond their initial training is clearly an integral part of the issue of standards in the service. Teachers are absolutely right to claim that total provision for in-service training is seriously below the necessary level in most LEAs. What is perhaps surprising is the higher education sector's failure to develop, jointly with the teaching associations on the one hand and the LEAs on the other, a realistic level of pressure for improvement. One reason why this kind of concerted action has not yet developed has been a disturbing level of misunderstanding between higher education and local authorities. The characteristic stance of higher education in general has been that it offers its courses in advanced study for teachers in the light of the academic criteria that pertain to advanced courses, and if teachers or their employers do not much like what is on offer that is the teachers' problem. Only very slowly is higher education coming to understand the potential of negotiated arrangements. LEAs are rapidly exploiting arrangements for courses and associateships of one term's duration as well as one year. Some are linking one-term secondments in series from the same school, developed jointly with a polytechnic for an action–research task carried out in three linked stages. LEAs are responding well to higher degree courses which require the student to present a problem facing his employer and devote the year's work to solving it – a model widely used in business schools but adaptable to school contexts on its own merits.

The dominance of secondment and part-time courses for which teachers take the initiative in applying is giving the further professional development of teachers a strongly individualistic character. That character begs a number of important questions. It puts those questions a shade dramatically to ask whether the initial training of all teachers should not be in two distinct parts, the second of them corresponding to the movement from an entry phase to a permanent–professional phase – after, say, two to four years on the job. For there are perspectives vital to long-term professional competence that initial training cannot fit in by reason of time and would not handle successfully because the students would not be ready. The prime candidates for inclusion in such a second stage would be some study of the ethnography of the classroom and its counter-culture (*cf.* Hargreaves, 1984); close analysis of the condition, as the pupil perceives it, of being what teachers so easily call 'no good at my subject'; the nature of classroom interaction and its relation to such matters as body language. For the secondary teacher's tendency to become absorbed in his subject has similar effects to the primary teacher's concentration on the pupil's growth and learning: both develop surprisingly large blind-spots about what is really going on in their classrooms.

The significance of the possible elements to be added to teacher training on an in-service or post-initial basis is that they apply to virtually all teachers. For that reason it is too haphazard to leave them to sub-options in diploma courses for which at most a tenth of the profession can hope to qualify. Nor does the foregoing list exhaust the matters which need inclusion in the training of all teachers. The obvious candidate here, and an urgent claimant for inclusion in all initial training, is some replacement of the universal folk-myths about leniency and severity in marking. There is a powerful tradition in secondary schools that assumes unthinkingly an equation between high standards and low marks. It is a tradition against which initial trainees need to be inoculated, but at present rational discussion of marking is held by many teachers to infringe the privacy of the classroom. So teachers have little or no insight into the weaknesses of practices which give each teacher a choice of norms and scatter, allow each one to use grades to mean what each one wants them to mean, and deprive pupils, parents, and even head teachers of any possibility of coming to know what marks and grades actually mean in a given instance. Correspondingly, they have no insight into the value of a standard mark-scale which is used for all public representation of scores, while individual teachers can use whatever raw-score variations they choose provided they are translated into common format for public use. Since a number of school systems in Europe have long been accustomed to such order in their marking practices (in Germany since 1813), there is some reason to think that contemporary British practice is a case of individualism run riot (Pearce *et al.*, 1985). To the extent that such disorder baffles parents, as it can be seen to do from any issue of a parents' lobby magazine such as *Where*, it does not generate freedoms for the teacher: it destroys them.

Promotion and accountability

The intense individualism that characterizes in-service training and developmental work among teachers is borne out in two further ways. The most obvious is the relationship between course-attendance and promotion. It is easy for the staffroom cynic to dismiss the practice of regular participation on in-service courses as the ambitious teacher's substitute for real achievement, and the profession probably does not exist in which promotion always goes only to those whose merits are those of achievement in substance rather than attainments on paper. At the same time, anyone experienced on the other side of the table soon learns to recognize and distinguish the assiduous course-attender whose in-service activity films over an otherwise inadequate record. More difficult and more important to identify is the able teacher whose substantive achievement reflects both a wider experience and contact in the in-service domain and the crucial ability to make effective use of them on return to school.

For it is in the area of disposal, of 'what difference did it all make?' that the individualism of in-service education as at present constituted raises the biggest questions. It is by no means uncommon to find a large secondary school, with a teaching staff of 80 or more, among whom as many as six or eight teachers have pursued advanced courses of some kind, part-time and full-time, diploma and degree, taught courses and formal research and interactive research – yet at no time have they sat down to discuss openly with the head of the school their collective perceptions of what the work signifies for the school. The teacher who after 15 years in the classroom gains a one-year secondment to take an advanced diploma may return to the school with a set of three or four important changes she wants to see implemented. But what arrangements are there to ensure that an individual set of perceptions is in any way made organic to the school as a whole or even shared formally with its staff? Failing such arrangements, what incentive is there for the teacher to maintain her loyalty to the school rather than seek a post elsewhere, only to find (in all probability) that it, too, is as skilled at tissue-rejection as the school she has left? These are generalized examples of what the in-service world has long recognized as the 're-entry' problem, which is now inevitably changing its shape. Hitherto most of the frustrations generated by 'tissue-rejection' have been discharged by the mechanism of promotion to other schools. The slowing down of movement in the profession, by sharply reducing the amount of promotion, is removing much of this pattern. Major in-service opportunities have become less and less the exclusive preserve of the potentially strong candidate for promotion. Schools must expect to have to manage within their own confines an increasing scale of changed perceptions and commitments among their existing teaching staffs.

These realities will increasingly assert themselves both as part of the ever-growing burdens on head teachers and as part of the problems of managing schools for which authorities will hold their head teachers accountable. It is always difficult, in the day-to-day pressures of a job such as running a school or taking part in the running of an LEA, to appreciate the magnitude of the changes that are taking place around us. But the typical tenure of a head teacher is nearer 20 years than 15, save for the smallest primary and secondary schools that become lower rungs on the promotion ladder. In the service of a majority of head teachers now in post the change in the head teacher's overt accountability has been dramatic. The overall scale of this responsibility in most secondary schools has now reached the stage where responsible observers recognize school leadership as a group rather than an individual function. Reporting their research into the appointment of secondary head teachers, Morgan *et al*. (1983) suggest this clearly, implying that no one member of a management team can hope to possess all the skills it will need. The recognition is one aspect of the relationship between promotion and accountability for which individualistic training of teachers, whether initial or in-service, cannot be an adequate preparation.

It is perhaps relatively easy to see the nexus between holding a top-management post, the available preparatory training, and the maintenance of standards in the service. It ought in principle to be much easier to see this link in the work of middle-management, at the level of heads of department and the like. In practice this perception is relatively rare. In secondary schools there are still numerous teachers in salaried head of department posts who reject completely the idea that this gives them any kind of management responsibility. In particular they see their special responsibility post as requiring them to provide necessary stock of books and equipment, to allocate resources and teaching spaces and duties, oversee internal and external examinations and the courses leading to them, co-ordinate departmental returns of marks or other records, and no more. This perception omits, as a rule deliberately, any responsibility for the work of the teaching staff of the department. In the case of probationary teachers the exclusion is overtly contrary to the terms of the relevant DES Memorandum, but heads of department who maintain this position are a diminishing minority. The majority, however, continue in most LEAs to be at a loss to know precisely what kind of responsibility for the work of their departmental staff is expected of them. Some LEAs have spelled out their answers: to observe them teaching, to discuss their teaching programme for each class once every term or year, to oversee their lesson preparation, to monitor the progress of their classes through the agreed scheme of work, to review their career development at intervals, and so forth. In other LEAs this has been done for particular subjects by the specialist adviser working through an annual heads-of-department conference or course. Where this kind of subject-based initiative has been taken, however, it is unusual for the advisers in other subjects to be formally encouraged to do likewise. Yet until this omission is repaired it will be impossible, alike in human equity and in law, to hold a teacher accountable for aspects of performance that have never been the subject of discussion with his immediate superior.

And in that simple word, *superior,* we meet the nub of the problem. For the individualism of teacher training and feeling in England arises only in part from the omission of anything to qualify it: it arises also from an ancient and honourable academic tradition where the collegiality of scholarship is bodied forth in a community of equals. In the grammar schools of the 1950s and 1960s this set of values was still alive: headmasters enjoyed immense public respect, but within their schools saw themselves as first among equals. Salary distinctions under the Burnham scales did not become a significant feature until the mid-1950s, and the full-dress hierarchies of the 1970s were a concession to the obvious realities of larger and more complex schools measured against the necessary public economy of the service. But the salary distinctions of the sixties did not bring with them any enforcement of accountability, and it is only now that that is catching up. In the current moves towards overtly managerial direction of schools, that catching-up must be expected to proceed more rapidly, more rigorously, with occasional casualties, and with some clear immediate and long-term benefits to standards achieved by pupils in classrooms.

The price of failure

We have suggested that the accountability of many teachers is made effective by being built in, as it were, by their training. What if that fails? What enforcement exists of the accountability of the failing or ineffective teacher? All county LEAs and a majority of the others have adopted agreed disciplinary rules and procedures, framed to implement the terms of the relevant legislation, notably the Employment Protection Act (1972). They usually distinguish between misconduct, gross misconduct, incapability, and incapability by reason of ill health, and set out what the employer can and must do in responding to such cases. In every local authority where such rules are agreed with the teaching associations they function as a backdrop rather than as a weapon. Head teachers and officers know how they work and act in matters of discipline with confidence and sureness of touch, knowing that if it becomes unavoidable it is possible to dismiss an employee, be it a teacher or any other, provided the procedures are followed and the evidence clear. This certainly lends clarity and firmness to an otherwise muddled area of management, and makes it possible to manage and resolve problems before they grow too difficult. Some simple and deliberately brief examples will illustrate the point.

A four-teacher school in a centralized but rural authority lost its teacher of reception and middle infants. The LEA assigned a probationary teacher who started work and was found within a month to have taught no mathematics. Her answer to the head's query was that she did not teach maths, did not understand maths, and was not going to teach maths. The headmistress took her aside and explained that she had a contractual obligation in the matter, and refusal to meet it would technically be misconduct. The head did not want to get to the stage of issuing orders, but this really was a thing about which no infant teacher had any choice. Within six months the newcomer had worked through her problem in a string of sessions with another member of the staff and was actually beginning to find reward in seeing her pupils overcome the difficulties she had carried throughout her own education.

In an urban comprehensive school of some size there were not very large numbers of candidates for GCE Ordinary level, but each year the head of English was able to recruit a set for English Literature. One June they went into the examination room to discover that they had been prepared for three set books but that only one of them was included in the paper they faced. The examination boards have ways of dealing with such eventualities without undue harm to the candidates. What seemed an unfortunate mishap assumed a different complexion when the same thing happened the following year. The head of the school consulted the LEA and issued a formal warning to the head of

English, describing the repeated error as incapability, and telling him that any repetition of the error in any degree within the next two years would render him liable to serious disciplinary proceedings. Two years later, nevertheless, a very similar blunder occurred with another English teacher's preparation of CSE course-work folders, for which the head of department was on his own admission responsible. The LEA asked the offending head of department to bring a friend or union representative to its offices and put to him that it was about to proceed formally to secure his dismissal as head of English, while offering him a basic-scale post. The union official advised him to agree to the arrangement in advance of formal proceedings, which the LEA was naturally very willing to abandon.

Our third example comes from a rural comprehensive school's mathematics department. A teacher of considerable experience in higher education overseas obtained a post at the school where a vacancy had occurred late in July. It was clear by the end of October that this lady possessed virtually no rapport with her pupils. She used a high-pitched and very loud voice while her classes mocked and mimicked it openly and vigorously. She planned her work in meticulous detail but was quite unable to execute her plans, because the pupils would not listen to her. Her academic distinction led the department to adjust her timetable so that she took a larger share of academic work with the sixth-form, whom she treated as higher education students and accordingly found wanting in knowledge and maturity. Mrs. Owen's confidence in her ability to win her classroom battles was a precise inversion of her prospect of ever doing so. Nothing disturbed her equanimity outside the classroom: she was utterly impenetrable to any suggestion that all was not well. The school approached the LEA inspector, who observed her at work for three lessons in succession on each of three visits, and in spite of long discussions made no headway. In December the LEA agreed to the head's wish to hold a formal hearing and a first warning was issued. Mrs. Owen's union official advised her to expect a second warning in six months' time and a proceeding for dismissal six months later. She went home and wrote a letter of resignation. The LEA agreed to pay her salary until the end of the sping term and she did not return to the school in January.

Freedom and accountability

It is easy to read 'accountability' as meaning simply a loss of freedom and to interpret the assertion of accountability as the crudest kind of managerialism. In practice teachers are accountable to pupils and parents as well as to their superiors, and in many respects head teachers see themselves as acting, if not on behalf of, then certainly in the interests of their pupils. That position will carry them a long way in terms of providing a rationale and justification for action they may dislike or expect to be unpopular or both. But while the network of accountability is a very real force in the English system, and has been so for many years, it is not and cannot be the whole story. For accountability has to work in hard times as well as good, and when painful decisions have to be taken it may be impossible to secure any decisions at all from a 'democratic' decision-making process. For example, a teaching staff accustomed to sharing in all management decisions may find it has to share in deciding how to apportion a substantial reduction in capitation funds for books and stationery, and it would be predictable that some teachers would refuse to take part in the discussion. This instance, which is not fictional, illustrates the necessary reciprocity between freedom and accountability. If the examples in this chapter appear to suggest that that reciprocity pertains only to assistant teachers, let it be said plainly that it pertains equally clearly to head teachers and parents as well as to children – as teachers are forever endeavouring to persuade them.

4
The Freedoms of the Service

This chapter is about the balance that prevails between the local education authority and the schools. I have sought to trace the origins of the traditionally limited nature of the LEA's activity, and re-stating the nature of that limitation here is necessary if we are to understand what 'balance' in this context means. We are long accustomed in the English system to refer to partnership, but much of this talk is rhetoric. Real partners enjoy working together, willingly submerge some of their own separate wishes and identities in the joint activity, and refrain from rubbishing one another in public. By that sort of standard the relationship between schools and their maintaining LEA is certainly not, in very many LEAs, a partnership. We are also accustomed, and not only on the head teachers' side of the matter, to assert the value of maximizing the autonomy of the school. We are less accustomed to recognizing honestly the constraints within which that autonomy has to work, some of which are placed by the necessary action of central government or of LEA, others of which are set up by the absence of such action.

It is easy for those outside the world of local education authorities to mistake the rhetoric of titles for reality. LEAs in practice exercise a very limited degree of authority over their schools. A simple illustration of this lies in so basic a matter as the appointment and employment of teachers. A minority of LEAs up to 1974, usually the smallest, appointed teachers to the authority's staff and assigned them to schools as vacancies arose. In recent years, however, especially with the easing of teacher shortages at a time when LEA office staff budgets were under intense pressure, basic teaching posts have been delegated to head teachers to fill, and the participation of 'the office' has been confined to senior posts, so that very often an adviser attends interviews for primary and secondary posts at deputy-head or head of department level, while the participation of governors will be for head and governors to arrange as they see fit. At headship appointments most LEAs depute a group of senior councillors to join a group of governors, advised by appropriate officers, and LEAs in increasing numbers require the chair and a casting vote to be held on the authority side. Once the LEA has appointed its teaching staffs, however, it will not as a rule maintain any more records about them than the payment of salaries dictates. Few authorities know the age distribution or generic levels of qualification of their teachers, or can say what proportion of their promoted teachers are women, and even fewer can identify the in-service training record of individuals. Most authorities, making a first response to the central government insistence that teachers should have qualifications matching their teaching commitments, are still discovering that for many PGCE-trained teachers the relevant qualification is not that of their first degree but that of their PGCE method course, which LEA records rarely specify. Against this kind of background the central government and local authority association proposals for new salary structures imply a level of LEA control which is not common at present. Such a background, extended to other aspects of routine management, provides the context in which we have to view the complex interplay between head teachers, assistant teachers, local authorities, external agencies of all kinds, and the professional commitment of teaching.

The place of the head teacher

The evolution of the LEA described in Chapter 1 involves a parallel evolution at school level. This is what historians of English education mean by describing it as not a national system locally administered but a school-based system resting on devolved administrative support. Space does not allow for tracing the detailed history of headship, which has throughout been one of dynamic responsiveness to external change. The pace of change varies over time and its pressure varies from one LEA to another and from one type of LEA to another. For example, relatively few county LEAs have had to address the needs of large concentrations of multi-ethnic groups, while few metropolitan district LEAs have been able to avoid doing so. That change of such magnitude is managed without wholesale replacement of teaching staffs tells us something important about the nature of headship in the system. Head teachers themselves would claim that this flexibility and professionalism is largely a product of the light-handed non-directive style of LEAs, but that view imputes to the LEAs more deliberation than may be justified. Most LEAs in recent years have refrained from a directive style for two interlocking reasons: they lacked the manpower and political backing to do otherwise, and they faced locally powerful teaching unions (including heads' own associations) able to exploit the weakness of the LEA that teaching staff were in short supply. The end of general teacher shortages, weakened local unions and the rise of political will to go beyond financial discipline brought a set of changes that many head teachers find taxing even to their powers of adaptation.

This freedom of the service to operate, and in particular to innovate, without significant control of important issues is usually cited as a virtue. Some of its effects, on the other hand, may be far from virtuous. The neglect of primary school science prior to 1978 is a good example, while the fate of primary school French is an even better one. Even where the latter was well-organized and effective, the reluctance of receiving secondary schools to build on it properly re-imposed that fracture between phases that its introduction had been partly designed to overcome. In more recent years the adoption of mixed-ability grouping has occurred in many comprehensive schools without adequate training and preparation, and often without enough thought for aspects of curriculum unsuited to it – and these omissions tend to be laid at the door of the LEA. Such an attribution is reasonable, but in the climate that prevailed before the DES curriculum circular of 1981 most LEAs would have felt themselves lacking the necessary power to intervene. Their advisory staffs were able to achieve a great deal without recourse to formal powers while the financial climate remained favourable, but, even so, repairing damage already done is harder work than preventing it. (It would be incomplete to omit mention of the clearly perceptible trend away from mixed-ability grouping in comprehensive schools in the mid-1980s.)

Throughout the era of expansion and long before it this situation made the brunt of teacher shortages and of change fall on the head. Examples are legion. In the years after World War II most heads who wanted to improve work in science by recognizing the new status of biology had to find spaces to adapt as biology laboratories by ingenuity and improvising. When schools became comprehensive very few LEAs relieved their heads of the daunting problems of re-training staff. In the 1970s a significant proportion of LEAs rationalized their provision of per capita funding for books, stationery and equipment, but overlooked the needs of major equipment items such as kilns for pottery rooms, lathes for metalwork and typewriters for commerce, and head teachers have had to find ways of funding these needs in the teeth of what many of them see as a deliberate LEA refusal to face realities. The logical completion of this devolution is formula budgeting, whereby all teaching and non-teaching costs other than loan charges are disbursed to schools on a formula giving a specified sum for each pupil, weighted for age: the school receives the global sum and has the responsibility of allocating the spending as the head and governors see fit. While that course entails a major change in head teachers' responsibility and freedom of action, it also opens the way, in principle at least, to the Swiss practice whereby a local community can agree to raise its own additional funding in support of its local school – which in a less tidy way is already happening. Such a development, however, exposes vividly the conflict between the head of a school as manager and the head as teacher.

For the governing tradition of the English system has been to see the heads of academic institutions as teachers first and heads afterwards, be the institution a nursery school or an Oxbridge college. Only in further education has the managerial function driven contact with classes out of the normal presumption of a principal's routine altogether, and in a minority of secondary schools the same pressures have had the same effect, but that there is much variation on the point testifies again to the head's autonomy. The rise of management demands has affected the route to headship in all kinds of school, however. Thus, it was not difficult in the 1960s to secure a primary headship without having been a deputy-head or even, in some cases, a primary teacher, whereas headship now often requires both deputy-headship experience and personal knowledge of the full range of work:

teachers without infant experience are less readily appointed to JMI headships and so on. In larger primary school headships and in the deputy-head and head posts in secondary schools many LEAs now find they can select only candidates with advanced qualifications, with experience (if appropriate to the vacancy) of very large schools or of work in proper management team structures. In recent years the available in-service provision has responded to the new needs created by these changes, and LEAs increasingly face the awkward implications. Thus, if headship now requires training, it is illogical to provide it after appointment; to provide the training for aspiring heads is either unacceptable, because it prejudges competitive selection for headship, or uneconomic, because it has to take in the likely candidates rather than the appointees. Worse still, the best practice in management development in the business world involves succession planning, which at present is alien to the way the network of interests in education operates.

The place of the head of a school in the maintained service, then, is increasingly one of concentrated responsibility. Society's demands and his authority's devolution of work become increasingly directed at his position. His own traditional rhetoric actually enhances this overload by claiming an autonomy which head teachers collectively see as threatened. But like many others in a service where real roles and accountabilities are confused by lack of definition and rhetorical assertion, head teachers can be all too easily represented as wanting to have things both ways. There are some things now assigned to them which probably should not be, other things assigned away from them that probably should be restored. In order to understand this seeming paradox, we need to come to terms with what the job involves.

Running a school

The terms *headmaster, headmistress, principal* (of a school) and their alternatives are not, in the English system, at all synonymous with the same terms in other educational cultures, and have no direct translational equivalence to the German *Schulleiter* or other continental terms. Indeed, the term *headmaster* means subtly different things as between maintained and private schools within England. Headship in the maintained system in England entails identifying an ethos, explicitly or otherwise, for the school to pursue; establishing a curriculum scheme within the narrow limits set by existing constraints; selecting, deploying and motivating a teaching staff to achieve that ethos and fulfil that scheme; identifying management tasks and creating the delegative and communicative framework for their performance; providing machinery for consulting and mediating pressures of opinion and aspiration among pupils, staff, parents and others; and showing a convincing human concern for people engaged in a demanding human task. Even that account of the functions of headship, though it may sound exhausting to the layman, will seem far from exhaustive to many heads. For it leaves out some aspects of the job, most especially its public social role, which go back long before LEAs were invented, to the church schools and the entrepreneurial secondary schools of a century and a half ago. This tradition is very much alive. It has four key features:

1   The local head teacher embodied, and was expected to be the embodiment of, a cluster of aspirations in society – about conduct, manners, 'educatedness' in general – which held out a promise that a child from a working-class home did not have to break into the aristocracy in order to break out from his home circumstances. Head teachers are still intensely conscious of this kind of public gaze, and are aware of it as strongly from ethnic minorities as from many social groups of native origin. In its extreme form this regard becomes a passing of responsibility that is properly parental to the school, which the *in loco parentis* doctrine of teacher responsibility has sadly fostered.

2   In spite of their great internal power, head teachers strive for a strong collegial solidarity with their teaching staffs, and unless they alienate it they usually secure it. Given elementary fairness, consistency and professional conduct, a head will be viewed as colleague as much as superior by many of his teachers. Even the knowledge that the head can strongly influence a young teacher's career enhances this, because such influence is not available to a non-teacher. Heads who behave unfairly or unprofessionally to their staffs are usually shown a degree of forbearance that outside observers find astonishing.

3   Head teachers enjoy a very unusual degree of immunity. Those aggrieved by a head's decisions have genuine difficulty about appeal: the authority is likely to be distant and very hard for the layman to approach, the governors are likely to see their first duty as supporting the head, and the skill of writing a persuasive letter to a Member of Parliament is far from universal. It is this difficulty, which many aggrieved parties see as a built-in obstructionism, that has fired many parental organizations and underlies the pressure for stronger parental representation on governing bodies. Such comparative immunity leads most head teachers to develop very sensitive antennae and feedback networks, but creates the danger that those long in the post may slowly lose real contact with the world of which they are so much the focal point. (Nothing of this affects the liability of a head to dismissal for gross misconduct, which is very rare.)

4   The head teacher has very great responsibility. A manager in industry or commerce in charge of a 100 or so adults and 1300 young people, a building worth £3 million at the least, with an annual turnover of £1½ – 2 million would be paid a great deal more than the £19,000 p.a. of the Group 11 head teacher in 1984 - 5. But by comparison with business managers of such status his formal accountability is low. Short of those catastrophic failures that bring dismissal, he can hardly ever be overruled, and then only in private. If the formal results are bad, the people held accountable will be the heads of subject departments, and even then they can usually cite the deficiencies of the school's intake (which nobody has tried to measure, as a rule). If there is formal inspection the school's staff and governors are more likely than not to close ranks against what all will tend to see, rightly or wrongly, as an external threat. That head teachers behave as if they were accountable, as they do, scarcely alters the structural reality of their limited formal accountability. What makes them behave accountably is a reflection of being in the gaze of a demanding public at a time when parents can usually take their children elsewhere. Arguably, that is a reality that the system's formal arrangements should take fuller account of.

What is said above about the social, professional and managerial aspects of the head teacher's position applies equally to primary as well as to secondary heads. It might be felt that the smaller scale of the primary school and apparently simpler curricular problems constitute a difference in kind for the position of the head. In reality this is not so: the primary curriculum is fully as complex as the secondary, since the monitoring of progress over the full range of the curriculum content falls firmly to the class teacher but needs interlocking with that of other classes and teachers. Moreover, the smaller scale creates problems of distance between assistant staff and head which if anything are harder to solve than those of the secondary school, and the sheer numbers of primary schools usually mean that visits from officers or advisers that might relieve the common professional loneliness of the head are comparatively rare. In many LEAs the idea of ensuring such a visit to every primary school every term is a pious hope at best, while most secondary schools expect to see some kind of LEA figure visiting the school once every week or two. If loneliness is the price of autonomy in the head teacher, it is a price that many heads regret having to pay.

The limits of autonomy

It may be helpful to identify more precisely the scope and limits of the autonomy of the school, as they have developed in the English system thus far. Such an outline is a necessary backdrop to an analysis of how the balance between school and LEA is undergoing change.

(*a*)   In its physical plant, it is the LEA that provides grounds, buildings and maintenance thereof. The scope for extension or improvement is determined almost always by the LEA's building budget, which above certain very modest limits is in turn fixed by central government control over spending. Even if a school could raise the funds for extensions, a maintained school could not build without both securing LEA approval for the plans in detail and getting the project into the list of DES-approved building within the LEA's capital spending limit. Most LEAs depend on heads to notify maintenance needs to them, and in many large schools this duty is delegated to a deputy-head.

(*b*) The LEA determines the teaching staff budget and lays down a formula for assessing non-teaching staff levels. A majority of LEAs have long used pupil-teacher ratios for teacher staffing, but there is a long tradition of staffing selective (grammar) schools more generously than secondary moderns, quite apart from the more generous ratios applied in sixth-forms. In many LEAs, moreover, until the arrival of financial stringency in the past five years the actual staffing of many schools reflected decisions made by area education officers, which often reflected the amount of pressure that individual head teachers could bring to bear. Only the imposition of cuts brought heads together to compare notes and forced the adoption of uniform ratios in such cases. The extent of local officer discretion is now very small, which has seriously restricted the scope for LEA-led curriculum development. One consequence has been that such schemes as groups of specialist advisory teachers servicing an area of small primaries, once a recognizable feature of the LEA landscape, at least in the larger authorities, are now to be found only as a result of special *central* government provision under such schemes as Section 11 (for meeting the needs of immigrant groups) and the recent Education Support Grants scheme of the DES. The ESG scheme epitomizes the problem of network subversion, whereby power (in this case in the form of grants) is exercised to subvert the proper working of the network or hierarchy of accountability.

(*c*) The LEA determines the school's budget for all other expenditure, usually on a basis which treats all schools in a given sector on the same formulae. To go beyond these limits is possible only by raising funds locally, e.g. from parents or at fund-raising events and activities. Few if any LEAs would regard it as within their powers to prevent head teachers from such fund-raising.

(*d*) All schools are bound to teach a curriculum which draws on the culturally accepted (and probably culturally determined) way of breaking knowledge into manageable units – in the English case by dividing it into subjects. The school, however, is at the intersection between the growth of new knowledge, which is quite as likely to develop into new subjects as into new areas of existing subjects, and the natural unfamiliarity of parents and other laymen with such developments. I vividly recall hearing a professor of metallurgical physics, asking a boy of 15 in 1944 what subjects he was doing at school; on hearing the answer he exploded: 'Biology! What on earth is biology, my boy? I would have thought a boy of your brains would regard that as general knowledge!' We see exactly the same tension in the conventional suspicion of psychology and sociology and even economics as inappropriate for teaching in school, although the professional objection to them is the aridly theoretical style of their treatment rather than any novelty. The way in which a given school resolves these tensions is a central issue for this book. It surfaces regularly in the debates about peace studies, sex education, multi-cultural religious education, dietary education (or, rather, the lack of it), and much else. The issue is not resolved by the conventional pieties about heads and governors being responsible for the curriculum: in LEAs up and down the land political figures view these issues as within *their* purview. So indeed many of them are, but to distinguish which issues lie with which level of responsibility is not simple.

(*e*)   All heads are bound by the other exponents of the way our culture structures knowledge, the corresponding structures of teacher supply (and teacher shortage) and of certification. The structure of teacher supply and shortage is fundamentally one structure: what generates teacher shortage is a set of decisions – e.g. to close courses offering training for infant teaching may generate shortages of infant teachers, while encouraging the change from woodwork and metalwork to Design Technology has 'created' the shortage of CDT specialists. The matching structure of teaching salaries and promoted posts interlocks with it, but neither structure is planned in relation to the other. Nor is there any planning of curriculum change which might permit planning of the recruitment and salary structures. It may be that to hope for planning of that sort is unreal – the history of manpower planning in teacher supply is not very encouraging – but in its absence the constraints created bear almost entirely on the individual head teacher. He has to fill his posts, and the possibility that this might not happen is the distinctive, recurrent head-teacherly nightmare.

(*f*)   Even if the head teacher can fill his vacancies, he is still at the mercy of the levels of professional skill and commitment that prevail among teachers as a whole and their responsiveness to the pressures that bear upon them. These pressures include, of course, their relative position in salary bargaining and the current and predicted relations between teaching unions, to which most teachers belong, and employing LEAs. Moreover, the professional skills and the commitment may be at odds with each other: primary school teachers may have a strong commitment to child-centred work without being particularly clever at organizing group work, just as secondary school teachers may be passionately in favour of mixed-ability grouping without having much understanding of how to manage individualized or small-group learning.

(*g*)   There are external constraints on curriculum also to be reconciled or circumvented. At present the most obvious of these is the increase of children with special educational needs in the ordinary school. But almost every policy innovation sets up constraints of some kind, some less easily contained than others – TVEI is a case in point, but pre-vocational education in schools is a better example because it has not carried the circumventing of obstacles (or network subversion) made possible by special funding. Pre-vocational courses have been widely adopted by schools, but have rarely been conducted with the course co-ordination and style of tuition they call for, and this causes 'tissue rejection'. Similarly, the pressure is on primary schools to deal properly with environmental studies and humanities on top of the new interest in science and the radical improvements in language and mathematics of the last decade or so. The primary head could be forgiven for wondering how it is all to be fitted in.

The typical head teacher is thus in a dilemma. He is too professional to see these new demands as improper, but is well aware of the limited nature of his school's resources for meeting them. His natural and traditional response is to seek protection for his autonomy – but this is a coded way of voicing what different heads see very differently. The problem is that head teachers are now accountable for too much that is outside their control or influence, and giving them more status or independence is not going to help. Curriculum is very complicated, and in the freedoms given to the English education service it has become complicated beyond imagination. We now need to explore these effects in more detail.

The curriculum tradition

Curriculum thinking and practice in England has always had broad intentions. When pressed, most teachers would define curriculum as the totality of concepts, knowledge, skills and attitudes that the school intends its pupils to take away with them. They also use the term very freely in more particular ways, as in 'the history curriculum' or 'the reading curriculum'. The confusions about such usage provide a happy hunting ground for academic thinkers. With less justifiable pretension, HMI have sought to superimpose on conventional notions of subjects the idea of 'areas of experience'. This began as a hazy derivative from a widely disputed branch of educational philosophy, suggesting that pupils 'experienced' such 'areas' as 'the linguistic', 'the aesthetic' and so on. The wording was always at odds with the insistent emphasis of HMI in other publications on the educational priority of activity in learning, since the idea of 'experiencing' such things as 'areas' implied to most readers of the HMI's 'Red Book' (DES, 1977) a passive posture for the pupil. The kinds of performances and outcomes that the 'areas of experience' approach to curriculum predicts remain obscure. Moreover, the original HMI documents strongly implied that the eight 'areas' constituted an exhaustive analysis. Certainly that is how LEAs and teachers understood them and HMI discussed them. But HMI revised the list: *The Curriculum from 5 to 16* (DES, 1985c) turned the eight into nine by adding, hardly to universal surprise, 'the technological'. What began by purporting to be philosophy has ended as another example of the process of accretion that has put us in our present difficulties.

The consequences of 'autonomy' and 'partnership' in the curriculum field include the following:

1   Papers issued for the 'Great Debate' (reprinted in DES, 1977) showed that LEAs in England provide almost every possible age of transfer between schools at one place or another. A pupil whose parents move house, for instance in search of employment, in two successive years can have the odd experience of attending the local final year of pre-secondary education three times in succession. This degree of local autonomy, which is political and administrative rather than primarily educational, is quite acceptable as proper to local government. Its curricular effects, however, are

destructive of the educational coherence of the service and damage the educational careers of many individuals.

2   The distribution of in-school time between the curricular claimants is not subject to any serious degree of check or control. The data in the HMI surveys (described on pp. 66–67) shows that within surprisingly broad limits head teachers are free to increase or run down particular subjects' teaching time at the expense of others. The compulsory element for all pupils (usually English, mathematics, RE and physical education) could range anywhere from less than a third of the total time to over two-thirds, and if the great majority gave such a core two-fifths of the week that fact does not alter the freedom to do otherwise.

3   Much is made of the need for each individual pupil to experience a 'balanced curriculum'. This is almost always taken to refer to the set of subjects the pupil is taking at a given moment. In practice very few LEAs have any machinery for checking whether their schools insist on this kind of balance, and if they had it there would be serious doubts about the political backing their officers would get if they tried to insist. The available evidence comes mainly from dissertations, and suggests that at both ends of the ability range curricular balance is readily sacrificed to other needs.

4   The notion of balance in the curriculum as something to be obtained, not in any one year but over a period of several years, is quite absent from the English system. It is found in almost every other advanced education service overseas. There is nothing objectionable to Swedish or German or Canadian eyes in a curriculum which gives children geography for two years and history for three, in the course of a six-year secondary scheme – but when a subject is in the timetable it is there on a proper basis of a teaching period every day. It may well be that five periods of geography in each of two school years will cover more ground more effectively than our present habit of two periods for three years with an option available for four periods for two more years. The curriculum debate in England does not at present attend to such practical issues.

5   The problem of movement between LEAs, and so between

school systems differently organized, is accentuated by the enduring problems over transition. In the LEA world the inability of infant and junior schools paired on adjacent sites to reach a harmonious linkage of their curricula is proverbial. The vast majority of secondary schools make some effort to smooth the path of each new intake by good relationships with their 'feeder' primary schools, but serious curriculum discussion across the divide very rarely attains the harmony or even basic mutual understanding that marks the pastoral aspects. In systems that operate a transition at 16 matters are much better in respect of vocational courses, but the position on the academic side is confused. Teachers of A level subjects in sixth-form colleges regularly complain that a given grade in the same subject at O level does not mean anything useful as a basis for planning the start of the A level course. The reason is that most O level candidates, or their teachers, can exercise choices of set books, historical periods, modes of assessment – choices which the same sixth-form college teachers regard as their absolute right in the sphere of A level examinations! This position throws strong doubt on the successivity demand habitual among teachers: there is something not quite logical about insisting that an applicant for an A level course in subject x or y must have a good O level grade in the same subject, and complaining in the same breath that the realities thus signified do not match their need. Teachers in most other advanced systems understandably prefer more explicit curriculum description to the shorthand of grades.

6   Rather similarly, our curricular arrangements are shot through with inconsistency about teacher qualifications. That a majority of lower-secondary English and mathematics is taught by teachers whose formal qualifications lie elsewhere was shown in the survey by HMI in 1979 (DES, 1979b). A panic-button reaction to allegations of falling standards leads the Secretary of State to demand that paper qualifications must match the subjects taught, and that degrees in certain suspect subjects should no longer qualify for teaching. Pushed to its full logic and sustained over several decades, that position would have kept permanently out of the service all teaching of English, geography, biology, economics, geology, computer studies, home economics (as distinct from cookery), and technology. The truth of the matter is more sensibly

recognized in the same Department's In-Service Training Grants Scheme, designed to improve performance in a range of curriculum fields, at least one of which (pre-vocational education) cannot by definition have teachers with first degrees in the field.

7   It is hardly necessary to rehearse here the almost total mismatch between the demands of industry and the output of the schools. The 'irrelevance' of the curriculum to the needs of industry is partly real and partly a constructed fallacy. The fallacy stems from industry's own failures. Personnel officers and middle managers have been staggeringly prejudiced and ignorant about CSE, and the dissertation literature is replete with evidence of their inability to approach school leavers with any insight into their capacities, because their testing procedures are (like GCE, be it said) geared to expose the candidates' *in*capacities. Industry has also itself moved up the employment market without realizing it, while the large-scale shift to extended education and to the service industries has made the articulate, socially polished recruit much harder to find. At the lower levels of the job market, too, employers have continued to demand a level of social obedience and personal deference that disappeared from real life decades ago, and to blame the schools for not trying to reproduce it. The sustained refusal of British industry to follow continental practice on the scale and funding of training lies behind a great deal of its use of education as a whipping boy. But the irrelevance of the curriculum is also real: examinations in English at 16+ are still overwhelmingly written, making the preparatory courses likewise, when above all else society needs a universal oral competence, and similar distortions of relevance exist in almost every subject.

8   The sustained and virtually unanimous verdict of HMI on the schools, recounted more fully in Chapter 6, is that the curricular experience of a majority of children in schools is a depressing mix of tedium and passivity. It is generated mainly by two pressures. One is the need for control, which leads to exercises and worksheets designed to make children work individually, in silence, in writing. The assessment that follows is based on the writing the pupils have done. (If it were based on their attention to and active participation in the exploration of the ideas or matter of the lesson, things might be very different. But that would entail

copying West German practice, and our ingrained xenophobia would presumably prevent that.) The other pressure is the compulsion to be, or to feel, academically respectable, in a context where that quality resides in properties of generality, verbalization and transfer to other specifics. This compulsion operates at school level to generate abstraction. A poem is apt to be studied not as a fine poem but as an example of sonnet form, an event in a physics laboratory is presented not as something curious to be explored and understood but as an example of So and So's Law (itself a generalized abstraction, like sonnet form). There is little or nothing in our curricular arrangements that resists or sets any limit to this grip of abstraction, which Hull (1985) describes exactly.

9   Next in this catalogue of curricular incoherence, we have to look at the individual. A visitor occupied a tutor period with a fifth-year group in a large comprehensive of high repute, and put a grid on the board. Along the top he listed the subjects, drawing a column for each. Down the side he asked each pupil in turn to sign in and mark the subjects studied. The second boy ticked mathematics, but said he was in a different set from the first boy, so everyone wrote in their set numbers. The visitor asked them to work out the average number of subjects and sets that any three of them had in common. Few could name three, none could name four. There was one set in biology that six of them went to, but otherwise they split up. Asked to comment, the girls were vocal: 'I only chose Art to be with my friend, but they had to go and put us in different sets!' 'I only learned my fourth-year maths from Jane here, and then they put me in a higher set than 'er!' The boys were philosophical, but they argued, very cogently, that if they did most subjects together they would work far better, and the teachers ought to put their energies into coping with that instead of into the option scheme. They were also, in a tutor group of lower band, quite clear that the option scheme was 'a cheat to give the toff kids smaller classes'. Yet we ask why our schools alienate pupils – and that alienation is the prime enemy of successful education.

10   The external examination system survives because it is utilitarian in effect, a key part of the social process of sorting entrants to the labour market. The vast expansion of entry for examinations at 16+ is in one aspect a result of the school system's urge to throw off this sorting role, which is now in course of being

reasserted in the 16–19 sector and its arrangements. The less prominent the sorting function at the 16+ level, the less constrained teachers can be about the syllabuses, but the National Criteria for GCSE issued in April 1985 have for the first time delimited that freedom. Introducing the new arrangements for GCSE entails a large burden of in-service training, which the Department of Education and Science has vested in the examination boards. Many in the LEA world would argue that such training should be led by the LEAs, since giving it to the boards will further the existing distortion whereby the examinations dictate the curriculum rather than follow it. Even within the GCSE system, as well as between its component boards and the non-school agencies like the City and Guilds of London Institute, the Royal Society of Arts Examination Board and the Business and Technician Education Council, the dominant pattern is one of competition. Clearly, examining boards that compete for candidates are inherently likely to minimize the demands they make on pupils and teachers in order to maximize their income. In the process, schools find themselves in need of a consumer advice service from their LEAs, whose officers in turn find that the advice sought urgently by one school is viewed by the next as an intrusion.

The disease and the cures

I have enumerated, without attempting to be complete, some of the ways in which our curricular arrangements exhibit the cost of the vacuum over curriculum policy. In this book I lodge much of the responsibility for that vacuum with the local education authority, partly because national control is inefficient and alienating of the commitment that sound curriculum needs. But it is a responsibility in which the electors, school governors, teachers, parents, and head teachers all share in some degree. There have been several partial attempts to remedy the disease of incoherence in the curriculum.

The most dramatic of these has been the Technical and Vocational Education Initiative (TVEI), lavishly funded by the Manpower Services Commission and operating at the time of writing in 62 LEAs. Each scheme is a pilot one in the sense that it is funded for five years, and at the end of that time each LEA will have some painful decisions to make about the future of the schools involved, as well as about the implications for the curriculum of all other schools. It is too early even to attempt a guess at what the decisions will be, but among the outcomes one or two are already evident: there will be a sharp and permanent change in the whole curricular consciousness of a significant minority in the profession, and not only in the subject fields mainly involved.

The second attempt to cure the curricular disease is of course the series of curriculum circulars from the Department of Education and Science already described. These may be very necessary but are anything but sufficient, since they address themselves to what is rather than what might be, and to considerations of policy rather than those of implementation, which is where most of the difficulty lies.

A third endeavour can be found in the series of papers by HMI under the general titled of '*Curriculum Matters*' – so far on English, Mathematics, and the curriculum from 5 to 16. Called discussion documents, their function is ambiguous. It is of course pious cant to claim that teachers in England or anywhere else will arrive at a coherent and agreed view of curriculum if they are given enough opportunity for discussion. The subject foundations of our educational culture preclude it. In any case, the real decisions are being made elsewhere, in the committees, panels and policies of the Secondary Examinations Council.

The fourth attempt at a cure is important as the only one to come up from the grassroots in schools. We are witnessing a large-scale process among teachers, not only of developing the social and personal education offered by their schools, but of seeking legitimacy and coherence for it. The commonest single approach is known as Active Tutorial Work, which began as a project funded by Lancashire, and subsequently by the Health Education Council, and has become one of the most influential curriculum projects of all. But the movement takes many shapes. Formative profiling is very widespread: thousands of young people take part in self-assessment and negotiating the documents that record their attainments and qualities. Records of Achievement began as one man's dream, suffered a sadly wrong-headed 'evaluation' for the Schools Council, and now have DES funding for a number of pilot projects. Few LEAs realize the scope and depth of this development in their own schools, but in many counties the schools without them are both few in number and characterized by a generic resistance to innovation. However strong this development, it can never gain legitimacy as a full element in the curriculum as the English tradition has defined it so far.

By far the most potent response to the curriculum problem is the GCSE examination due to begin in 1988. The General Certificate of Secondary Education replaces a norm-based, competitive examination with one based on explicit criteria: vague syllabus and myth are replaced by explicit requirements the pupil and parent can understand. In subject after subject the consequences of this and related changes are dramatic, and in many schools the routines will be transformed. The changes pose serious problems of adjustment and funding, and create well-founded anxiety among teachers. But as well as being a single system, GCSE will be based on explicit statements of what candidates can achieve who gain specific grades. The first round of results, in 1988, will reveal how accurately the grade-criteria judgements have been made.[1] If their pitch has been even a shade too steep, everyone will say how badly the system is performing. If their pitch is slightly too lenient, everyone will say how unfair the old system was. Yet that stage lies beyond a large-scale task of retraining teachers into a wholly new world of interpreting not syllabuses but statements of criteria, of assessing not passes and fails but match to criteria. The oddity and the excitement in the work now being planned and directed by the Secondary Examinations Council is that if it succeeds, the real need for formal public examinations will disappear within a decade. Even so, a complete success for the SEC would not put right more than a proportion of the ills that beset the curriculum.

The chief reason for this guarded conclusion is that the new secondary examination system will operate directly on the secondary schools without more than marginally engaging the LEAs, while within the secondary schools the influence of the changes will extend only to the teachers directly involved – and fully a third of secondary teachers never teach GCE classes at all. Moreover the GCSE system is deliberately designed to minimize the 'backwash effect' so notorious in GCE today, so that curricular decisions will go on being required about the work of years 1 to 3, and of course about what subjects are pursued by which pupils. The effect of these five attempts to cure our curricular ills, then, taken together, is more likely to be an increase in the burdens on head teachers rather than a reduction.

Towards some solutions

The directions in which the service needs to look for real and lasting solutions are surely three. First, the process of evolving curriculum programmes for the schools of an LEA needs to be given permanence, teacher participation, renewal and political legitimation. In each LEA, that is to say, the curriculum needs specifying on a lasting basis, in documentary form, by a process in which teachers take regular part. That process should be permanent: if an LEA has an agreed curriculum for, let us say, history in the lower part of the secondary school, the document is likely to have been the product of two years' work. After a period of a few years it will need renewal, and so for all the other such papers. It would be wise for such arrangements to respect the local school organization: another LEA will have its curriculum guidelines for middle schools, and so on. Above all, when the documents have been produced, they will be subject to endorsement at political level – and if the representatives of the people wish to insist on changes, that is their very proper right. In exercising that right, the politicians would be endowing the documents with a weight, and the curriculum with a coherence, that we now lack.

Our second need is for a very significant change in the way teachers are prepared in their initial training in the field of pedagogy. Many aspects of this change are already under consideration in the relevant White Paper and other documents (DES, 1983c). But those changes will lose their maximum effect if the emphasis in training does not focus insistently away from what the teacher does (teaching as classroom performances) towards what the teacher gets the pupils to do. This change has been largely achieved in the primary sector, but to bring it about in the teeth of old and deep-seated habits in secondary staffrooms is very difficult.

Our third need is for a searching change in the focus of our assessment habits in classrooms of all kinds. When coupled to properly developed curriculum guideline documents, sound classroom assessment takes place during and at the end of every lesson. It is still unusual, for example, to find language teachers who record which pupils have taken part in the oral commerce of the lesson, and it is rare to find English teachers who can identify after a lesson how many pupils, let alone which ones, have taken no part in a 'discussion period'. The freedom to be idiosyncratic about assessment in routine class practice is, like many other of the freedoms catalogued in this chapter, part of the luxury of individualism we can no longer afford.

Note
1   The introduction of grade criteria into GCSE examinations has now been postponed.

PART TWO

Quality in the Service

The next three chapters are concerned with the mechanisms which ensure the maintenance of quality in the service. At LEA level the principal mechanism is the authority's inspection and advisory service. In many LEAs this is of relatively recent origin, and manning levels, tasks and deployment are very variable from one LEA to another. However, LEA advisory staffs number between four and five times the strength of HM Inspectorate, which is described in Chapter 6 and is shown to have functions both smaller and greater than those commonly attributed to it. Chapter 7 sets forth an account of the ways in which schools may be held accountable in detail for the quality of their work. This part of the book argues that the need for the LEA to be seen to be maintaining quality in its schools can readily be met, but that this would require political endorsement of the procedures employed and a change, in some LEAs a very marked change, in the management of the advisory service. It is also suggested that the standing of HM Inspectorate has enabled LEAs to rely on it as a guarantor of quality to a far greater extent than its numbers or style of working has justified, and this reliance accounts in large measure for the weakness of some authorities' advisory services in the past.

5
The Advisory Function

The pragmatic local authority

The outline given in Chapter 1 of the growth of LEA advisory services reflects the very pragmatic nature of English LEA work. The LEAs brought these groups of officers into being at widely varying rates, for widely varying ostensible purposes, and there is no available evidence that any of the local authority associations thought out what advisory staffs were fundamentally for, still less what the numbers and structures were that met the needs of an LEA. Perhaps more strangely, there is no evidence that the chief education officers gave the matter much collective thought either. One factor in this seeming oversight was that advisory manning was ever a sensitive topic, in some eyes an index of a chief officer's success with his committee, in other eyes exactly the reverse. The absence of coherent analysis of the purposes of one of the largest single categories of the LEA's own officers also played its part in further variegating the tasks that advisers were given, and in preserving their variety of designations. Even today it is difficult to make firm generalizations about what LEA advisory staffs do. This is apparent in the best available statement, issued by the advisers' own association (NAIEA, 1983):

1   A Local Education Authority Inspectorate or Advisory Team is a group of experienced officers charged to assist the Authority with the monitoring and improving of educational standards.

2   The team's first responsibility is therefore to gather an overall and detailed picture of all the educational establishments (at

all levels of their operation) within its purview.

3   The picture will be gained principally by visits and direct observation (e.g. of classroom practice) and will be the basis of all subsequent action. Inspectors/Advisers must therefore have freedom of action to decide when and where they will visit; as representatives of their Chief Education Officer they have no need to wait for an invitation.

4   If a first advisory responsibility is to become informed about the education provided in the Local Authority, the second is to use this information as the basis of advice to those whom it may benefit – the CEO (and through him elected members), Education Officers, Head Teachers, Classroom Teachers and others – so that the service to all, from young children to adult students, can be as effective as possible.

5   The third responsibility is to use this information to guide the provision of relevant advisory support for the schools and other establishments. This support will come in a variety of forms, including for example extended work within a school or the provision of in-service courses for a large range of teachers on such diverse topics as the management of large schools or classroom techniques for new teachers.

6   These three duties are common to all Inspectorates/Advisory teams. Other tasks receive varied stress in different LEAs, but are also important in advisory work and provide additional ways of monitoring and improving educational standards. They may well include:

   (*a*)   the conduct of surveys and formal inspections;
   (*b*)   involvement in staff appointments and staff deployment;
   (*c*)   providing advice on building design, staffing and other policies;
   (*d*)   work with School Governors and
   (*e*)   giving personal and professional support to school staffs.

7   It should be noted that the task of an Inspectorate/Advisory team as a whole is not necessarily the task of each and every member. Some specialization is inevitable. Planning and

co-ordinating the work of individual Inspectors or Advisers is thus a crucial part of the role of the team's leader, the Chief Inspector or Adviser.

The omissions from this list are as interesting as what is included. There is no mention of curriculum innovation, although less than ten years earlier the only well-financed research so far instituted on advisory staff (Bolam, 1978) was into their function in innovation. Nor is there any hint of the adviser as the formally authorized specialist officer in a curriculum field, employed not only to help and support teachers but also to shape and mediate the authority's policy for that field. No mention is made of any interlocking with Her Majesty's Inspectors, in spite of the view, evinced by many HMI and accepted without apparent challenge by many local advisers, that on curriculum policy matters it is for HMI to propose and the local adviser to dispose. These are not inadvertent omissions: they reflect the attempt of the statement to embrace the many differences between LEAs. The NAIEA definition of the three responsibilities common to all advisory teams may be readily accepted, together with its set of five tasks common to most but not all of them. However, we should certainly add two others. Curriculum development and innovation has been among the priorities for many advisers for two decades. Drawing up or negotiating curriculum guidelines and policy statements is increasingly prominent among their duties. These ten tasks fall very unevenly: some inspectors may have work under all ten headings, others may encounter only two or three. In some LEAs building design is assigned to specialist officers and teaching appointments to education officers; in others there are as yet no agreed disciplinary procedures for teachers – and in the absence of professional research it is impossible to say how many authorities assign which tasks to whom. It is clear from small-scale inquiries (Pearce, 1984, NAIEA 1974*ff*) that with the exception of servicing governing bodies a majority of advisers in most LEAs perform most or all of these tasks. The weight of the work changes over time, in some tasks imperceptibly but in others dramatically, as in the sudden drop in school building work in 1982–4.

Before looking at each of these functions in some brief detail, it may be helpful to clarify the issue of nomenclature. A majority of advisory staff are called Advisers. Perhaps a quarter of the 1,850 or so advisory staff in the English LEAs are designated as Inspectors, and where the title is used it usually applies to the whole team. Only a handful of LEAs have a rank–and–file of Advisers with senior posts of Inspector. The designation does not imply any distinction of function: advisers may inspect, and do, just as many entitled Inspector do not in practice conduct inspections. Such officers differ, however, from Advisory Teachers, who do not usually have an office base outside a school and do not comment formally on the quality of work seen. In practice most teachers refer to all three simply as 'advisers', which identifies how they see them.

What advisers and inspectors do

1　Knowing the schools

All advisers are experienced teachers, but they are much more than that because they accumulate knowledge of many different schools. It is their habit to start in the classroom: few advisers will base a judgement of a school on what they see from walking round or talking with the head teacher. Their personal observation will always take in both the many lessons they see and the school context in which they see them: the condition of the staffroom is as telling to the experienced eye as that of the toilets or the corridors. If inspectors sometimes appear preoccupied with the surface or decorative condition of schools, it is because they know that the habitués become used to not noticing, but the little noticed squalor will influence pupil attitudes. There are some things that only advisory staff ever notice – for example that in school A the fifth formers do not even look up when their ineffective head walks past, while in school B, in contrast, the noise in the teaching block ceases within two minutes of the start of afternoon lessons. The range and acuteness of the antennae that advisory work develops in most advisers frequently surprise teachers, although there should be nothing surprising about it. Part of this acute sensitivity, however, lies in both suspending judgement and concealing the judging eye.

The heart of advisory visiting, then, is in lessons, and all advisers know that teachers will feel threatened by their coming – though even the most case-hardened adviser never quite loses the anxiety about visiting a school for the first time. Classroom visits are also expected to yield some profit to the teacher, however small, and every adviser knows this too. Perceptions about what constitutes profit, however, can easily become confused. Some teachers become so anxious that their emotional expectations require a criticism from the visitor if they are not to be disappointed. Reciprocally, some advisers are so anxious not to appear threatening that they come across as merely 'wet'. Given the English tradition of closed classrooms which the teacher's own in-school superiors never intrude on, such anxieties have to be recognized. In open-plan buildings it is much easier for the visitor to feel, and indeed to be, unobtrusive.

Every classroom visitor seeks to be unobtrusive. Advisers seek to reassure, and the explanations that the visit is 'just routine' or 'doing my rounds' or 'covering the patch' are usually the simple truth. Where there is a specific reason for the visit an adviser is wise to give it. Advisers usually refuse to collude with a head who wants a report on a single teacher. Such a request has many a time become a review of a whole department that left the head with as much to remedy as the department. Advisers also try to be at a lesson when it starts: lesson openings are always revealing. Once there, some will want a chair at the back, others will want to read the exercise books; some will sit still throughout, others will circulate while the teacher does so – and which the visitor chooses is usually deliberate. Some advisers talk readily to pupils, others not; some talk with them about their work, others about the subject and the approach. Advisers very rarely 'take over' a lesson: as teachers they have heard too much staffroom indignation about this practice among HMI, and teaching today is too carefully prepared a business for off-the-cuff work to be of any value. In any case it tells the adviser much less than the talk with the teacher afterwards. But advisers do not need telling that their presence modifies what they observe. Nor, however, do teachers need telling that their pupils' and their own bad classroom habits always reassert themselves, usually before the lesson is ten minutes old, whatever care has been taken to dress things up for show. The timing, tone, volume and frequency of 'Please Miss' from a single pupil reveal too much, unawares, for a visitor of any experience as a teacher to be deceivable.

Gaining advisory knowledge happens after the lessons as well as in them: the talk with the teacher is as varied as the teachers. It will very rarely include a negative judgement, and even then the adviser's skill lies in bringing the teacher to reach it for herself. It may invite an initial assessment and go on from there with questions, some factual, some about matters of judgement: why are the boys and girls so separated, why this rather immature book with this class, why move from reading to writing without any discussion of the connections, why no activity by the children to apply this concept, did you mean to end five minutes early (or late), what can you do with the disruptive boy in the back row, and so on. As often as not the teacher is asked about something she had taken for granted or not registered as significant. Often the talk has to be brief, until break or lunch-time offers time for more. No doubt many such conversations will happen during a playground duty before schools learn to provide time and space for them. A small proportion will have to be professional rebukes for shoddy work, and style again varies: some advisers are frank but amiable, others frosty and disposed to convey disapproval by omitting to express any approval. Where the messages the adviser has to convey become repetitive, there is the basis for an in-service course.

Often the adviser's message is one for the head teacher, about rooming or resources, support for a young teacher, unjust timetabling, avoidable inconvenience. It can be quite difficult to convey the right degree of approval to a young teacher doing well in intolerable conditions, and the right degree of anger to the deputy head who has unwittingly imposed the conditions, without leaving them puzzled at the difference in the messages. Advisers are of course paid to be somewhat harder to please than the rest of educational humanity, but they have their full share of the teaching profession's habitual reluctance to make adequate use of praise. In a period of low morale among teachers, much of it stemming from the gratuitous dispraise heaped upon them from political and media sources for many years, advisory staff have no interest in being rigorous for rigour's sake: they seek not to rebuke but to improve.

Advisory staff have several other ways of adding to their store of information about the schools they deal with. The most important, probably, is exchange with their own colleagues. LEAs vary enormously about this. I have heard of but never identified one where all advisers had to write a report limited to 5–10 lines on each visit, and each report was filed with others for the same school, the secondary files were circulated each school holidays for the advisers to read, and each summer a list was passed round of schools each adviser had not visited. Such tidy discipline appears to be unusual: there are some advisory teams where no report is required on a visit, although their number is now fast diminishing, but the accumulated files of reports are usually seen as for the sole use and information of a particular education officer. Many teams, both those that write visit reports and others, hold regular meetings to review schools, and hold monthly or termly conferences where a great deal is exchanged. Apart from the formal reporting, which is often practised in a style of studied neutrality, advisers tend to avoid writing their knowledge down. Much of it is personal, acquired in confidence; most of it is transient, relating to circumstances that are constantly changing; and much of it technical in a way that is inaccessible to non-specialists: their reluctance to write such knowledge down is understandable, and may be strengthened by the conviction that written documents are an instrument of bureaucratic management, whose goals are inherently inimical to the professional interests of teachers – or such is the perception of many advisers.

The absence of recorded information can mean that advisory teams become very fragmented in their knowledge of a school. Unless advisers can develop in other ways a strong sense of their own colleagues' need to know, and can rely on using a common base in which direct personal contact with most colleagues is likely at regular intervals, their feeling of belonging to any kind of team may become a piety that causes only a rueful smile.

2   Using the knowledge

The ways in which advisory staff in an LEA make use of the knowledge they acquire is closely bound up with the ways in which a team is organized. The depth and intricacy of the knowledge will be more apparent after we have looked at their other tasks, each of which will illustrate some of the many ways of using advisers' knowledge.

3   *Supporting the schools*

Some concrete examples first:

(a)   A teacher wrote to his Area Inspector to say that while he was a biologist he was having to teach a lot of physics, and he wondered if the LEA could assist with the costs of the Open University courses he was following to help him. After replying, the inspector asked his science inspector colleague to explore, and the teacher was seconded for a full-time course designed for biology graduates wishing to train for physics. (The shortage of teachers qualified in physics and chemistry is still serious and will become much worse.)

(b)   A junior school head in a country town prided himself on having the best local primary in the LEA's 9+ reading assessment. After two successive failures to achieve this, he asked the primary adviser to help. She visited the school, spent 20 minutes or so in each classroom (with teachers she knew quite well), talked with them over lunch-time coffee, and set up with the head teacher an after-school staff session in one of the classrooms. When they met, the adviser asked each teacher to describe precisely what she did about reading, starting with the first year classes. It transpired very soon that although all eight teachers were following the school's guidelines, their interpretations of them varied more than they realized. Thus, one had fully adopted the advice to hear children read much less often but for much longer passages, while the others had not thought this very important, and when children had to go back to being heard every week they felt demoralized. A second session was necessary, of course, to work out agreed practice, but the adviser was not needed for that.

(c)   A girls' grammar school in a large northern LEA had long had cause for concern about its mathematics department. At the headmistress's request the mathematics adviser and his advisory teacher colleague spent three days in the school, observing nine teachers for five or six lessons each. The root of the trouble, they concluded, lay in the head of department's lack of guidance about what being a subject leader meant. They laid out a list of tasks she needed to carry out, and suggested some deadlines in series for them; in reserve, supplied to the headmistress, was a set of tasks for the other holders of scale posts in the group, which were negotiated over the ensuing year. The adviser kept regular watch, and nine months later introduced the teachers to the idea of individualized learning packages. It took well over a year for the promoted teachers in the department to adjust fully to their new roles, but they did so. In the process, the headmistress had to find the answer to the question why it was only mathematics that had to come up to snuff, and in due time all departments found themselves facing similar requirements.

(*d*)   Tockleston Primary in 1980 had five teachers and about 110 pupils. The head was a diminutive, wiry and sociable man who had been in post ten years and was almost untouched by in-service training, curriculum review, or any serious idea of the duties of headship in respect of curriculum quality. That year two of his staff left and the adviser, himself a recent arrival, saw a chance. He offered to help with the new appointments, and the governors were happy to leave the work to him and the head. The adviser began by asking for job descriptions, after which it was not hard for the head to identify the relevant applicant from fields he would previously have scanned for 'good chaps'. The Scale 2 post, now for language as well as games, brought a gifted young woman, the Scale 1 post a probationary teacher the adviser would be supervising anyway. It took nearly two more years for the steady feeding-in of new ideas – a language scheme, revision of the maths scheme, a syllabus for topic work, all of them sought as part of the continuing work of local courses, and much else – to persuade the difficult but locally prominent woman who had been deputy head for many years that it was time to retire. The new deputy was a young man with his own career to make and a flair for science. At the end of four years nobody closely connected with the school could or would deny that a transformation had taken place, but not even the headmaster suspected that back in 1980 the primary adviser had been waiting to start a process still continuing.

(*e*)   Pawless Secondary School is an anomaly. Its LEA opted in the late 1960s for a first school, middle school and upper school form of organization, but the total school population in Pawless and its surrounds did not justify that structure, so it retained its

5–11 primary and its 11–16 secondary, the leavers going on to post–16 education in the town 14 miles away if they wished. The headmaster at the time of the reorganization had fought with desperation to prevent the anomaly happening, and had been away following a heart attack later the same year. Ever since his return he had virtually left the conduct of the school to his deputy, a skilful teacher whose administration yawed between tyranny and duplicity. The head eventually retired, and in the last two days of term removed as his personal property every piece of furniture in his study, every file he had ever kept, and all but the most personally private of his deputy's files. The next day he wrote a series of letters, in which he addressed to each of his more long-serving members of the staff a vitriolic catalogue of deficiencies and misdeeds – and he copied each letter to the Chief Education Officer and to his successor. The CEO was away on holiday and returned in mid–August. The only officer available for discussion of the Chief Education Officer's letter of guidance was an adviser. The new head and the adviser arranged for each recipient of a letter to see both of them formally, with a colleague or a union representative if they wished, as a reassurance that the new head's resolve to reach his own judgements was genuine. The deputy head had been depicted very damagingly in some of the letters, and demanded to be transferred to another school. The adviser was able to use his connections with a college of higher education to arrange admission to a higher degree course (with a management element), for which secondment for the year was granted. Much chastened, he became a head of department elsewhere on a protected salary for his remaining few years of service.

(f) In a small sample of LEAs[1] visited in July 1984, 16 out of 18 advisers for primary education were expecting to offer or organize, in the academic year following, short courses for specific groups of primary school teachers. The target groups included teachers responsible for all the infant work of a school (i.e. teaching the school's only infant class), heads of infant schools, heads of infant departments, teachers responsible for language, teachers responsible for art or display, head teachers of small schools (on guidelines for science in most cases). Five were also expecting to arrange courses of some substance for newly appointed heads, deputy heads of larger primary schools, and the like.

These examples are not fictional, although names and places have been disguised. They illustrate the great diversity of forms that 'support for schools' can take, and the diversity of the schools and situations that the support needs to cater for. The form, timing, duration and location are all variable, and advisers develop sensitive intuitions about whether to suggest a visit to another school (and if so, which one) or to propose an after-school session with a teacher from out of the area, or to arrange a teachers' centre course, or even (albeit rarely) to buy in supply staff for a day to release a group of teachers for a planned set of visits. The point to be made is that 'support' is not a euphemism: advisers are not in the business of leaning on teachers, or of feeling offended if teachers do not take up the opportunities on offer. A great many of these support responses take the form of in-service courses, and most advisers learn from hard experience that they cannot afford to devote personal time and energy to teaching courses themselves: the planning demands too much time. So they are constantly seeking for teachers who combine the necessary professional expertise with the much rarer gift of being able to address teaching colleagues acceptably and to learn from their mistakes in trying to do that. Teachers are rightly a very demanding audience for the in-service trainer, quick to provide him with the evaluation of not coming again, and even very good teachers of children have to learn a new art with adults.

The kinds and size of groups of teachers the adviser aspires to support will vary from one LEA to another, but may include whole staffs, the subject heads of the whole LEA, and many more specialized groupings. Support to teachers as individuals is described in section 8 below.

4 *Surveys and formal inspections*

These are dealt with in Chapter 7.

5 *Staff appointments and deployment*

Formally teachers in most LEAs are employed by the authority, and the appointment is made on the recommendation of the governing body. (Aided schools, however, have the power to appoint vested in the governors.) Practice varies a great deal, however: some LEAs expect heads and governors to do all the selections, though few go this far in devolving powers, while a few still expect to make most teaching appointments 'in the office'. There are still some authorities which look to fill primary headships without letting the candidates visit the school, but this is becoming rare. In a large majority of LEAs, teaching posts on the lowest salary scales are devolved to the head and governors, and many boards of governors leave the task to the head, while more senior posts require the involvement of a representative of the chief education officer. In the large majority of cases this will nowadays be an adviser, and a growing proportion of authorities operate explicitly stated appointment procedures, which provide a secure framework for all concerned. To judge from their actions, most LEAs reject the view expressed in the past by HMI and echoed in the Rayner Scrutiny of HM Inspectorate (DES, 1983d) that such work is 'administration' and thus not appropriate for advisers. On the contrary, most advisers would claim that while there is little merit in using advisers for every basic grade appointment, their participation at other levels has a number of advantages.

First, the head teacher will not usually know the schools from which leading applicants come, but the adviser will often have seen other applicants from the same schools. Secondly, the vacancy for a specialist is likely to be outside the head's own sphere of expertise. Thirdly, a head in doubt whether to appoint at all can seek a detached view on the quality of the field as against the quality of recruits available generally. The adviser's presence lessens any odium attaching to decisions for or against internal applicants. Where governors want to ask technically improper questions it is often easier for the adviser to prevent this than for the head. Being present at interviews helps advisers to keep track of needs for in-service training. The teacher appointed, especially to headship, expects a working relationship with an adviser he has met at interview and makes assumptions about this that greatly ease the adviser's path.

It is easy for disappointed candidates to suppose that the adviser has had a decisive voice in an appointment. In most cases this is inherently unlikely: governing bodies and heads do not readily cede one of their most cherished powers. Advisers do not have appointments in their gift and do not want them so. The interview, however, is the outcome of a longer process, starting with a job-description reflecting hard thought about the kind of school or department that is wanted. (That most job-descriptions are perfunctory suggests a need for management to become more professional.) Culling a file of applications will often involve an adviser, for a senior post at least, as will short-listing for interview. But the adviser who invests many hours in a single appointment cannot afford mere personal prejudices: they are easily spotted by the ordinarily acute governor or head, and undermine the reputation for detachment that is the adviser's main claim to be heard. In many authorities it is on the construction of confidential references that the adviser is likely to have significant influence, but most advisers are ambivalent about such references. If one has to enter a reservation, the adviser who drafts it is under a professional obligation to ensure that the teacher concerned knows the substance of what is being said. That does not stop a teacher making many futile applications: some find it difficult to believe that such reservations have any effect or are more than very minor. But in most authorities the teacher whose applications are getting nowhere will be able to find out why if he approaches the relevant officer. Personal prejudice or captiousness about selection does happen among members and governors, but that is part of the price for a service grounded in the community and its due political process.

Much has been written about interviewing and its limitations as a way of selecting head teachers (notably Morgan *et al.*, 1983). Most demands for improved techniques are academic: selection for senior posts in a public service is a political act even if it is rarely a party political one, and thus an exercise of power, which its holders are not going to cede to some technique. The most serious criticism to be made of current procedures is not that they are muddled and still less that they are irresponsible: it is that the pressures on the time of those involved prevent adequate preliminary planning. If a group of governors and members are to select a 'long list', they surely need to decide what they want from the apppointment before they see any applications. Such decisions entail some understanding of the school in question and its needs, and set limits to the preferment of purely personal favourites. Other faults remain widespread too: laymen have to be told more plainly of the dangers of letting interviewing panels be too large, and the proportion of senior posts going to women remains unacceptably low even if relatively few of them usually apply.

The advisory function in job-selection is inherently prone to misunderstanding. The disappointed are bound to suspect conspiracy or stupidity occasionally, and may quite naturally impute more weight in such decisions to the professionals they know than the laymen they do not. Appointing panels cannot give reasons for appointing X without implying reasons for not appointing Y, and they will not do that publicly. In many LEAs, however, advisers who assist with interviews regard the talk with each unsuccessful candidate as one of their most valuable opportunities – to encourage promise, explain defeat, salve hurt pride and, above all, demonstrate the human concern of the authority. In addition, allegations against advisory influence over promotion are in many instances a cover for quite different concerns and feelings.

The coming of sharp falls in school rolls has changed all LEAs' management of their teaching staffs in order to keep their numbers in line with public policy. Teaching unions have long advocated that this was an opportunity to reduce class sizes, without fully realizing the financial demands involved or the research evidence that class size, of itself, is not a simple index of success. LEAs have managed reductions in teaching manpower by internal transfer, early retirement, voluntary redeployment, and the use of temporary appointments to fill vacancies that arise when a reduction is to occur in the foreseeable future. Extended use of secondment can also help, by taking the teachers concerned out of the labour market for a year and by giving them a new range of scope for redeployment. In such ways the English LEAs have achieved a remarkable record for managing staff reductions without recourse to compulsory redundancy. In some LEAs the personnel work involved is done entirely by education officers. In most it is shared widely with advisory staff, who can often suggest matches between a teacher to be redeployed and a possible post. In a few LEAs redeployment has been deputed entirely to the advisers, at the expense of much of their other work until the crisis was over – an extreme instance of the tendency for LEAs to use their advisory staffs as a mechanism for adjusting to change.

6 *Providing advice*

In September 1983 a new head teacher took over a comprehensive school which had been run for the previous 12 years like a grammar school of the 1950s. The cult of headmasterly autonomy had made advisers overtly unwelcome, and the senior staff learned to hide and circumvent their problems. The new head, rather unusually, had taught in maintained schools but had been a deputy head in an independent school. He wrote at the end of his first month to his District Education Officer with a list of problems. Was he free to begin moving metalwork and woodwork in the direction of design technology, and if so would the LEA provide the expensive equipment? What could the authority do about the 16 manual typewriters lying unusable for want of spare parts in a store cupboard? Replacing the burned-out elements in the pottery kiln had been delayed for two years: were there safety factors involved? The school had won a microwave oven in a competition but had not used it because a governor thought it unsafe: were they right? Was it possible to remove a serious blockage in a fume cupboard? Was there any officer in the authority who could tell him how his school's examination results compared with others? In reply, the officer said he had copied the letter to six of the county inspectors, who would respond direct within two weeks.

Each of the head's questions is technical. Obtaining an answer had the effect, however, of exposing many more problems. The metalwork shop provided several examples of unsafe machinery and working practices. The case for trying to maintain a business studies department in a medium-sized comprehensive school four miles from a good college of further education had to be questioned entirely. The teachers in the art department could not use the kiln, but none of them had trained in ceramics anyway. The microwave was safe enough, but the school was unique in the LEA in still teaching cookery to the exclusion of home management. The fume cupboard was unblocked within days, but the school's insistence on three separate sciences for all pupils from entry at 11 to the age of 16 was a source of serious difficulty for many pupils and teachers. The inspector concerned with the examination results reviewed them with the head, then with the heads of department meeting, and in due course with the governors.

The narrative illustrates the nature of advisory expertise in two ways. The advisory staff exists, among other things, to be a repository of technical expertise on matters that any responsible employer needs to guard against, be they matters of health and safety, welfare of people, sound use of resources, value for money or simple good practice. It also exists to testify to educational standards in whatever way happens to be appropriate and relevant. There are two criteria of relevance in advice to a school, however: apart from the obvious one of need, as in cases where a school is putting pupils at risk, there is a test of applicability. It is no good offering advice that those you advise have no hope of acting on, or even advice they cannot act on easily. Thus, the metalwork teacher will know about machine guards, but may need a copy of the necessary catalogues and some help with funding. Which of the art teachers goes on which ceramics course will need to be negotiated, but part of the negotiation involves finding the department a qualified specialist who can cover the absence. The run-down of business studies needs to be negotiated not as a run-down but as a transfer to the college, with the school's teachers offered training and transfer or some other constructive outcome.

The adviser is not there merely to offer the advice that is asked for, although some teachers and heads do not like the asking of questions that dig below the surface problem to the more substantive issues. To view the adviser as merely a respondent bearing goodies will overlook the main part of what, implicitly if not formally, most authorities employ him to do and to be: a surrogate, in respect of his special field, for formally stated policies. We have seen that the nature and structure of LEAs in general is not conducive to policy formulation at curriculum level: elected members and education officers alike prefer not to be drawn into issues of curriculum. In many instances the emergence of curriculum issues that members and officers cannot (or will not) solve has been the precipitating factor in setting up a new advisory post. The device permits the LEA to manage policy issues as if they were technical ones and preserve the fiction that curriculum questions are delegated to heads and governors. Almost every adviser of any experience has encountered the problems that arise as a result, which can best be illustrated by examples.

First, in the years after the Plowden Report on primary education the great majority of junior schools consisted of rows of closed classrooms where children were instructed in rows of desks. The unanimous weight of professional opinion in initial training of teachers, among writers and the still small numbers of primary HMI and advisers, and many recently trained rank-and-file teachers, endorsed the Plowden advocacy of child-centred work using small groups and with access to specialized spaces (such as 'wet areas'). These principles required open-plan layouts, and many authorities designed and built new schools accordingly, much helped by DES models. Some heads and teachers simply had to adapt, but not a few buildings were reconverted into 'classrooms' by the resourceful placing of cupboards. Most, however, adapted with flair and skill, much helped by advisers who at that date included few primary specialists, had little or no formal endorsement, and found themselves often bitterly and unfairly attacked as the main source of the unwelcome innovation.

A second example concerns science: should it be organized up to 16 as three subjects (i.e. physics, chemistry and biology) or as two, such as physical science and biological science? In several LEAs the large majority of secondary heads have accepted the pressing need to move from three divisions to two (and thereby greatly increase the take-up), but have been prevented from gaining LEA adoption of this as policy by the resistance of a handful who, retaining three sciences, will be likely thereby to 'scoop the pool' of academic honours in the form of Oxbridge scholarships, access to higher education, and the consequent parental preferences and recruitment. The majority of heads, in more than one LEA, has begged the authority to impose the two-subject solution, but only one or two had acceded to the request when the issue was taken to a higher place by its endorsement in the DES Policy Statement in 1985. Even then, the conflict places a heavy burden on the LEA adviser who seeks adoption of the new policy without political endorsement by his authority.

A third example occurs in the developments in personal and social education already referred to, most of which seek to compensate for the narrowness of the examination-centred curriculum. In one LEA, two dozen schools had committed themselves to Active Tutorial Work; eight were deeply into programmes of guidance and personal counselling; others had evolved their own schemes where a cumulative record of each pupil's interests, achievements in and out of the classroom, and the like became the basis for a self-evaluation that was negotiated with and endorsed by the tutor. Careers education, too, was developing from giving information to providing a degree of guidance. All three developments reflected the same underlying need, and schools opted for one, other or even all of them without realizing that many others were on the same track. An adviser who sees this kind of pattern and acts to facilitate exchange of experience has to operate with little or no endorsement from the LEA – unless there is already in being a machinery for bringing curriculum issues before members.

As these examples suggest, it is easy for an adviser who seeks to facilitate curriculum renewal to imply a policy position on behalf of the LEA. This is why a machinery for contact with members has a significance for advisory staff that it did not have in the days of consensus educational politics. Relatively few LEAs provide for this: education committee members too often observe, after a rare discussion of a curricular issue, that it is pleasant to 'actually discuss education for once'. The responses to Circular 14/77 showed that in most LEAs the *de facto* source of curriculum policy is the advisory staff. Without political legitimation their position with each school has to be negotiated, and in some schools that will not be possible in any case – because the head will wish to know the policy status of the advice. My own professional experience happens to have been with an authority which developed a Curriculum Working Party drawn from all parties and serviced by a group of inspectors and officers. My inquiries in other LEAs suggest that there is abundant contact between advisory staff and members, but it is unofficial and selective. The particular mechanism I have worked with did not seek formal policy statements on major curriculum issues as a rule. It monitored the important DES and HMI documents, heard LEA inspector commentary on each, dealt with HMI inspection reports, and discussed the central issues of the day in an amicable dialogue. The inspectors learned to understand the layman's concerns and prejudices, the layman learned respect for the inspectors' knowledge, and a negotiated, shared outlook emerged which gave the whole inspectorate confidence. The particular instance is unlikely to be instantly suited to other authorities, but the principle involved is one of great significance for the advisory function.

7 *Working with governing bodies*

Only a small proportion of LEAs appear to require advisory staff to service governing bodies, and they limit each adviser to two or three. Advisers without experience of the work view it with anxiety, but those who have done it often find it valuable. It brings lay governors a broadened outlook which can in time transform community support for the service. It often forces the adviser into finding answers to governors' questions about aspects of the LEA's work he would otherwise know nothing of.

8 *Personal and professional support for teachers*

Teaching is a demanding occupation and creates every kind of stress. Even in the successful, promotion is attended by anxieties, and the continuance of success does not happen of itself. In the successful and unsuccessful alike there are needs for personal counsel about career development or relationships with colleagues, most of which teachers can recognize for themselves, so one part of the support function concerns responding to needs that teachers bring to the adviser. Very few advisers receive adequate training for this counselling role. When the problems that teachers bring are those of acute stress, depression and unrecognized mental illness, the omission of such training leaves advisers feeling exposed and uneasy. But it is entirely understandable that teachers should turn to the adviser in many such cases: he is a figure they know, without the involvement of the head teacher, accustomed to being very discreet.

As with policy advice, however, the passive stance is not enough. The typical adviser accepts an obligation to identify and where possible meet the professional development needs of 'his' teachers. In the example cited earlier of the new head with six specific questions for his district officer, the home economics inspector had chafed for years that no contact was permitted that would enable her to start alerting the teachers to the changes taking place about them. Many instances of this alerting occur in the context of discussing promotion, since the good applicant needs to know what expertise will be expected by the appointing school. Because schools tend to be self-isolating, this advice may often surprise. The marked rise in levels of academic qualification among applicants for senior management posts is a case in point: career advice by advisory staff has often become a discussion of appropriate advanced courses. But one of the rewards of advisory work is to see the professional progress achieved by teachers who have found career advice worth taking.

Teachers seeking individual advice will usually be those considering a move after three years in a first post and those aspiring to headship or deputy headship. The typical adviser also expects to find in his 'case load' a small additional element, the time-consuming and distressing category of teachers calling for support: those experiencing difficulty in the classroom. There is little evidence on the frequency of incompetence in teaching. An Inner London study (ILEA, 1984) gives a figure of between two and five per cent of teachers in inner-city secondaries, but my own survey (1984) found a tiny incidence in county and metropolitan district areas by comparison. The nature of the problem also varies widely, as do the solutions applied. Of the 30-odd cases I have known in any detail, only half of them in my own LEA, most suffered not from laziness but from trying too hard, and it was possible to help them through to competence. Of the 30, four left teaching, grateful to have been pushed to a decision they saw they should have taken long before. Two came to dismissal, one of them gaining reinstatement on appeal. The notion that teachers cannot be dismissed is a myth, but LEAs vary in their readiness to attempt it: only a majority have agreed disciplinary procedures in operation under the Employment Protection Act. The procedures entail a lengthy sequence which cannot even begin until the school and the adviser have tried many strategies of support – much observation of teaching and analytical discussion of it, visits to other schools, modifying room layout or timetable or the teaching materials. Most teachers in difficulty need help with class control and management, the mundane but essential ground rules of where to stand, how to be audible, how to use eye-contact, naming, silence, and all the tricks of the classroom trade that body forth the teacher's self-confidence. Most weak teachers know their weakness and respond to open discussion of it with relief, but going beyond this to serious improvement needs hard work from the teacher and often some toughness from the adviser – a toughness impossible to offer if the LEA has no willingness to convert the support, should it fail, into resolve. Weak teachers are also, contrary to some myths, not of any particular age-group, subject, or type of training, but many of them prove to have significant problems of health or family difficulty.

9 Curriculum development and innovation

In the era of expansion the notion of curriculum innovation had a certain self-consciousness about it, as if it was itself new. And indeed it was so. It is now possible to see the DES-funded research on advisers and innovation (Bolam *et al.*, 1978) as part of the process by which this function of advisory staff became domesticated and lost its self-conscious status. In the subsequent ten years advisers and inspectors generally have come to accept contact with and support for innovation as one more among the many tasks between which their time is divided – both to restrain unwise innovation and to foster well-designed schemes. It is a process that has been helped by a diminution in the number of curriculum development projects on the Schools Council model, where the essential vehicle was a body of published materials intended for use independently of the discussion, in-service training, in-school domestication and related processes that real innovation is now seen to need. Those adoptive projects that survive tend to be either taken up into the conventional world of published books and materials (whose purchasers may not be aware of the degree of innovation once embodied in them), or based on strong local support groups, often clustered round an LEA adviser who provides small but vital fragments of funding or access to courses and conferences (as in the case of 'Geography for the Young School Leaver').

At the same time the past five years have seen the rise of a new model of curriculum innovation, in the form of the Technical and Vocational Education Initiative (TVEI) and other schemes like it. In their organizational structure, two features combine: significant external funding is provided for the LEA, with very precise definitions or conditions, and the authority appoints an officer to supervise its spending. The TVEI Scheme was the first to combine these elements, which derive from practice in continental education and some branches of industry, but the later Education Support Grants scheme of the Department of Education and Science has adopted it. Indeed, where the TVEI contracts normally involve a single co-ordinator post, some of the ESG schemes go much further: that for records of achievement in one authority carries with it no less than four full-time posts led by a co-ordinator. Such schemes embrace the rural primary curriculum, primary science, mathematics at primary and secondary levels and other areas of curriculum. Since their leadership entails the appointment of at least 200 and possibly as many as 600 posts, many of them on permanent contracts, this new category of quasi-advisory staff is growing up without any serious thought being given to their collective impact on the LEAs or the advisory staff whose duties will (yet again) be extended to take in their supervision and deployment.

10   *Curriculum guidelines*

Many LEAs now have sets of substantial documents setting out the objectives that teachers seek to pursue in various curriculum fields. In the more progressive authorities the vast majority of primary schools already have their own documents for policy in language, mathematics, science and topic work. Numerous LEAs have similar documents for reference use in all primaries. A smaller number have complete curriculum coverage for the secondary school up to the age of 16, and many can offer very detailed guides in major subjects. In the case of English, there are at least 50 which run to more than 100 typescript pages, a large handful of them over three times that. It is often said that the value of such paper is to those who do the writing, but the best of them provide a massive support to teachers – in the case of English and drama, for example, the Avon LEA's guide is influential far beyond that authority's borders, and deservedly so, for it is direct, imaginative and realistic.

The typical process by which these documents are prepared is for the adviser concerned to select and convene a group of interested teachers. If he is wise, he will canvass the list of possible names with the locally influential leaders of teaching opinion and may possibly invite general applications. Some groups are funded by the LEA to have several working days on release for the work; some have to work in after-school sessions; some can operate in residential settings run by the LEA. The drafting will be by teacher members and sometimes the writing and editing will end in the hands of a teacher chairman, but the adviser will have to present the document to the chief education officer and, if he sees fit, to committee. Even if the committee approves it, however, such a document can have no more force in the English system than the assent of teachers will give it. This is in striking contrast to the status of the *Lehrplan* in most schools in West Germany, which is authorized by the Land parliament after a very similar process of development but becomes the basis of all teaching, assessment and textbook design. (It is also in contrast to the position of the *Programme* in French schools, which is frequently ignored and sometimes subverted.) Even so, many LEA guideline documents in England become strong influences, partly by offering expert guidance to teachers whose confidence in their own expertise may be limited, partly through their use in in-service training, where their professional and local provenance gives them great weight.

The management of time

This account of the ten tasks that fall to advisers has been unavoidably spare, and divides the work up with more tidiness than most advisers know. The tasks spill over into one another all the time: is talk with a teacher about a newly adopted reading scheme part of in-service training or teacher support? Such questions are also questions of definition which different advisers will answer in different ways, even in the same LEA team. The list is already long, at ten headings, but is not exhaustive, yet for many advisers the job embraces perhaps only five or six of them at most: it is the secondary general adviser who will most readily experience the fragmentation and constant movement from task to task that is inherent in so long a list of functions while being expected to constitute the LEA's mechanism for adjusting to change. More seriously, the available evidence suggests that LEAs in general, and their teams of advisers, are extraordinarily bad at setting priorities for advisory work. The results are predictable: teachers and schools perceive advisers in shadowy, fleeting fashion, and advisory staff themselves experience a grotesque degree of overloading.

The teacher's perception of advisory staff has become something of a favourite for master's degree dissertations – to list even a

portion of them would overweight this book's References. Their
findings are frequently of limited value, often because the
researcher has looked at one LEA without appreciating the
diversity of advisory practice, but they have in common three
points on which most or all studies agree. First, advisory staff have
much more complex and interesting functions than the researching
teachers appear to have expected prior to their research: the
classroom teacher's perspective, and even the head's view, is
limited to seeing a small fraction of the total. Secondly, although
only a few dissertations admit this explicitly, it is clear that even the
assembling of the perceptions of many teachers and heads will not
provide more than a very partial picture of what is usually called
'the adviser's role'. Thirdly, this literature is emphatic that advisory
staff in almost all LEAs are very seriously overworked, since
virtually every demand on their time and attention is felt by
teachers to receive less than its professional due.

   There is not very much solid research evidence about what
advisory staff experience themselves, but such as it is it abundantly
confirms the impression of serious overwork. In a short account of
a consultancy with what on internal evidence is Kirklees in 1982–4,
Small (1984) describes how a team of 15, whose quality he clearly
came to admire, was formally committed to an 11-session week for
a working year of 42 weeks, but was in practice working a
15-session week (a session being half a working day), or an average
of 650 sessions in a year against a contract that implied 440 sessions.
Small's account is interesting in another respect for showing how
the members of the team at the start of his consultancy had a set of
individual goals and priorities so divergent as to make the notion of
a 'team' the hollow euphemism it is in many other LEAs. From a
slightly earlier date, Williams' (1981) inquiry in the West Midlands
provides a scathing condemnation of the failure of the six LEAs
concerned for encouraging their advisory staffs to adopt a broad
function in the schools, and in the same breath both imposing
exacting and at times intolerable burdens in the office, and
expecting advisers to sustain the dual demand with wholly
inadequate levels of support staff. As a former education officer,
Williams comes from a tradition given to understatement, but on
the workload and working conditions of the 50-odd advisers he
surveys he concludes forcibly:

The enduring impression . . . emerged . . . of a cadre of inspectors in a stressful situation and experiencing increasing frustration over a self-perceived inability to achieve and maintain an appropriate balance between office and field work.   (p.19)

The incessant widening of the advisory brief is evident in Williams' fieldwork in 1981–2, when the flowering of the adviser-led in-service work was still not at its fullest and among subject advisers meets predictable resistance. But Williams observes:

As there had been little conscious, planned preparation or training for these duties and responsibilities, interest in and support for them was somewhat tepid . . . (*ibid.*)

It is a picture that the writer of one MA dissertation about teachers' experience of advisory support described with understandable asperity: 'The LEA office really seemed to treat the advisory staff as an administrative dustbin.'

My own survey[1] in 1984 selected LEAs which represented county, metropolitan district and London borough authorities, but avoided those surveyed either by Bolam's research in 1972–5 or by Williams. Interviews with the hundred or so officers and advisory staff confirmed the conviction borne of long service as an officer of NAIEA, that what Small and Williams reported in their observations was all too representative. If a trend could be perceived, it was that a small proportion of LEAs were appointing chief advisers who saw the problem and responded to it much as Small describes, building on a corporate process of establishing priorities and seeking to manage their advisory staffs. In those authorities where this pattern was present, and in only one case out of the five in question was there not a chief adviser, the real motive for seeking to manage something as inherently unmanageable as a group of inspectors was to protect them. For the inspectorate without positive management is exposed to a lethal combination: its members share a professional commitment which routinely becomes a low-status reluctance to say 'No' to a demand, while the demands for their highly prized knowledge and skills are unfiltered by any firm priorities. More than one LEA has advertized advisory vacancies with the point that the job-satisfactions lie in observing the achievements of others, but there is a fine line between that and a sustained, unadmitted loss of self-esteem. Advisers fight back by taking ever more strenuous refuge in their subject specialisms: they can see the threat in responding to 'general' tasks as clearly as anyone, but for many advisers in recent years their conscientiousness has brought only stress, breakdown and the early retirement of the allegedly valued skills.[2]

Many advisers and inspectors are reluctant to see their work discussed. Some, indeed, will resent its public exposure in these pages. At one level this reflects the sound perception that a low profile protects their discretionary time. The same low profile makes many advisers accept inappropriate working conditions without complaint. In the management of time they often prefer a muddle which leaves them some control to any more orderly priorities controlled by others or by the group. In consequence most of their clients and superiors regard advisory time as indefinitely extensible. Elected members in particular need to beware of assuming that advisory staff can be turned over to major new duties without effects elsewhere in the system that they had not anticipated and will not like. The self-reliant independence of advisers makes them ambivalent about being led, but Williams' 1981 study and my own more recent one found most respondents welcoming or seeking firmer leadership. The next chapter is not uncritical of HM Inspectorate, but HMI are very tightly managed. They also maintain a significantly higher proportion of their school–time hours in classrooms and derive much status from that. Local authorities might ponder these features in considering how and how far to guide their own inspectorates.

A further argument for positive management of advisory staffs in the face of their own reluctance to adopt any priorities but their own is the risk that advisers may become marginalized. The adviser whose skills are in very strong demand, so that he is quite unable to meet the calls on his time, lives with the knowledge that some callers will give up trying and make decisions he will later have to unscramble, e.g. in buying unsuitable microcomputers or robotics equipment. Most advisers, however, find their contacts with schools initiated by themselves, not the school, and find the response of 'their' subject teachers warmer than that of the head. Accordingly the subject adviser tends to identify with his or her subject, often at the expense of the general secondary expertise that the schools may need. Where the adviser is explicitly there to evaluate but there is no formal inspection procedure this alienation from the school can take in even the subject teachers as well. At the office end, the poor and often symbolically isolated housing of the advisory staff is reinforced by the common nexus with the administration, where the officer who calls in an adviser to solve a problem will usually be of lower formal (i.e. salary) but higher informal status. This turns the adviser into authority figure at the school and minion at the office, both of them roles he has sought to avoid.

However, let me stress once again the diversity of practice both between differing LEAs and over time within the same LEA. The uncertain definitions of advisory function that prevail in many LEAs make it peculiarly susceptible to short-term variation. But the unique LEA whose chief adviser requires one primary visit for every secondary one from all his subject advisers is as unusual as the one whose advisers spend more time on formal inspection than on everything else put together. So my endeavour to represent this diversity will not exempt me from claims in many LEAs that advisory life is not there as I describe it. Underlying that surface experience, nevertheless, are structural features of wider validity.[3]

Notes

1   The sample was constrained by time: only the month of July was available through study-leave from my LEA. It was necessary to study counties, metropolitan districts and Outer London boroughs, and it seemed wise to study one of each kind in some depth, adding sufficient other examples to provide a check on the representativeness of the set. In the event I visited officer and adviser colleagues at later times also, interviewing in all 88 advisers for an hour or more and 15 officers including three chief officers. The thrust of the interviewing was to establish the constraints on performance of the advisory function and the way those constraints interlocked with such features as self-image, local status, formal support at policy level, training, team management, etc. Having come to know numerous advisers during six years as an officer of NAIEA between 1976 and 1982, I was seeking an updating of impressions rather than any formal inquiry. The findings, necessarily impressionistic and tentative, are set out in Pearce (1984) and underpin the present text at numerous points. The impression that the largest urban authorities such as Sheffield, Manchester and Birmingham are different from the smaller metropolitan districts, in respects which parallel their differences from county LEAs, would bear closer study.

2   Advisory time can be studied by classifying its use in a simple matrix: all advisory work is either discretionary, i.e. done at the decision of the adviser, or non-discretionary, done because the adviser is required to serve (e.g. at an appointment interview). Advisory time is also disposed either in consultation or otherwise: the adviser may or may not be consulted about his diary. The matrix thus becomes:

	Discretionary	*Non-discretionary*
Timing consultative	A	B
Timing urgent or imposed	C	D

The individual adviser's position in the matrix reflects the teacher population he or she has to serve. In most county LEAs, for example, the adviser for languages, music, home economics, CDT or drama may have 250 or fewer, and will usually have most work in the A cell. The adviser for English, mathematics or science, working in the same size LEA unaided, may have to serve more than 500 and will have much more B–cell work. The general adviser will have most work in the C and D cells, and is able to keep some of it in the C cell by reason of the seniority that being a general adviser usually brings. It is the pressure of non–discretionary work involving urgent or fixed timing that makes the general adviser a shadowy figure to subject teachers.

3   As this book was being finished, the Department of Education and Science issued a draft statement on local authority advisory services. Its purpose was formally to keep a promise of such guidance given in an earlier document by the Secretary of State. Its intention was to give a description of the functions of advisory staffs that would bring them greater recognition and security. The statement's account of advisory work is broadly similar to that given in more detail in this book, and includes a number of indications of good practice. In particular, it states unambiguously the case for general adviser expertise and makes a strong bid for widening the scope of advisory work in further education. Unfortunately and perhaps inevitably, it does not come to terms with the resulting mismatch between these general advisory demands and a largely subject-based force: it is too hesitant about training, vague about manning levels and quite inadequate on the need, which is felt by advisers everywhere, for leadership by chief advisers who come from advisory experience. For all that, the draft statement is a landmark in the recognition of advisory work. It signals the complete rejection of the idea that HMI could ever be adequate to the needs of the LEAs on their own. To those who share even a small part of the view taken in this book about the place of the LEA the statement is very welcome indeed.

6
Her Majesty's Inspectorate

It is necessary to digress from my central argument. The accountability of a school to its maintaining LEA can be ensured by a number of methods. Some of these are virtual formalities, while others carry some genuine weight. Sadly, the head teacher's annual report to the governing body will usually be an example of the former kind. A full inspection, or a systematic review of some part of the school, will carry more weight, and if it can be followed up properly it may be quite powerful. Inspection by a local authority's advisory staff and full inspection by HMI may equally be weighty or ineffective: it depends on many aspects of the situation. But the ways in which LEA inspectorates operate are deeply influenced by the past and supposed present practice of HMI. Indeed, it is hardly excessive to say that for many or even most teachers the very word *inspection* denotes only the HMI model of full inspection to the exclusion of any other. The influence and status of HMI in the eyes of many teachers are out of all proportion to the frequency of real contact between them, as we shall see, but it is an influence that LEAs in general and their advisory staffs in particular have never been able to ignore.

The fear of duplication

HMI originated as assessors of what children knew and the state of school buildings, in order to certify entitlement to government grant. For over three decades until 1895 they reluctantly enforced the Revised Code which imposed payment by results on teachers, and after 1902 gained a powerful influence on local authorities, especially those many LEAs that had no school board inspectors to inherit. The principal vehicle of this influence was the full inspection, a ritual calculated to intimidate teachers and overawe the LEA. Whether these effects were intentional or not, there is abundant evidence of the withering contempt in which LEAs and their staffs were held by HMI before the First World War. The growth of LEA organizer staffs from 1916 onwards led the forces of 'retrenchment' in 1921 to question whether these staffs did not represent a duplication of the HMI service. The Board of Education's riposte, which appeared in book form as part of its Annual Report for 1922–3, referred to the aim of using the 368 HMI then in post to visit every school in the land once a year and to inspect it every three years. It was clearly hinted that this was a duty quite beyond the calibre of the 532 such officers employed by the LEAs – a charge that would more accurately have alluded to the latter's curriculum range, which covered largely those subjects viewed by HMI as of too low a status to merit coverage from London. Triennial inspection was to remain a pious hope: even in 1922 more than a quarter of elementary schools outside London had not been reported on for three years. Secondary schools gradually but steadily became more numerous, but the number of HMI was not adjusted accordingly. In the 1950s few grammar schools were inspected more than once in a decade. By 1968 we find the head of HM Inspectorate admitting to a Commons Select Committee that the aim of cyclical inspection had long been abandoned in favour of 'better' ways of monitoring the service: 'Some schools,' observed his recent predecessor, 'will never ever be inspected.' The notion of HM Inspectorate as the nation's chief guardian of educational standards lay in ruins, but it suited the dominant interests of the time, especially the teaching unions and the LEAs, quietly to overlook the fact.

HMI themselves had never been eager to claim any such status, although the inactivity of the LEAs in the matter thrust it upon them. The Board of Education was equally undeceived: its Permanent Secretary wrote in 1927 that 'We must look to examinations rather than inspection to check, test and secure the efficiency of public education'. It was a realism that endured, not least in restricting the establishment of HMI to only 400 in the 1950s and very little more during the era of expansion. The insistence of the teaching unions, the local education authorities and public opinion also endured, however, that HMI were the only proper guardian of standards. The fear of duplication recurred at Westminster in the late 1960s, by which time LEA advisory staffs had grown to more than 1,250 posts. The House of Commons Select Committee on Education and the Arts held lengthy hearings, at which the teaching unions and, more decisively, the LEA associations insisted that the work of HMI was indispensable and no duplication of local advisers and inspectors. The MPs do not appear to have explored why there should have been such unanimity, and concluded that the alleged duplication of functions did not exist. Not surprisingly in view of the uncritical consensus that enwrapped them at the Commons hearings, HMI let the number of full inspections of schools go on falling, so that shortly before the next study, made in 1981, only a score or so of secondary schools were being inspected each year.

The issue of duplication would not go away. The scrutinies of government expenditure conducted by Sir Derek Rayner from 1979 onwards included one of HM Inspectorate, which was conducted by a civil servant from the Department of Education and Science. The task was given woefully inadequate resources, so that the inquiry wholly failed to grasp the distinctive nature and scale of LEA advisory staffs. The present writer provided much of the evidence of the National Association of Inspectors and Educational Advisers to the inquiry, and found, just as the same body's witnesses to the Commons in 1968 had done, that the absence of any central bank of information about LEA practice was a serious handicap. The Rayner Scrutiny concluded (DES, 1983d) that the high level of trust enjoyed by HMI among all concerned parties justified their continued existence. It suggested that HMI should relate to LEA advisers rather as consultants relate to general practitioners, and neither group was pleased by so inept a parallel. The report recommended tighter management of HMI, and the result was a sharp increase in their workload. In consequence the ability of HMI to build a cumulative local knowledge of the schools is fatally undermined: without time to deploy at their own discretion HMI increasingly depend on LEA colleagues for information. This situation in turn destroys the rationale of the distribution of HMI in divisions and districts, since HMI generally can spend only a tiny proportion of their time in their 'home' areas.

The additional time obtained in this way was directed almost entirely into increased full inspections, but some of it went into writing. From about 1976 onwards HMI had adopted a higher public profile, asserting a more critical stance in their pamphlets and stressing their professional independence from the Department of Education and Science. The same period saw the LEA advisory staffs become more vocal and self-assured about their place in the scheme of things, and the question about duplication received its answer. The Department issued in 1983 a Policy Statement (DES, 1983e), which among many oblique statements declared plainly that to identify the special targets of HMI at any time 'one looks to the Government's policies and initiatives'. A parallel pamphlet (DES, 1983f) announced to parents and press that HMI inspection reports would henceforth be published. Turning HMI into an instrument of central policy once more (as one of several functions, be it said) certainly resolves the issue of duplication. HMI themselves continue to see their inspection programme, composed of regular visiting as well as full inspections, as a routine monitoring of the service. In the context of centralist policy and the more assertive stance of HMI themselves on curriculum and pedagogy, such a view is one that teachers and LEAs can hardly be expected to share: 'monitoring' is hardly as selective as that term suggests.

Recruitment and deployment

Virtually all HMI are experienced teachers, and their average age on appointment is about 40. Most will have been exceptional heads of primary schools or subject departments, some have been deputy heads or even heads of secondary schools, a handful are former LEA advisers, and a similar pattern can be found in the inspectorate for further education. HMI are formally civil servants, and their salaries are attractive. Retirement at 60 is obligatory and pension provision is good. Selection is by interview after public advertisement, and only a small minority is recruited by any sort of invitation, mainly to cover recondite fields. Most new HMI are now posted very quickly to an area where they cannot have been known as teachers, with no choice over the area and very little consideration for spouses in employment who cannot move (not a few HMI have to maintain a second home in consequence). The new recruit is provided with a 'mentor' who oversees his first year, providing a number of training tasks and reviewing early attempts at mainstream HMI tasks. The selection process for HMI is usually one of formal interview only, carried out in a fashion quite as amateurish as that castigated by research into selection of secondary heads (Morgan *et al.*, 1983). It is to be expected that some recruits prove ill-matched to such distinctive work: many HMI confess to having been quite unprepared for the scale of writing work involved, still less for the editorial ruthlessness with which their writing will be handled. The selectors do now make plain, however, the weight of the workload and the gravely unsocial nature of its hours.

The training of the new HMI is only partially lodged with the 'mentor'. The Inspectorate mounts in-service courses for itself and is beginning to make use of the growing range of training provision outside the educational world, as are some LEAs. For a group which undertakes a range of in-service courses for teachers HMI seem surprisingly reluctant to re-examine or provide training in in-service technique, so that while there are splendid exceptions, many DES short courses are still wedded to the lecture-and-discussion model of in-service work that many LEAs discarded long ago. Unlike most LEA advisory staff, HMI regularly join one another's course teams, across subject and specialist boundaries, as part of their own training.

The recruit, once posted, becomes available for the full list of assignments plotted centrally for all HMI one term at a time. Typically, HMI will find themselves assigned to inspections for as many as eight or ten weeks out of a twelve-week term, in as many different locations with completely different teams from week to week. Within a year or two the onerous duty of Reporting Inspector will occur once or twice a year, and for primary specialists more frequently. The remaining time will be available for getting to know schools on the HMI's local 'patch', which for a major subject may be no more than one substantial LEA but for a minority interest may be a large region or even more. Most such visits last for a single day, and the purposes may be wider than observing subject teaching. HMI may be looking at buildings, pastoral care, the use made of Section 11 funding for multi-ethnic education, specific projects such as those for Low Ability pupils or for TVEI. If subject teaching is involved, an HMI in English or mathematics may visit a large school where there are 12 or 14 teachers in the subject. He may visit six or seven in the day and be accused of selectiveness, or all 14 and be charged with superficiality! Such accusations are familiar: HMI and LEA inspectors alike become used to the harsh judgements of teachers who see only single aspects of a multi-faceted job. Many experienced inspectors can learn a great deal about a class and a teacher in ten minutes, but the length of a visit reflects what the inspector is seeking to know.

The meat of the term–time programme of most HMI lies in full inspections. HMI have always been aware that these visitations have a ripple effect – the centrality of the HMI model in this book's consideration of inspection is a case in point. The deployment of HMI into ever-changing teams is in practice constructive: so far from undermining the Inspectorate's unity, it fosters a common experience of collegial work under regularly changing leadership. The key feature of all HMI inspection work is the hidden but essential process of letting a collective judgement emerge. The individual HMI is repeatedly thrown into close proximity with colleagues who rely on his or her judgement in a specific subject field. When a full inspection is in process the inspectors begin to formulate their provisional perceptions from the start and test them out against each other's insights and evidence. They thus learn from experience to let their colleagues' perceptions inform and be qualified by their own, to allow the collective judgement to evolve and shift as the evidence accumulates. The effect is a constant training, a discipline in awareness of the whole curriculum that few other educationists acquire. Much the same holds for their writing of reports. This basing of judgement on a consensual reading of precisely factual and quotable evidence becomes habitual for all of HMI's work.

The HMI model of inspection

Teaching combines privacy, autonomy and immediacy to an unusual degree. No act infringes these three properties so completely as inspection by an unknown observer. Full formal inspection applies that infringement on the scale of the whole institution, and does so within a limited span of time. Such a ritualizing of inspection causes the maximum of anxiety to individual teachers, and the mythology that it was all very confidential and 'secret' has endured. It is only in recent years that teachers or heads have felt it proper to describe the experience of full inspection in the educational press. In spite of their anxiety, however, teachers rapidly discover that HMI are mostly personable and amiable, and may find it hard to grasp that these attributes may mask a rigorous professional. When HMI turn out to be critical some responses of schools and teachers are predictable enough – to seek another repository for the blame (especially the LEA, or its enforced limiting of resources), or to ignore it all and hope it will go away. Such responses are often strengthened by conspiracy-theory notions, quite groundless but held all the same, about why the school was selected for inspection. If HMI can be caught out in even the most minuscule error, the fact will in the psychology of the staffroom offset a thousand well-founded asperities.

It is small wonder, then, that HMI set out above all else to be factual and accurate in arriving at a secure judgement. The information sought in advance is extensive and detailed. The coherence between that information and the observations made in classrooms is consistently close. In view of the pace and intensiveness of the process, HMI have a good record for accuracy, and their judgements are soundly based in the observed facts of a school as well as consistent in stance from school to school. The criteria that constitute that stance are set out in the next section. The judgements made in a full inspection rest on a significant sample of the school's work. Thus, two HMI inspecting a ten–class primary school over four working days are likely to have fully half a working day with each class teacher from one or other inspector. In a secondary school of 1,800 pupils and 95 teachers, a team of 18 HMI engaged on a full inspection for 5 working days will usually observe some 400 or more of the 3,100–3,200 lessons in the timetabled week, or between 12 and 15 per cent of the total. Most teachers seem to find the judgements of HMI solidly factual and almost always fair-minded, if at times a touch opinionated and prone to concentrate on minutiae. At the end of the process the Reporting Inspector meets the head teacher, sometimes with the deputy head(s), outlines orally the team's findings, and invites correction of errors and misapprehensions.

The next stage of the process will see the Reporting Inspector invited to attend a meeting of the school's governors and give an oral outline of the developing report. The outline will have covert messages for the professionals present that most laymen will miss, but the head teacher will have heard them more explicitly (which is not to say he will have grasped their full import). Many a governing body has been well pleased with a report which in printed form has seemed unexpectedly critical. One reason is that the oral account only deals with subject departments by way of setting up examples, but another is that in reporting to governors HMI try not to undermine local confidence in a school. The final report is published anything from four to eight months later, to the school and LEA two weeks in advance of issue to the press. A full inspection report on a primary school and a 'dipstick' report on a secondary will usually be in the range between 1,200 and 2,000 words, while a full inspection report on a large secondary school can be anything up to ten times as long. The wise LEA will prepare a press release in 'printable copy' form that summarizes the report and comments on key points only, but some local newspapers will print a report on a primary school in full.

Publication of HMI inspection reports is still a novelty. The 1983 Policy Statement (DES, 1983è) said firmly that teachers, schools and LEAs were free to challenge the findings, and this has certainly happened, especially with the 'dipstick' form of inspection introduced in 1982. This uses a team of four or five HMI to review the general character but not the subject teaching in detail, in a visit which in a secondary school will last three or four days. It leads to an oral presentation to governors and a shorter form of report, and there is an analogous 'short form' for primary and middle schools. The leadership of the Inspectorate appears to believe that this procedure helps HMI very much by greatly increasing the number of schools inspected. It appears unaware that it also damages HMI greatly: the use of a small team alienates the teachers of subjects not represented in the team, for whom HMI expert in other subjects are by definition not competent to observe and judge them: teachers do not see any compensating gain in the team's penetration of the school's character and merits. This very fact testifies to the grip of the conventional HMI model of full inspection as something covering every subject with a specialist: any other practice is apt to be rejected as third-rate, and the school feels it has been undervalued.

The dual model raises a further problem by making teachers dubious about why their school has been selected for either kind of inspection. HMI repeat ad nauseam that selection is made by a computer, unaware that teachers now know that that only posts the question further back: who programs what sort of criteria into the computer? The Policy Statement admits that a few inspections are made in special circumstances, and teachers in all schools are apt to look for reasons that might 'explain' a given selection. The truth is more prosaic: the computer is programmed to provide coverage of a representative range of school types, locations, sizes and other variables obvious even to non-statisticians. But anxiety makes the prosaic less credible than it needs to be. Teachers and LEAs alike will know, only too well, whether their inspection is a special case: if they are not sure, they can assume it is all routine, and they may as well settle for minimizing the stress on themselves and the tedium for HMI.

Does full inspection have any effect? When reports were kept confidential it was not uncommon for a head teacher to allow a report to be seen only by departmental heads, who saw only the sections concerning their departments. This is no longer possible: the total ethos and curricular performance of a school now have to be faced by everyone in it, and the LEA has obligations about follow-up less easily evaded and much more easily enforced. At the other end of the scale, firm approval from HMI can bring marked and lasting benefit to a department's morale, especially if HMI can so far lay aside their studied moderation as to confirm their praise in print. Too often, however, HMI reports in the past have fallen into the trap of citing rather trivial complaints which prove more memorable than their carefully phrased judgements. Thus, a school's craft teaching was criticized severely as narrowly based in wood- and metal-working skills; two years later the position was unchanged, but everyone who was asked about the comments of HMI could remember the broken trip-switch they had found on a lathe and the broken pair of goggles. Even where a published report is severe about boring and undemanding repetitious classwork, the local authority may be unable to do much about it if the school staff and the head are disposed to leave matters as they are – and neither the governing body nor HMI themselves will be able to do anything effective about it. The LEA's inspectors will also be helpless unless they carry a quite unusual degree of political endorsement. At its best, full inspection by HMI can have valuable but limited effects on a school, but in the absence of other major factors for change such effects will be the exception rather than the rule. Paradoxically, the effect on other schools may be as great, and we shall see why in the next section.

The expectations of HMI

It is reasonable for professionals engaged in assessing the work of other professionals to make their criteria explicit. Until the decision to publish their reports, HMI had never done this. The shared values of teaching were assumed to suffice. Since mid-1983, however, reports have appeared at a rate of over 200 establishments a year, and HMI have issued a series of summaries of findings (beginning with DES, 1984b, 1984d). Analysis of numerous individual reports suggests that the effectual criteria employed by HMI are six in number:

1   *Plant*   HMI observe the adequacy-for-purpose and condition of educational buildings and grounds in relation to the demands made on them by curriculum and the needs of pupils, with the well-justified belief that shabby buildings invite their users to treat them shabbily.

2   *Match*   HMI are closely interested in how well the work that pupils are asked to do is aligned to their aptitudes and abilities (in all their variety). In particular HMI look for evidence of firm expectations by teachers at both ends of the range of ability as well as across it.

3   *Pedagogy*   HMI expect the school to engage its pupils, at all levels of age and ability, as active participants in their own learning. They are relatively uninterested in teaching in any performative sense: their concern is with what the pupil does rather than the teacher. They look for learning that is active, oral and questioning rather than passive, silent and receptive. They seek real problem-solving in place of token exercises and formal drills.

These priorities rest on large-scale observation of pupil performance: HMI have seen quite enough good work of this order to be confident that the demand they make is reasonable.

4 *Progression* HMI seek patterns of work planned to yield a real movement, that the pupil is regularly made aware of, from week to week, term to term, year to year, school to school, in an overall curriculum where balance and breadth make the progression found in each area coherent and ordered.

5 *Professionalism* HMI expect teachers to do the jobs they are appointed to do: they are impatient of heads of department who do not manage or lead, appointments carrying emolument but not duties, status but not responsibility, structure but not meaning.

6 *Climate* HMI have very sensitive antennae for the quality of relationships in school, between pupil and pupil, teacher and teacher, as well as between teacher and class. They view a supportive and reassuring climate of good order as significant, not only for the personal and social education of the pupils, but for the delivery of an effective curriculum.

Each of these headings is suceptible of an essay in itself, but what matters about them is the way in which they interact. If there is a dominant theme in HMI reports it is in the relationship between Match and Pedagogy: the outstanding weakness identified in hundreds of reports concerns the use of undifferentiated, whole-class methods and materials with classes set up and defined as mixed-ability. This practice must fail the test of Match for the most and least able alike ('teaching for the middle'), and because whole-class methods lead to passivity they must also fail the test of Pedagogy. While more primary schools appear to pass these tests than other kinds, a proportion do not, and a majority of middle and a large majority of secondary schools fall short of what HMI know, from repeated observation, that teachers can achieve. It is in disseminating these criteria, which carry the stamp of HMI's repute and authority but can readily be endorsed by their own professional staff, that LEAs are in a position to give the practice of inspection by HMI immeasurably greater influence on the schools HMI do not inspect that on those they do assess. It is a radical as well as a rigorous educational stance that HMI propound, for all types of school.

Her Majesty's pamphleteers

The experience of repeated observation of classrooms leads any inspector into generalizing strategies. LEA advisory staff will often find it easier to address widespread bad practice by setting up local in-service courses that will canvass better approaches. This option is not open to HMI on any substantial scale, but they have developed their inspectorial findings in pamphlet form to excellent effect. If HMI are oblique and opaque in many of their inspection reports, their pamphlets can be astonishingly direct. The 1984 paper *Slow Learning and Less Successful Pupils in Secondary Schools* is a forceful indictment of initial training and typical staffroom habits of thought. The easy slide from faulty planning of work or careless record keeping into the facile labelling of children as 'not good at my subject' is exposed firmly as the slipshod and unprofessional fallacy it is. Other pamphlets have the same quirky skill of saying very severe things in a wholly unexceptionable fashion, and in a compressed brevity that all writers can envy. *Girls and Science* (DES, 1980b), *Ten Good Schools* (DES, 1982a) and *Music in Primary Schools* (DES, 1983a) are not the cautious and conservative stuff of officialdom. In many such papers HMI can be seen openly supporting the innovative radical against what is obliquely identified as a deadening conservatism, and inviting others into similar adventurous initiatives. The use of professional papers issued free with very wide circulation has been brought to a fine art by the Further Education Unit, often with striking innovative effect, and HMI have done the same with some of their pamphlets. Others, however, and these include most of the more penetrating papers of value to in-service courses, have been published through HMSO with little publicity and their pricing has seriously restricted their influence. There is some contrast between such writing and inspection reports, where a report that may strike a head teacher as amiably approving can turn out to refer to 'narrow' and 'limited' approaches as many as 20 times (and similarly for seemingly gloomy ones): if inspection reports seem written in semi-code, the pamphlets are very much 'in clear'.

HMI pamplets, then, embody a strong advocacy of innovation and updating of practice. They can do this with a clear conscience: HMI are not asking schools to do what they do not do themselves. Many individual HMI have been recruited specifically for their quality as innovative teachers; the service is not one without its characters; its recruitment and promotion of women have been greatly strengthened in recent years; a proportion of their DES short courses have shown flair and imagination. And the whole impact of HM Inspectorate has been enormously increased by the conduct of surveys. In the mid–1970s HMI began planning their inspection of schools on the basis of statistically controlled sampling of schools, and added to their normal inspection methods the use of systematic data–collection methods and data–processing. In each main type of school they also carried through a programme of survey visits that were not designed as full inspections but yielded information and judgements that contributed to the surveys. The outcome was a series of published Survey documents of weight and influence – *Primary Education in England* (1978), *Aspects of Secondary Education* (1979), middle schools (1983) and first schools (1982). These papers provided many head teachers with a basis for reviewing the practice in their own schools, and many LEA advisers and inspectors followed up this use of them energetically. The influence of the surveys has varied: on primary schools, especially in the science field, the impact of the relevant Survey was dramatic, while the Secondary Survey was little read. The surveys collectively show the same search for quality, lucid illustration of examples, undogmatic readiness to see educational quality in strange guises, and insistence on solid factuality of judgement. They are among the best examples of the range and depth of HMI's work in writing for publication, an important and growing part of their functioning.

Limitations of the HMI model

The established regard for HM Inspectorate's way of conducting full inspections is apt to overlook some limitations:

1   The criteria used by HMI are traceable, as we have seen, but for any given school facing an inspection they are likely to be

inexplicit or even quite mysterious: relatively few schools or LEAs have found out and disseminated the available information.

2   Although inspection reports and publications alike show HMI collectively as having an identifiable stance on most key educational issues, there is a careful avoidance of any formal commitment or 'policy'. The individual HMI is quite free to express an individual view, or dissent from the stance of an HMI publication. And HMI are under no obligation of any sort to take cognizance of advice that teachers may have received from their LEA or its advisers.

3   Whether they constitute a profession or not, teachers are experienced and self-reliant people: influencing their practice for the better calls for respect and time. The pressures of a one-week inspection are not conducive to this. Teachers repeatedly report the experience of finding that the brief talk they had with the inspector on (say) Day 2 was not followed up by the 'proper' talk they expected but proved to be the only contact they had. Relatively few of the full inspections by HMI that have provided the experience culled for this book have escaped the problem of teachers finding the printed report very different from what they thought had been said to them at the time by HMI.

4   A one-week inspection is a snapshot of a dynamic institution, and is inherently likely to underrate the importance of change already being generated. Many schools have reported HMI as recording short-term and temporary problems as if they were permanent features, and LEA advisers have become used to finding minor HMI complaints corrected or outdated before the report appears. This limitation may well be a necessary price to be paid for the fearless candour of HMI about inadequate buildings and funding.

5   HMI have to leave follow-up to others – but those others are not party to HMI's judgements, still less to their criteria. There is regular regional contact between subject HMI and their adviser colleagues, but it is amiable collegial talk rather than the serious debate of criteria, as a rule. Nor has the occasional discussion led anywhere to proposals to include an LEA inspector as an observing

member of an HMI full inspection team or to arrange the kind of posting to an LEA that is becoming known to DES officers.

6 The full inspection activity of HMI is only part of their duties, but it stamps the work of HMI, in the eyes of the schools, as inherently distant and intermittent, very much a come-and-go service, the results of which are on offer on a take-it-or-leave-it basis. This devalues the influence of the whole service. The Department of Education and Science has sought to find a way round this problem, by requiring the LEA to report within three months what it proposes to do about each inspection report. LEAs have responded very variously: I have seen responses running to a 70-page schematic presentation of each and every comment made on a small secondary school, point by point, with the LEA's existing position on each point in a second column and its future intention in a third. At the other extreme another LEA has responded about a very large secondary comprehensive in a letter of less than 300 words. (The DES has not seen fit to guide LEAs on which kind of response is appropriate, which suggests that its officers need a better understanding of the tight manpower position in LEA offices. Such secretiveness over what is wanted is no longer characteristic of HMI, but HM Inspectorate and the Department it serves are distinct bodies with different practices in many respects.)

The decision to publish HMI inspection reports was taken unilaterally: any consultations involved were limited and unpublicized. Perhaps as a result, the decision missed an opportunity. In those LEAs where inspection occurs on a regular basis, it is not uncommon for the reporting inspector and relevant education officers to sit down with the staff of the inspected school after the report has been published, to discuss where the school goes in the immediate future and what action might be available or proposed through the LEA. This discussion almost always improves the teachers' insight into the report and the inspectors' commentary, and enables the inspector to undermine the inevitable tendency of some teachers to misread or misrepresent a report by selective quotation. It is an example which would serve HMI well, and in the present state of teaching opinion and morale would be no more than a fair parallel to the presentation to governors.

The advisory function

Teachers and heads are often frustrated by the habit of HMI, when asked for advice, of referring them to the LEA. This reflects the fact that HMI see themselves as advisers not to schools but to the Secretary of State. With the run–down of DES courses to relatively small numbers, the advisory function of HMI is now exercised largely through their publications, and the ability of HM Inspectorate to recruit considerable intellectual and academic expertise makes for some impressive work. The problem is to bring teachers to read it.

HMI have significant advisory functions at LEA level. Each LEA is assigned a pair of District Inspectors, one for schools and one for further education, whose duty is to monitor what his colleagues find in the authority's schools and to meet the chief education officer at intervals for discussion. In the larger LEAs such discussion will also occur at area level with officers and advisers. The LEA response is variable: in one the chief officer will have his chief inspector with him, while in another the local advisory staff may find themselves taken to task on the basis of inferences from such conversations. The interlocking of HMI perceptions and local advisory observations of the same range of schools has never developed as fully as it might have done, because HMI have felt a constraint (in their own terms a very proper one) over being too closely engaged with local colleagues. The overwork that now besets HMI means that they can now no longer provide much information or first-hand knowledge of local schools, which in the past LEAs found very valuable, and the provision of information now tends to move in the other direction. The old reliance on HMI in this context no doubt provided plenty of CEOs with any excuse they may have needed to restrict the numbers of their own advisory staffs, and its cessation is one cause of the steady rise in advisory appointments in LEAs undergoing intense financial stringency.

One part of the growth in the workload of HMI relates to the growth of interest and funding in curricular areas not previously of much concern, or in aspects of provision that cut across local authority boundaries and may not be of very much significance in the scheme of things in a single LEA. Examples include the provision for under-fives in the rural counties and the need to explore various ways of relating nursery provision to parental support. Analogous areas of study for HMI include the use made of Home Office grants for the education of what the relevant legislation called immigrant children; the integration of children with special educational needs in ordinary classes; DES-funded projects like that for pupils of low ability; the use made of special grants for advisory-teacher support for rural primaries, primary science, mathematics and the like; the TVEI scheme, and so on. These developments are apt to show a good deal of variation from one local example to another, and the cross-fertilization that HMI can provide is at least as useful as their evaluation. Each of these and a number of similar schemes will have been filtered through HM Inspectors' advice at the time of their planning, and some of them owe their existence to in-house initiatives from HMI who have identified a need that can be met in no other way. This is a type of advisory function with which the LEA adviser is familiar.

HMI act as an advisory service, however, chiefly to the Secretary of State and his Department. Policy proposals go through the typical civil service process of securing expert comment, and the influence of HMI is perceptible in some cases quite clearly. For example, the sophisticated calculation of the length of full-time in-service courses in recent annual In-Service Training Grant schemes reflects very well-informed judgement about what can be done for head teachers or their deputies in 20 days, for science teachers in 35, and mathematics leaders in 30. The advice of HMI is not accepted invariably, and is sometimes sought alongside that of other parties: it is hard to see the retrograde scheme for Merit and Distinction certificates in GCSE as having survived a commentary from HMI. In many respects the advice of HMI is secured not by formal consultation but by assigning inspectors to other bodies and tasks: validation of courses for training of teachers and selection of bids for the TVEI scheme are examples. HMI are also the Department's (and thus the Secretary of State's) field service: as the Rayner Scrutiny report spells out, ministers, MPs and the various branches of the DES generate large numbers of questions, requests for information, and advice on problems or complaints. HMI are expected to provide expertly written responses based on detailed local knowledge at very short notice and in the face of all the other pressures on their time. Full written records of every visit, kept in good office order, become one of the basic values of the HMI's job.

Assessing the local service

At the end of the 1970s the break-up of the Inner London Education Authority was firmly on the political agenda. HMI were instructed to review their coverage of ILEA, fill a few gaps in the visiting of the previous four or five years, and assemble the evidence in a single report on the Authority's educational provision. When it received the report, ILEA insisted that it be published (DES, 1980a). It was severe about many aspects of the schools, especially secondary, and on some aspects of the authority's management, but it did not provide the opponents of ILEA's continued existence with the ammunition they hoped for. Even so, ILEA's head teachers and officers collectively did not respond very positively: it fell to a later period to attempt an adequate assessment of ILEA's problems, and the Hargreaves Report (ILEA, 1984) is an impressive demonstration of the merits of self-evaluation over external inspection. Outside the capital the report by HMI caused some annoyance by its assumption that an LEA's inspection and advisory staff is only doing its job if it is inspecting: non-HMI readers could not be expected to know that for HMI the term 'inspection' covers all school visiting as well as the conduct of formal inspections. LEA advisory staff for their part have been reluctant to admit that they too are inspecting whenever they are in a school on whatever specific business. The ILEA report of 1980, however, was to have a wider effect.

The DES Policy Statement on HMI (DES, 1983e) endorsed the use of HMI to provide a selective professional audit of provision in an LEA – what political leaders called 'giving an LEA a full inspection', although so misleading a phrase is not one to make HMI very happy. LEAs as diverse as Dudley, Wiltshire, Haringay and Norfolk have been assessed since then, and the practice is continuing, covering some three or four authorities each year. HMI found it unwise to base their procedure on a calling up of inspections made over the previous few years: the number of full inspections was extended for a short period to gain a current picture, and the number of HMI concentrated in one LEA for a few months is quite large. The ensuing report is apt to be short and pithy, rehearsing the financial provision, the general quality of schools, and the nature of the relationships between schools and officers. Most such reports have alluded to in-service training and to the local inspectorates, but HMI appear to have become less dogmatic about both of these as they have learned more about the subtler variations. Some of these surveys obviously run into difficulties: the reports take anything from under one year to over two years to appear, and even then they do not say very much that local political and educational leaders do not know. HMI can and do show a splendid disregard for local political factors: Norfolk was castigated for having the most under-manned advisory staff in England, while on the London borough of Haringay the report was severe about a number of projects dear to the local political leadership. All seven of the reports issued so far judge on the basis of evidence in classrooms, giving formal policies short shrift if they do not emerge in action. It is too early, however, to see what criteria, if any, HMI employ above the level of the individual school.

Such professional audit is clearly useful, and publication is a necessary part of showing that the accountability of LEAs is in place and working. The question to be asked is whether HMI alone are the right body to conduct it. Only a handful of HMI have served as LEA advisers or education officers. Nothing in HMI's experience equips them to assess the organizational cultures of LEAs: they know nothing of how LEAs function and little of their relationships with schools. It may be that such evaluations should be conducted jointly with the Audit Commission, which recruits senior LEA officers on secondment and already carries at least as much weight with local authorities as will the attempts of HMI to judge LEAs.

HMI and LEA advisory staffs

There has always been a marked difference in status between HMI and their local counterparts. The difference in salary is minor compared with the difference in the perceptions of heads and teachers, but such contrasts are now rapidly diminishing. Some of the reasons have already been explored: the workload, enforced mobility and suitcase living of HMI make the job less attractive now that the LEA alternative, where it is politically secure, is available. Teachers are coming to see the LEA adviser's link with resources as potentially more rewarding. The growth of LEA advisory staffs to professional standing and coherence is closely related to the occupation of more and more advisory posts by teachers with comprehensive experience, and to other factors explored in Chapter 1. This kind of change is uneven and some attitudes change only slowly: there are still a few HMI who view their LEA colleagues with ill–disguised contempt, and some LEA staff treat HMI with an undue deference.

The diminishing contrast between the two services does not extend, however, to the way their time is deployed. There are 380 sessions in the statutory school year. Most HMI expect to spend upwards of 250 of these in classrooms, and even those with 'office' or headquarters functions will put in a substantial number. An exhaustive study of the available evidence about LEA advisers (which includes Williams (1981), Small (1984), and private communications from 15 LEAs and three subject associations of advisers) suggests that fewer than half the LEA advisory force would achieve 250 sessions in classrooms and many would regard 150 sessions (or four a week) as something of an achievement. They would claim, with some justice, that the now massive scale of advisory involvement in local in–service training gives advisers a depth and frequency of contact with teachers that makes figures about classroom presence misleadingly incomplete. At the same time, a new chief adviser coming to a team from outside will do well to secure a monitoring of his team's use of time. As with HMI, time in classrooms can be measured against the sessions of the school year or against the total hours the inspector works, and the two yardsticks are very different.

The principal difference, then, between HMI and LEA advisory staffs lies in their use of time and the way that use is managed. Few things are more difficult for most LEA teams than arranging dates when all the members are available. It is contrary to the tradition and practice of a large majority of LEA teams to impose anything like the diary commitments that HMI take for granted. If HMI are no longer to be relied on for routine coverage, even at a superficial level, it might be supposed that LEAs have now undertaken to ensure it in a reasonably systematic way. It is in reality not yet possible in a majority of LEAs to assume sound, routine advisory coverage of the schools and believe that every school has received appropriate visitation at known frequencies. Nothing has been done by central government to persuade local authorities to provide this coverage in place of HMI (who ceased to provide it half a century ago). The reluctance of central government to insist on such coverage has made the need for it into a victim of the localism and self-interest of leading members and chief officers in the LEAs, who naturally resist being told how to spend their money, especially when the result would modify their own freedom of action. It is surely time there was a basic code of practice, negotiated between HMI, DES and chief officers and chief advisers of LEAs. The alternative would be for the Department to follow the example of the Department of Employment, which issues a detailed guide on the recruitment, training, deployment and functions of local careers services.

The consolidation of LEA advisory services is incomplete. In view of the financial constraints of most of the period since the 1974 reorganization this is understandable. Their relationship with the schools on the one hand, with HMI on the other, has been occasionally confused by changes affecting HMI and their relationship with the schools. HMI attach great weight to their 'independence'. What this refers to is their integrity of professional judgement. Thus, although the Secretary of State can decide not to publish an HMI document, by tradition he cannot amend a word of it. The idea that 'independence' refers to the role of HMI *vis-à-vis* government policy is a misapprehension, but it has left many head teachers and advisers baffled by the apparent aggressiveness of many of HMI's educational demands. HMI are indeed independent in speaking as they find; they are anything but that in being instruments of policy. The strong tone of much HMI writing has left many LEA advisers feeling that their own calculated supportiveness is becoming undervalued, and not enough is said or done to convey the message that the two are properly and necessarily complementary. Where the LEA has accepted the inevitable arithmetic – HMI in very recent years have been giving full inspections to some 200 schools each year out of a total over 34 *thousand* maintained schools – its advisory staff has found from bitter experience that full inspection is an exceedingly heavy user of time. The search for alternative procedures such as guided self-evaluation is not simply an easy way out: too much other good work was at stake for cyclical inspection to be an automatic option. We shall explore these alternatives in the next chapter.

The final consideration concerns the effect on political and professional opinion of the existence of HM Inspectorate. HMI perform a very complex and demanding set of tasks to a remarkably high level of achievement: that is not in question. From the 1950s onwards, however, the actual contact of HMI with teachers and schools, whether in full inspections or otherwise, was infinitesimally smaller than almost all LEA councillors and chief officers believed. As the service expanded, the disproportion between reality and myth grew ever wider. But the layman's faith in HMI, the natural antipathy of the teaching unions to inspection, and the reluctance of LEAs to incur additional spending all worked in the same direction, to restrict the development of local inspectorates which would do the work most people thought HMI were doing. This process operates to this day. Where it was overcome and local inspectorates did develop properly, the mystique attaching to HMI discouraged local teams from formal inspection, even where they bore the historic title of inspector. Local advisers and inspectors naturally sought legitimacy in the role of teacher's supporter and friend. It is hard to escape the conclusion that for many decades the quality, standing and supposed availability of national inspectors has been, all unintended, the main barrier to the development and standing of local ones.

7
Models of Inspection and Review

The purpose of this chapter is to outline the alternatives to the HMI model of full inspection that have been evolved by LEAs and schools. Practice is very diverse, so that an exhaustive list is not possible. We are concerned here only with activity that involves more than the single teacher and that involves some representative(s) of the LEA. On the basis that effective accountability has to be seen to be in operation, self-evaluation conducted entirely within a school does not qualify for this discussion. The advisers involved will usually be in groups, but may be used singly in a consultant capacity. There are five essential terms involved:

Inspection   a study of a school or part of one, within a defined period, by officers appointed for the purpose (i.e. not seconded teachers) who report to the LEA or its chief officer.

Review   a similar study, usually confined to a department or section, with the reporting addressed to the teachers and the head.

Self-evaluation   a systematic review of a school by its own teachers, with or without participation by LEA officers or advisers, leading to reporting, formally or informally, to the authority.

Appraisal   periodic conduct of formal discussion of performance with the employee's immediate superior, leading to an agreed evaluation of the period in question and setting of goals for the ensuing period.

Assessment   the use of the machinery of appraisal for the purpose of determining entitlement to salary additions or promotion.

These definitions are offered for convenience to chart the discussion, but some caution is necessary: LEAs and teachers freely use 'inspection' as a label for what is here called review; 'self–evaluation' is widely used as an approving label for almost any procedure which leaves out or excludes LEA officers or advisers; much of the public debate about appraisal rests on a conflation between what are here distinguished as appraisal and assessment. In principle it is possible for all five to be operated so that Sockett's two requirements are met: my definitions do not imply approval or disapproval of any of them. The mythologies of staffrooms identify full inspection as an event, dramatic or even traumatic in the recollection. Appraisal is also an event in the sense that any one teacher will usually experience an appraisal interview once a year. Review, however, may not be so easily identifiable in terms of time: some LEAs consciously set out to maintain continuous review by planning where their groups of inspectors visit, but to avoid giving the school the feeling of a timed inspection by distributing a given school's subject or faculty review visits over a period of two years. These variations reflect the individualism of LEA practice and the compromises that arise from local consultation. Almost the only things they have in common are a not always conscious desire to escape from the damaging aspects of the HMI model and a wish to ensure that teachers regard them as fair.

What inspection is for

More baldly than most strategies of accountability, inspection matches Sockett's two requirements with apparent simplicity: to maintain and improve quality and to show that this is being done. However, improving the establishment being inspected makes four requirements:

1   The criteria employed by the inspectors must be explicit or already shared by the school.
2   Inspectors and inspected must believe by the end of the period that their accountability obligations (e.g. to pupils and to one another) are reciprocal.
3   The inspected must accept the fairness and accuracy of the

inspectors.
4   The remediative action found necessary must be inescapable.

We have seen that of these requirements, in the case of HMI, the first is problematic and the fourth unattainable. The publication of inspection reports certainly persuades laymen that improvement of quality is taking place, but there must be some doubt about the reality behind this acceptance. In the hands of an LEA inspectorate, the doubt about criteria remains, since few LEAs have given any public indication of what they think a good school should be like or of the more specific criteria in their inspectors' minds. A local team, however, can hardly escape the remediative action arising from its reports, and similar considerations affect the other branches of the authority. If the LEA inspectorate has publicly described a science block as disastrous for teaching, the LEA's Sites and Buildings branch can hardly ignore the matter entirely.

It has been a favourite argument of teaching unions that the LEA inspector cannot be 'independent' or 'objective'. We have seen the sense in which HMI can properly claim independence, and the position of the LEA adviser is identical: if the intention is to impugn the adviser's integrity, the teachers represented by unions that have advanced the argument do not appear to share such suspicions. Some residual claims are made that the local inspector will inspect in the light of mere personal foibles. The argument applies just as much to teachers and can be set aside as factitious or brought into the open and tested by proper debate. Teachers more often argue that inspecting and advising on promotion ought to be separate functions. At bottom this rejects the authority's right to manage, and most laymen would ask whether promotion advice could come from a better source than one who has seen the candidate teach – and if he has seen only some of the applicants teaching he has to say so: no system of promotion is perfect and any system produces disappointed aspirants.

A more serious argument alleges that local inspection will favour teaching that adopts the advice given when the inspector is not inspecting. This, it is implied, makes him judge and prosecutor in the same case. If the LEA employs the inspector to improve curricular quality, he must advocate the promotion of those who adopt his advice, other things being equal. But the approval of those who follow advice also characterizes HMI, whom nobody criticizes for it. Head teachers too face this conflict, and can often be reluctant to insist on observing and inspecting before reaching judgements about their own staff, while being quick to attack inspectors who appear to do the same. In any case, inspectors and heads alike rest on a vital, extensive, if unexamined consensus about what constitutes good educational practice, and arguments like these point above all to the need to examine and discuss it properly.

Inspection in LEA practice

Those LEAs that have adopted the HMI model have so far been a minority, and have not always perceived how the local context modifies it. Unlike most LEA inspectors, HMI make no formal recommendations, few LEA reports are ever published, and the inspectors have to live and work with the inspected teachers afterwards, as well as deal with the deficiencies they have found. These facts enforce a directness of style on LEA reports very far from the obliqueness of HMI-speak. Thus, in a primary school report, HMI may refer to 'the need to pay more regard to co-ordination of the work of the various classes . . . and . . . support the head teacher's search for coherence in each subject area'. A typical LEA report would describe things more directly:

> The staff prefer to work as separate individuals and have resisted the head teacher's efforts to weld them into a team. The responsibilities attaching to each post on the staff should be reviewed and their holders required, in future, to co-ordinate the work of their colleagues accordingly . . .

To those who can decode HMI-speak the message is substantially the same, but the difference in tone is characteristic. Naturally enough, HMI tend to view the LEA style as clumsy, while the HMI style sometimes strikes LEA officers as positively arcane.

LEA practice of full inspection is frequently different from the HMI model in not requiring the inspectors to be present for the same defined period. This is often intended as a way of reducing the strain on the school, a view that most heads and teachers dismiss as naive, or as a way of reducing the tendency to window-dressing, a view that underestimates totally the inspectors' normal capacity to penetrate the surfaces of what they are observing. Some LEA practice attempts to conduct inspection without putting anyone in charge of the team or the process. In reality any formal inspection compels prior decisions on four key issues, and they in turn dictate that someone needs to be in charge:

1   Are the lessons to be observed selected by individual subject inspectors, or is a timetable necessary to ensure a reasonable coverage of classes, ages, teachers etc?

2   Should the non-classroom aspects of a school's life and work be left to the team's sensitivity or assigned in specific parcels to individuals to look at?

3   Is the reporting process one of asking each inspector to go away and write his piece to a deadline some time ahead, or should it involve discussing provisional impressions each day with a view to developing a coherent view and an early report?

4   Is the team to register and report serious problems (e.g. safety risks or teacher incapability) as part of the inspection process or through separate action?

In all four issues the experienced inspectorate will have discovered that the second alternative in each case is much to be preferred. For example, an inspection may uncover an ineffective teacher. It is not possible to meet the problem in an inspection report: that would infringe the teacher's rights and would prejudice duly constituted disciplinary proceedings. But what inspection and such proceedings have in common is the principle of disclosure: inspectors habitually assert the rule that statements *about* a teacher must also be made *to* that teacher. This applies to inspections both at the level of the individual teacher and at the levels of department and school, which explains why a reporting inspector (like HMI) goes over the whole draft of a report with the head teacher. It both prevents the report being subsequently discredited by inaccuracy and serves notice of the improvements to be required in due course. There is no alternative to the principle of disclosure if teachers and inspectors are to maintain the professional trust which alone permits their contact to be effective.

The inspector's methods

Inspectors do not have a uniform or standardized methodology. Outside classrooms the aspects of a school to be observed have been listed by many LEAs in the form of checklists, and the Surrey list (Ingoldsby, 1976) is a typical good example. Such a list serves to ensure that an inspecting team does not miss anything of obvious importance, but is not exactly a sensitizing agent. Nor is such an agent needed: inspectors visit many different schools, and this alone renders them highly sensitive to what Shipman (1979) calls 'traces' – the signals that a building gives of the quality and style of the life of its occupants. Looking at a school after hours is a study in such traces: the orderliness of the desks and chairs, the age and quality of the display, even the matter left on the blackboards and many other details tell the inspector much about what to look for in the school day. The body language as well as the speech of exchanges between teacher and pupil in corridor or playground are far more revealing, taken in the mass, than most teachers realize: they must be, since teachers often seem surprised at how much HMI and local inspectors pick up from simply walking the school.

Within the classroom the inspector's method is likely to be individual and in many cases not very explicit. That does not imply either dogmatism or muddle. Inspectors are just as likely to find a new classroom stressful as the teacher finds his presence, and a deliberate openness of mind is a necessary precondition of seeing what is there. Moreover, the inspector whose reports have been dissected by teachers or governing bodies soon learns not to be muddled. To approach a classroom visit with preconceptions or obsessions is uncharacteristic in any inspector, though doubtless it can seem to happen now and then. But a checklist of all the signals there are to register in a classroom would be unmanageable. The inspector observes the display and the positioning of the furniture; how pupils move in and out, and what their body language reveals of their attitudes; how long it takes to settle to work; how pupils behave behind the teacher's back; what proportion of them take part in the oral commerce of the lesson (and whether the teacher keeps count of this, as he always should but almost never does). The relationship between the task set, the way the pupils set about it, and how long the least motivated keep at it will reveal a great deal about 'match'. The style and pace and placing of the teacher's questions, his readiness to forgo closed questions, the patience of the class while a pupil articulates a response to an open question – these are revealing about pedagogy. The teacher's own preparation notes, or the lack of them, and the departmental scheme of work, or the lack of one, will be revealing about structure. The domains in which HMI look for evidence – plant, match, pedagogy, structure, progression and climate – all draw in some degree on classroom observation, and the three core ones among them can draw on little else. The judgement of progression is the most difficult of the six, and usually calls for close questioning, often of pupils as well as of teachers.

The process of classroom observation, then, is one of constant selection from a mass of constantly changing evidence. The focus will usually be subject-specific. Thus a scientist will look for the balance between passivity under exposition and activity in real problem-solving. A linguist will listen for the pupils' oral confidence and adequacy of accent. An English specialist will look for structured connections between class discussion and writing tasks and for a suitable match between books being read and the abilities of the class. But much classroom observation makes no subject demands: a specialist in any subject can see when a class reader in English has some reading far ahead and others not following at all, and an inspector of any subject can assess a sixth-form Economics lesson where the teacher is speaking for all but one of the lesson's 40 minutes. The subject inspector observing a teacher for the first time also has to establish his subject credentials before moving on: he is under some compulsion to make his opening question or comment at the end of the lesson into one which at once establishes his shared knowledge and shared values as a specialist alongside the teacher. It is that same establishing of community of values that demolishes the tension in the teacher, that makes every staffroom, at the end of the first morning of a full inspection, resound with the feeling that 'this isn't so bad after all'.

Inspection and research

What then are the claims of inspection to constitute a form of evaluation with the sort of validity and objectivity that evaluation aspires to in the research community? Inspection does not look for the kind of validity required of academic evaluation, and if it were to do so it would require to be out of all proportion more expensive and elaborate. Nor can inspection profess the statistical reliability demanded of attainment tests or research procedures – again because to seek it would radically change the nature of the activity. What inspection seeks, as I have suggested, is to negotiate its own professional acceptability much as the research community negotiates the validity and reliability of a given research procedure each time the designer puts it forward. If the negotiation is very devolved and informal, it still takes place, even when the teacher being inspected knows the adviser in other contexts very well. Part of the negotiation requires the inspector to be open to information from the teacher that what has been observed is untypical: the teacher who conveys that 'this is my difficult group' or 'this period they come from PE and are always over-excited' is negotiating for indulgent assessment on perfectly proper grounds – to the extent that the claim made is true and relevant. The inspector will have to judge that for himself in the light of all the other evidence of the teacher's response to the class.

The same applies to the suggestion that inspection cannot be a valid procedure because no two inspectors would see the same realities if they were to observe the same lesson. That is not quite the point. The inspector is seeing a sample and is seeing it selectively, as is not in dispute; but he has also to establish with the teacher, before or after his observation of lessons, that his perceptions are not unreal and in substantial degree match the teacher's. The teaching profession's demand that inspectors be 'objective' means that they should be detached from purely local dissension, fairminded, showing good will and without petty obsessions – and that they should be seen to have these attributes. It is very striking, however, that the anxieties on these grounds widely voiced by teachers about the growth of LEA inspection in the late 1970s have almost entirely ceased. These considerations do leave one complex topic that still needs ethnographic research: we know nothing of the nature of the processes by which the myriad observations of a team of inspectors become generalized into a judgement, and how the thousands of possible pieces of evidence become ordered to sustain it.

Review

A great many LEA advisers have taken part in some kind of review process. Some arise from requests from head teachers to 'run the ruler over' a department, perhaps stimulated by recognition of a problem. Properly conducted, a review needs a minimum of two inspectors and a minimum of two working days, and in a school of any size three days. Typically, an adviser for science will recruit his colleague for mathematics and possibly the adviser for Design Technology, and they will spend three and a half days observing the work, in a secondary school of, say, 600 pupils, of 11 or 12 teachers in those subjects. At best they can hope to see each teacher for three periods, but will cover a variety of work and by questioning will find out much more. The leader of the group will rehearse their impressions with the heads of department and the head, and will go away and write a report or a letter setting out a small number of attainable goals for the three departments over the next two years. If the head teacher cares to attach deadlines to each of these goals, he is free to do so. The document does not go to the governors, still less to the education committee, but both bodies need to be told of the review, and of its essential outcomes.

This kind of activity lends itself to numerous adaptations. The inspectors do not necessarily have to be present at the same time, although it lends weight if they are. They do not have to do their observing continuously for whole days, provided the teaching staff know which days will be involved. (It is less than fair to withhold this information, but it creates less anxiety if the precise choice of lessons is not set out in advance.) Like inspection, review is not putting individual teachers on trial: it is evaluating the performance of a group or a whole staff. Variations on a basic pattern of review described above do not all have to be in the direction of less formality. In some LEAs the inspectors are assigned to subject and faculty teams, between 12 and 13 in all, each one three or four strong, each inspector belonging to three or four teams. The year's work is then programmed so that every secondary school in the authority receives a visit from a Review Team of some kind once a year. The teams are formed only for the purpose, and any one inspector may be called upon for no more than six or seven reviews in the year. As a strategy for ensuring that accountability is seen to be pursued it has many merits. As a device for the effective deployment of inspectors who by temperament are intensely individualistic it has the virtues of giving them a useful training, a wider curriculum perspective, and a limited constraint on their use of time.

Experience of review by advisory staff is now widespread in many LEAs, although it does not always go by that name. Advisers speak warmly of its value to them as offering a chance to work with immediate colleagues, and as permitting a degree of openness with teachers that no formal inspection procedure can encompass. There is an obvious problem with review as a procedure: unless it is formalized, as in the Review Team machinery outlined above, or by recording its outcomes formally to committee, it is easily impugned as cosy and lacking in rigour. If such a charge is merited, its burden must lie less on the advisers who conduct reviews and more on the officers and members responsible for policy who have omitted to spell out what they want the review procedure to do and to be. Once again we are back to the vacuum of curriculum policy in the LEA.

School self-evaluation

The change in the climate of opinion in the mid–1970s brought numerous signs among members of education committees of the intention to institute some degree of formal inspection by the local authority advisory staff. The available evidence suggests that while a majority of LEAs dipped a toe in the water between 1976 and 1979, not very many kept it there. The dramatic reduction in the influence of the teachers' unions that was taking place nationally at this time (Salter and Tapper, 1981, Ch. 9) was matched by a similar containment in the more solidly conservative LEAs, but union opposition, however muted it may have been, was not the reason for the faltering of the drive towards inspection. As will be clear from previous chapters, full formal inspection on any scale, let alone on a cyclical basis, was beyond the administrative capacity of most LEAs. Even if the advisory staff could have managed it, no sub–committee of elected members would welcome, or indeed be able to handle, the sudden addition of a score of full inspection reports to their agenda in each committee cycle. The most alert education officers perceived that the current fashion in higher education for self-evaluation as a procedure for use in schools had something to offer. There was a difference between self-evaluation as an exercise for the individual teacher and as a procedure for the school as a whole, and it was in the latter guise that many LEAs were to explore it. It was in many cases not so much a matter of heading off the threat of formal inspection, although it could be represented in that guise to attract the endorsement of the teachers, as a search for a procedure that would meet both of Sockett's requirements without being unmanageable. This pragmatic basis has characterized school self-evaluation wherever it has become institutionalized.

Historically the first LEA to venture into school self-evaluation was Inner London, and although its original scheme appeared after the storm about William Tyndale Junior School had broken, the documents had been in preparation for some considerable time. In the light of the strictures of the Auld Report (ILEA, 1976), the self-evaluation scheme that appeared in *Keeping the School Under Review* (ILEA, 1977) seemed innocuous enough. But this short pamphlet was to have great influence on many other LEAs. It was in due course revised and filled out, with separate versions for the differing phases of school, but these retain their original form as checklists of questions for heads and teachers to ask themselves. Their use in ILEA schools remained voluntary for some time but has now become compulsory.

The example was to be quickly followed. When a senior officer of ILEA became Chief Education Officer in Oxfordshire, that authority developed a similar pamphlet (1979), and Solihull's checklists for primary (1979) and secondary (1980) sold in large numbers to other LEAs exploring their own schemes. The lists of questions posed in these later documents were longer and more exhaustive, but there emerged a second generation of self-evaluation guides by 1982, among which the simplest is that from Stockport (1982). This literature is reviewed in some detail by Shipman (1983), and the original ILEA document is reprinted in McCormick (1982). The flow, however, has stopped and the incidence of self-assessment by schools has declined – according as the teachers' consciousness of serious public criticism has declined (which is not to say that teachers are unaware of low public esteem for the service). A conscientiously conducted survey (Elliott, 1981) showed that while a majority of LEAs discussed a move to self-evaluation, and 21 had issued guidelines, only one or two had sought to make their use obligatory. The same reluctance to insist has befallen the close alternative developed by the former Schools Council known as GRIDS (or Guidelines for Review and Institutional Development in Schools), which reflects a wider problem in its tentativeness over recommending the use of an outside consultant. Numerous groups of schools have used GRIDS with an adviser as consultant, but will be able to continue doing so only in the rare cases where the LEA has built that use of the adviser's time into its normal planning, and has thereby accepted that form of self-evaluation as policy. Securing decisions with policy implications of that kind is something advisers very widely find difficult: chief officers show a reluctance about them that, again, reflects a policy vacuum over curriculum. The topic and its literature are well reviewed in Nuttall (1981).

There is a lasting problem with self-evaluation, which the practice of co-evaluation with an adviser only accentuates: how is it to deal with a teacher who has serious weaknesses and either cannot or will not recognize their existence? A self-evaluation by a group such as a primary school staff will preserve its solidarity at the price of a collective dishonesty, or vice versa, in such cases. A co-evaluation will shift the problem to the adviser, who will have to choose between the spirit of the evaluation process and the interests of the ineffective teacher's pupils. In practice an authority has to respond, but it does so by a separation in time between the self-evaluation process and the action over the individual. The management of these matters becomes more necessary and more delicate in very small schools, where action over a teacher can be action over a third of the staff, but it has to be action by the LEA based on the assessment of the LEA's own officers.

The Oxfordshire practice

The first LEA to make school self-evaluation a requirement was Oxfordshire in 1980. At first envisaged as a cyclic process taking four years, it required each school to:

review their statements of aims and objectives, to gather facts, opinions and observations on which to base their self-evaluation, to hold evaluative discussions and to write their school report . . .

(Brighouse, 1984)

The schema for the school report was set out by the LEA, and it may run to upwards of 20 pages for a primary school, 60 or more (sometimes much more) for a secondary. The report goes to the governors, who add their own comments if they wish, and then to the Evaluation Panel of elected members. In the initial scheme (1980–5) a member of the panel visited the school, and the full Panel, head teacher, chairman of governors and appropriate officers met to discuss the report. Engaged in reviewing nearly 300 schools at a rate of perhaps 15 each term, the Evaluation Panel acquires real expertise. The process has developed a further stage, where officers and advisers discuss identified needs with the staff of the school before the report goes to the Panel. In the second cycle (1986–91) the process is to be modified, so that a sub–group of the Evaluation Panel joins with officers and advisers for a visit which combines both purposes. The full panel thus meets only once a term, when issues arising from numerous visits can be teased out. The second cycle will also seek completion in five years through shorter reports and some changes in detail (Brighouse, 1984). The arrangements appear to have proved their worth with heads, teachers, governors and elected members, in spite of having to be operated at a time of very severe reductions in the authority's headquarter's man-power. The system places the onus of evaluation on the teaching staff and other parties to the life of a school, in ways which clearly reduce the element of threat and greatly enhance the status of professional as against utilitarian evaluation.

The Oxfordshire scheme is widely known elsewhere through the 'pink book' issued in 1979, *Starting-points in Self-Evaluation*. In practice the schools tend to work from the guide to the format of the report issued by the authority and agreed with the teaching unions. The format has made many reports heavily factual, and descriptive rather than evaluative, but the head teachers have come to value highly the direct contact with members, for a full hour for each school, that incorporates the evaluative discussion at the heart of the scheme. It gives the head teachers face-to-face experience of the values of their ultimate employers, making a felt reality out of what would otherwise be a paper exercise. The members for their part gather much more than facts or evaluative judgements: the meetings facilitate soundings on major issues as well, and policy formation benefits enormously for such first-hand contact on a basis of a shared task.

The Oxfordshire scheme will have to operate for the life of at least a further cycle (i.e. from 1986 to 1991) before its full value can be assessed, and it is one of the problems of local government that such fundamental policy initiatives can be overturned with a change in political control. It clearly meets both of Sockett's requirements of accountability procedures and with no small benefits to spare, but it is also costly in time and manpower – as, of course, is any other effective approach to accountability.

Appraisal

The process of reviewing a manager's performance with him or her once a year is long-established practice in many branches of industry, commerce and the public services. The guidelines issued to senior managers for the conduct of annual appraisal of this kind have been widely disseminated and studied in the educational world, and in many LEAs a substantial proportion of head teachers have adopted some form of it. So common is it outside teaching that one may well ask why it has not been general before this within it. The answers lie in the power of the teaching unions up to the mid-1970s and the gravity of teacher shortages since then – shortages which endure even now in some subject areas and are only just below the surface in others. But part of the answer lies elsewhere: appraisal is a process in which the formal superior, the appraiser, sets out to get the subordinate, the appraisee, to do most of the talking, to reach his own evaluation of the year's performance, to work his way to a dispassionate judgement of strength and weakness. The appraiser who in other phases of the job habitually exacts deference from subordinates finds this role in appraisal difficult, and the subordinates find it almost impossible. Appraisal, that is to say, will not work where head teachers are autocratic or tyrannical. The coming of appraisal to teaching symbolizes plainly the great change that has come over the nature of headship.

The widespread adoption of commercial models of appraisal in schools has assumed that managers (e.g. deputy heads, heads of department, etc.) can find the necessary time for an hour and a half's interview with anything up to ten or twelve teachers with no release from teaching and no effect on other duties. The provision of training in appraisal interviewing is not often thought of in such circumstances, either, but the serious flaw in most thinking and practice about appraisal of teachers is one which has received virtually no attention: it is surely unreal to think of appraising a teacher without any element of observation of his performance in the classroom. The business model can rely on performance measures from the out-turns of the plant or manpower being managed, and it is only in that context that manager-appraisal has any meaning. The notion that teacher-appraisal can be a significant contribution to the profession and its competence without observation of classroom teaching is an invitation to window-dressing: it must put a premium on those aspects of teaching which influence the non-observer – classroom silence, elaborate work-sheets, abundant written work, sedulous detailed marking, voluminous 'notes', complete and timely paperwork, being a bureaucratic 'good boy'. In short, unless appraisal is observation based it is likely to make the actual conduct of classroom teaching *worse*.

There is a difference, of course, between appraisal of teachers and that of head teachers, to the extent that the latter can and should be appraised in respect of their performance as managers – but the relevant criteria are complex and difficult to make explicit. The academic debate about appraisal has concentrated in large measure on the issue of who does it to whom, and has largely assumed that head teachers and teachers are alike so far as this question goes. The fact of the matter is that head teachers are employed by their employing authorities to manage their schools, and to that extent it is for those authorities to decide who does the appraisal of their management. Very few LEAs would in practice reach any decision of that sort without consulting the head teachers themselves, but this consultative practice should not be allowed to obscure where responsibility lies.

Appraisal of head teachers raises acute problems for LEAs. The reason lies in the disproportion between the number of officers engaged in 'management' and the much larger number of head teachers to be 'managed'. This disparity is eagerly exploited, of course, by the advocates of head teacher autonomy, who have canvassed alternative appraisers such as retired heads, seconded heads, chairmen of governors, the head's own deputies, his assistant staff, and others. Few of these options are compatible with the LEA's own accountability, and until the problem is resolved the appraisal of head teachers must be viewed as easy to propose but far from easy to implement.

The notion of peer–group appraisal is not, of itself, any guarantee that bad practice will be checked or good practice endorsed. Paradoxically, it is the superordinate status of the appraiser that underwrites the process, not only by the deployment of superior interviewing skill (where present) but also through access to supplementary resources or training. The best compromise to have been proposed in the LEA situation to date uses a qualified triad: head teacher A appraises B, who in turn appraises C, and one of the three each year is appraised jointly by the appropriate other head and an officer or adviser of the LEA. Even here, however, the process needs to observe the procedures of formal appraisal by insisting that the appraisee provide the necessary preliminary papers and write up the agreed outcomes: ill-prepared appraisal interviews bring the process into disrepute and waste everyone's time.

It is important to be clear about what appraisal cannot do. It will not provide a way into mentioning to weak or lazy teachers those deficiencies that they will not admit or that their superiors do not have the courage to mention. It will not provide a way of identifying and removing ineffective teachers: that requires, under the law, a proper disciplinary procedure – and LEAs have ample experience of disciplinary action that works well and does not alienate teachers.

The coming of appraisal, with or without any link to salaries, exposes in acute form the dangers of the traditional posture of the LEA as facilitative rather than managerial. For the worst of all worlds in appraisal would be an outcome where the LEA had no role whatever. How assistant teachers are appraised is not a matter that can be left to the goodwill and good sense of individual head teachers. Appraisal will need to rest on a programme of training and a body of basic procedural guidance to head teachers and their 'middle managers'. Teachers are also entitled to some guarantees against the use of appraisal by head teachers who see it as machinery for asserting their authority or wish to treat it as an empty formality. This points to some agreed scale of participation by the authority's inspectors at each level in the profession.

The prospect of a salary structure for teachers that sweeps away today's finely graded distinctions and incentives also points towards appraisal on a professional basis as a central focus for the distribution of the thousand-and-one tasks that keep schools going – not as ways of burdening teachers, but as a means of recognizing merit and guiding staff development. The interlocking of a new salary structure with appraisal offers a dramatic change in the way many schools are structured and managed, but it would be naive to suppose that appraisal can take the place of the incentives provided by the existing salary structure.

A deeper issue lies in wait. Arguably, appraisal cannot be 'value free': an officer, governor or member appraising a head teacher must have some preconceptions or values about the nature of a good school and hence of successful headship. It is just these preconceptions that LEAs habitually avoid teasing out and like to refer or leave to their 'partners'. The curriculum circulars and the demand for appraisal are both signals, which society at large clearly endorses, that the LEA itself cannot escape not only being an active partner but also the obligations of being the senior partner.

Assessment

The difference between appraisal and assessment is that the latter is explicitly linked to salary, in the form of merit awards or of progression past an efficiency bar. Such bars have a long and discredited history in the management of many kinds of quasi-professional group, and no precedent in the case of teaching in England. The oft-cited analogy of Lowe's Revised Code is a false one: not even the lunatic right is suggesting that teachers be paid on the basis of their pupils' test scores. The proposals have been ineptly made and just as ineptly received: a moment's thought suggests that they are incapable of being implemented effectively. If teaching unions were capable of such a ruse, they should enter formal discussions with every appearance of seriousness, and wait for the management side to discover how totally impracticable assessment of teachers must be. The reason emerges from the calculations later in this chapter under the heading of the 'Arithmetic of Accountability'. The union side can reasonably claim that an assessed teacher should be observed on two separate occasions, and a medium-sized LEA with 6,000 teachers is going to have to find observational manpower to do this – if assessment is once every three years, 2,000 teachers a year will require 4,000 sessions, which is equivalent to half as many inspectors as most LEAs of that size employ now.

The value-for-money lobby is likely to react by increasing the pressure to privatize education in some degree. If teachers cannot be paid according to their performance, their schools should have to gain their pupils competitively, runs the key argument. This situation already holds good: schools everywhere know they are in a market economy and will survive only as they build and maintain a reputation that attracts pupils. Only one factor is missing, the political will to close the school that fails to attract enough customers. It is pertinent to note here that for LEAs and DES to fudge the closure issue does have implications for curricular quality, and the parental and local lobbying that surrounds such proposals is not conducive to sound judgement of the curriculum or quality aspects.

A variant form of review

The two characteristics of appraisal that set it apart from other forms of assessment are its one-to-one nature and its reliance on a known and predictable time-scale. It is worth exploring the use of the second of these in the context of other forms of assessment. It is not, of course, practicable to deploy small Review Teams on a cycle which ensures, for example, that every school has its science work reviewed once every five years: that would require a level of manning far beyond present manpower. But it would be possible to plan a modest programme of full inspections in a way which takes advantage of the certainty of time-scale found in appraisal, and at the same time removes the uncertainty of criteria that bedevils most inspection. Under such an arrangement, the LEA's inspectorate would make its criteria clearly known, and would communicate the intention to inspect, not a few weeks but fully a year in advance. The school thus has opportunity to study the criteria for itself, to consider how they are matched by what goes on in its classrooms and departments, and to modify its practice in time for the changes to settle down. The inspectors are then looking at a school with a preliminary account from the head of the changes recently made, and are seeing one in a dynamic relationship with their criteria. The static postures of a school either second-guessing what the inspectors want to see, or hoping against hope that its traditional habits will stand examination, are thereby swept away.

Such an arrangement is the logical development of the position in a number of LEAs where the inspectors' checklist is published and the curriculum guidelines of the authority have been developed jointly between inspectors and teachers. It would associate naturally, too, with the practice of a number of LEA inspectorates over plant: unlike HMI, some LEA inspections regard structural and decorative aspects of school buildings as outside their remit. The tendency of local newspapers to pick on such criticisms of detail in HMI reports and overlook the real substance suggests that in publication conditions HMI would be wiser to do the same, making comments on plant direct to the LEA.

Inspection relying on published criteria and a long notice period would be open to two objections. One is that the authority for the inspectors' criteria should not be merely that of their own judgement: criteria would require the sanction of the employing authority, which logically would entail curriculum policy decisions taken by councillors who at present avoid or devolve them. Their inspectorates might enjoy such a devolution, but cannot afford to accept it, since a school of good local standing could reject the criteria – and without explicit member support the inspectors would be helpless. The other predictable objection is that it would give the teachers the sense of being under a long, threatening shadow. Teachers accustomed to annual individual appraisal do not feel this. Teachers who have experienced full inspection in one school and find they have moved to another only to encounter full inspection again do not find the second one threatening. The objection is in reality a demand to be excused external accountability.

The arithmetic of accountability

The various forms of audit explored in this chapter strike differing balances between Sockett's two requirements: some provide information about the maintenance of quality rather more firmly than others, and some focus on improvement more than others do. What is clear is that any serious approach to formal accountability demands a considerable investment of manpower. Oxfordshire has had to adjust and adapt its manpower at education officer and adviser level as its evaluation system has developed and its real demands have emerged over time. It is perhaps obvious that any chosen method of maintaining the LEA's responsibility for curriculum quality will have calculable consequences for its professional manpower. Nevertheless, there has been no published indication that any LEA has sought to make such calculations. The attempt to make models of the deployment of advisory staff is worth making.

At the level of the individual school the arithmetic of appraisal, if it is conducted properly, is revealing. The industrial experience is that appraisal interviews that do not exact proper preparation and last at least 1½ hours are in the medium term not worth doing: they bring the system into disrepute. If each appraisee thus demands a minimum of three hours of senior or middle management time, a school of 85 teachers is adding a significant element to its own workload. At the level of the LEA similar calculations apply, but the assumptions and variations involved are much more complex. If an appraisal system for head teachers is to invest three to four hours of officer or adviser time in upwards of 300 schools for appraisal alone, and at least as much in the necessary follow-up, 1,800 working hours is equivalent to an additional session each week in term time for nine or ten officers or advisers. Broadly similar calculations apply whatever particular approach to evaluation is adopted, although full formal inspection is by far the most consuming of time. This book has referred at several points to the way in which advisory time is apt to be treated as the authority's widow's cruse, and it may be useful to suggest a way of calculating and planning its deployment.

An arithmetical model is suggested in Appendix A (pp.212–3). It asks the user to make his assumptions fully explicit and apply to the model whatever practical realities his own position throws up. It requires the user to take 13 separate steps in the calculation, but the decisive ones are of course the early decisions about deployment priorities. The model is reversible: the user can decide how much visiting coverage is wanted and derive the advisory establishment required for it; or he can start with the existing establishment and obtain the priority decisions necessary to enable it to maintain a given level of visiting, and so forth. What matters in all this is that those who manage advisory teams should appreciate the pressures on them and offer them realistic leadership over their use of time.

The decisions which make the greatest difference to teachers and schools, and which bear most directly on teaching quality, concern classroom visiting, selection of senior staff and in-service training. Most advisers who take part in staff selection claim, in my view rightly, that it is their single most influential means of improving the quality of schools, especially at primary headship level. Its time demand, however, is finite and relatively stable. The balance between visiting and in-service work is a constant tension, and the unchecked growth of the latter is a potential threat to the adviser's credibility. Since, in principle, the skills and labour of short courses can usually be delegated (and many advisers are expert in fostering such skills in teachers), while the observational work of the inspector cannot be shared in that way, it is the classroom visiting that should have its irreducible priority in the use of time. Against a background of this kind of thought and planning about the manpower for inspection and review, the local education authority should be in a position to make ordered, rational decisions about which approach to explore.

Postscript

After this chapter was completed, HMI issued their survey *Quality in Schools: Evaluation and Appraisal*. It summarizes some of the extraordinarily diverse practices among schools and LEAs, drawing repeated attention to the point that many schools have undertaken self-evaluation in ways that called for support or response from the LEA and did not receive it. The emphasis in this chapter on possible forms of LEA response rests on much the same gloomy assessment as HMI's about how far most LEAs are doing what they should be doing. Similarly, its insistence on classroom observation as the only proper and professional basis for appraisal is reflected in the factual observation by HMI that there seems to be very little of it taking place (DES, 1985e).

PART THREE

Towards Solutions

This final Part seeks to bring together the consequences of seeking a professional model of accountability in the service as it has developed to the present. Chapter 8 starts from the premise that LEAs cannot logically hold schools accountable in the absence of curriculum policy, and explores what different levels of curricular policy making might seek to achieve. It is contended that the elected members who constitute local education authorities need to engage with professionals in exploring curriculum issues, and to be enlisted by professionals in securing political endorsement of their curricular priorities. The closing chapter explores the interaction between schools, advisory staff and elected members in a professional model of accountability, and suggests the characteristics to be sought in the accountable school.

8
The Nature of Curriculum Policy

The purpose of this chapter is to explore what precisely the notion of 'policies for the curriculum' might mean, not so much in the abstract terms of curriculum theory as in the daily realities of the curriculum delivered in classrooms. The exploration will consider how far existing education authority practices, and in particular their predominant mix of reliance on advisory staff with tacit endorsement, can meet the need for curriculum policies. An attempt to identify the levels in the professional and political hierarchy at which particular curriculum policy decisions have to be taken leads to some uncomfortable conclusions about the existing arrangements.

What does 'policy' mean in the curriculum context?

The practices of a school are guided, in the present state of the English maintained system, by a complicated network of influences on curriculum, and previous chapters have suggested that it is simplistic to see the changing balance between such influences merely as a struggle for control. Whatever else may be said of curriculum, it is not easily susceptible of control in any limited sense, as the sad history of the French system since the Second World War demonstrates repeatedly (Legrand, 1983). Particular parts of curriculum display differing degrees of openness to control, but if we look at the realities in schools dispassionately we also find that the cost of *lack* of control varies too. If our underlying curricular values include any reference to social equity, or to maximizing the gains of pupils in accordance with their capacity to benefit, the costs of non-control have to enter the argument, but there is a striking paucity of attention to those costs in the voluminous academic debates about curriculum. Those same debates can also be surprisingly unreal in the assumptions they make about what actually happens in real classrooms and schools.

First, the era of expansion was also one of consensus about the subjects of the curriculum, but it was not a particularly thought-out consensus, still less a consistently applied one. Religious instruction was, uniquely, enshrined in statute as compulsory, but it has figured as a conscientiously taught subject in a steadily diminishing number of schools, and as a respectable discipline it now touches a minority of secondary pupils for a minority of their time in school. Why this is so is not our present concern. Merely, legislation does not guarantee curricular reality. The Primary Survey of 1978 found a serious lack of science work, by contrast, and the drive to remedy the lack was to enlist vast numbers of heads and teachers and advisers. Curricular reality does not require legislation.

Secondly, there was a concerted and skilfully led programme of development of French teaching in primary schools that originated in a handful of LEAs in the early 1960s. It commanded widespread support among parents and teachers, and many education officers endorsed it without access to specialist advice. Considerable resources were devoted to it, but the experiment failed: when the evaluation research was published, what was left of it virtually collapsed. Leadership outside the schools does not always guarantee curricular reality. In contrast, the spontaneous growth of personal and social education is now beginning to secure the legitimation of being labelled as a 'subject' (usually with the label PSE). Curricular reality does not always require leadership outside the schools.

Thirdly, at the level of the individual pupil the pattern of the curriculum can present acute contrasts between rhetoric and reality. The current problem of using microcomputers is a case in point: head teachers assent firmly to the need to ensure the best educational use of the hardware – and agree to quarantining their microcomputers in a computer studies department where the other subject departments cannot get at them and the hardware is used for teaching that brings the pupils little or no marketable learning. A deeper example of the same problem is the use of option schemes for fourth- and fifth-year pupils in secondary schools. Most secondary managements now recognize that they do not have the resources to furnish the sort of subject choice and the freedom to combine choices that is needed to satisfy the most demanding articulate parent: decisions are necessary that may make it impossible to offer German to a pupil who insists on music, or geology as well as geography to a pupil who insists on chemistry and physics. But most secondary schools now experience regular instances of parents who play one school off against another in order to bargain for option arrangements not provided in the scheme. The school that adopts all the best advice and insists that every pupil must do a science may lose some bright pupils to a neighbouring school that does not, and so for every other diminution of the total choice on offer in the days of plenty. (That private schools have never offered total choice does not alter the case, of course.) There is no way in which these patterns of curriculum choice can be harmonized without some sort of agreement or policy at LEA level – and to harmonize does not necessarily mean to standardize. There are of course other arguments, explored elsewhere in this book, for reducing the diversity of the central curriculum, and the coming of the GCSE examinations will enforce some degree of this, but on present indications few LEAs will acknowledge the need to lead their curricula rather than have their schools be led by one or another's entrepreneurial practice.

A rather different way in which curriculum policy operates through its absence is in the longitudinal form of the curriculum. History has brought the typical 40-period week to extreme fragmentation, as schools have struggled to provide timetable room for an ever growing number of separate subjects, whose status and separateness is created not by the structure of knowledge but by the social construction of a new subject as the force which defines a new grouping of people, gives them a raison d'être and in due course endows them with legitimacy, both academic and economic. This process has happened with geography and biology in this century, and the analogous separation of science into its alleged three 'sciences' has followed the same route. There is reason to suppose that if LEAs had exercised properly defined policy-making powers over curriculum, these changes would have happened very differently. At some point authoritative laymen would have stopped to ask if such fragmentation was desirable, and whether a subject claiming two fortieths of the week for four or five years might not be better off with four fortieths for two years, less diffusion and less forgetting, as in most other advanced countries. This form of the issue is likely to assert itself with a new urgency in the guise of pressure for modular forms of curricular planning, which in a somewhat haphazard way the examination boards are already beginning to accept.

There is less doubt about the issue of balance in the sense of the set of subjects forming the individual pupil's curriculum at any one time. HMI and LEA reports alike identify many instances of pupils whose personal curricula seriously lack balance, suggesting that their schools do not take enough care to prevent such choices. In reality schools are often the victims of their own systems. One example of this is the school which prides itself on accommodating every pupil's full range of choices: the satisfaction of fitting the choices into the timetable can distract attention from the need to judge the choices as a set. Another example, more common perhaps, is the deft way in which pupils play off parts of the school's system, securing a nominal set of choices and then, after the timetable has been constructed, negotiating changes with subject teachers which the form teachers or group tutors do not hear of until it is too late to block them.

Such problems of balance are readily manageable if the will is present. The same cannot be said of curriculum progression. The interfaces between schools remain enduringly difficult parts of the curriculum scene, and LEAs have tended to turn a blind eye.

In the absence of curriculum policies appropriate to each of several levels of decision-making, interest continues to focus on innovation. For those who see the inherited curriculum as a dead hand, innovation tends to induce a knee-jerk reaction in its favour – a tendency which once caused the spending of vast sums on language laboratories quite unsuited to school use. For those who see curriculum in terms of what they themselves knew at school, innovation induces equally knee-jerk reactions against the 'new fangled'. Into this intellectually empty plain lined by its opposed factions the determined empire-builder can move with alarming speed. Computer studies has been established as a 'subject' at school level when that was the last use of microtechnology the schools really needed. Where the territory is already colonized the matter is more difficult, so that although 'metalwork' and 'woodwork' were moribund and inert, they were there, and Craft design and technology is displacing them only slowly, making temporary alliance here with art and design, there with electronics. The uncertainty of where to classify CDT illustrates well the tension between the need for order in the curriculum and the need for openness to change. Striking the balance between these two needs poses once more the problem: how may we locate decisions on curriculum policy without increasing the present confusions or destroying the vitality and responsiveness of the service?

At the level of the local authority the price to be paid for such lack of curriculum policy is paid by pupils and teachers. Members and officers have concerned themselves chiefly with other forms of cost – roofs over heads, teachers in front of classes, meals and maintenance. One of the endemic effects of this diversion of managerial concern away from curriculum is that the managers involved are left with an archaic model of the curriculum process. In turn, therefore, the responsibility for crucial non-teaching costs is shirked, schools are under-funded for ancillary staff and the proper boundary between equipment funded by the authority and equipment paid for out of school capitation funds is fudged.

Even the concern with institutional costs is not always pursued efficiently. In some LEAs neighbouring institutions offer, with no restraint from the LEA, identical pre-vocational courses to 14–15 year-olds in one school, to 16-year-olds in a second school, and to other 16-year-olds in a college of further education. The traditional location of foreign language teaching in the schools, coupled with an elitist set of assumptions about how fast to proceed and to what objectives, destroys our national self-confidence about languages, when a rational analysis would vest almost all such instruction in further education when students have an adult motivation. Again, schools continue to teach the office skills of an outdated technology and feed the market for single-skill certificates, when leaving the whole field to further education would drive much of the private college work out of business. Inspections of single schools, of course, will not pick up these gaps in curriculum policy.

Head teachers worry most, however, about protecting minority subjects that can survive only if subsidized. In most schools, including grammar schools, music, Latin, Greek and some other subjects are taught in small sets subsidized by over-size sets in other subjects. But this is a surface sign of a wider problem: LEAs generally have backed off 'curriculum-led staffing' largely for financial reasons, and schools have seen this as a cowardice. But most LEAs have a committee machinery ill adjusted to facing curriculum issues seriously or in depth. Curriculum policy is penalized by the priority given to financial and legal issues. Primary school closure is a good example: the simple facts are that only the rarest skill can effectively teach more than one year-group in one class of any size, while any school of less than five teachers must suffer from some quite serious weaknesses in its curricular range – many primary experts would put the minimum figure at seven. These curricular realities tend to be set aside in favour of the quite untested mythology about 'knocking the heart out of the community' and local parental lobbying. This happens not because anyone involved is blind or craven or lacking in goodwill, but because most LEAs have no formal machinery for looking at curriculum policy, and many of those that have anything like it fail to treat it seriously enough.

Policies and intentions

There are inevitably some grey areas surrounding curriculum policy issues which shade off into other considerations – the size of primary schools is one example. These shadings are important because the long-standing habit of a consensus era is to subsidize a negligent or inefficient management structure by reliance on personal relationships. Advisory staff are naturally at the crux of this process. At one extreme, we find the so-called 'democratic' schools described in several instances by their former head teachers, such as Countesthorpe, Madeley Court, Sutton Centre and, in different ways and degrees, William Tyndale and Risinghill. In each of these cases, as with the much larger number of schools which followed similar histories but did not go over the brink into media notoriety, the relevant LEA advisers faced an insoluble dilemma. They might personally have had much sympathy with the school's aspirations, but they knew, beyond all peradventure, that there neither was nor could be any political legitimation for their actual performance. For the adviser, then, the issues become tactical – how to fend off parental and in some cases political anxiety, how to dissuade the school from giving needless hostages to fortune, and how or whether to precipitate crisis. To put the problem another way, advisers and inspectors could feel inwardly certain of what the councillors they served would tolerate, but instead of being able to express these limits firmly to the school they had to become party (in some cases unwillingly) to a conspiratorial game of calculating with the head teacher what the school could get away with. If the school staff fell victim to beliefs that political plotting against them was going on, even this degree of communication might not be possible.

At the opposite pole is the case of the school whose management by the head teacher is so autocratic and rigid as to cause serious 'personnel' problems with teaching staff, real difficulties with largely innocent pupils whose only fault is to have caught the suspicious eye of the head, and such division between parents that nothing is done – except to provide a claque of endorsement when public pronouncements about discipline and high standards emanate at the annual prizegiving. Here too the adviser most closely concerned with the school is well aware, intuitively but (and the difference is crucial) not on any explicit basis, that this is not a kind of school ethos the councillors would endorse – but in the absence of any explicit policy about school atmospheres he is powerless to speak. If the lack of clear preferences over school climate extends to vagueness or prejudice in the process of selecting new head teachers, the authority that finds itself with such problems has only itself to blame.

In both cases the adviser and education officer who have to deal with the problems day to day can have recourse to some procedures: the LEA is not totally powerless. In one north-country instance a series of teachers had left a school without new posts to go to, and one of them, out of the blue, announced the intention to sue the LEA for constructive dismissal. Before the case reached a tribunal the LEA held a hearing, reinstated the teacher in another school, and persuaded the autocratic head to accept early retirement. One metropolitan district LEA has a group of three long-standing members of committee who make 'visitations' designed to ameliorate such problems. A few still rely on the seniority and awe of the chief officer in person. A number of authorities have had recourse to the sometimes transparent device of the full inspection, and should not have been surprised if the teaching staff of the school to be inspected viewed the option as politically motivated rather than (as was more often the case) a professionally protective move. In rare cases the inspection has been by HMI, who found some embarrassment between their repeated claim to be independent of government and their use by government in such instances as Sutton Centre and Countesthorpe – a use now recognized in the DES Policy Statement about HMI.

The step which the LEA most wishes to forestall is the publication in the press of indications of serious trouble. This is not a cowardly wish for concealment, but a hard-headed certainty that public confidence in a school is indispensable. A school may be as good as anyone's ideal, but if parents or pupils do not have confidence in it the quality will go for nothing. But if LEAs had thought out what kind of ethos they wanted to see in their schools, had a policy of sorts about school atmosphere and style of management, head teachers would know where they stood, and applicants for headships who did not endorse such a policy would cease to be candidates. Hence, such troubles would be rare, and more easily managed when they occurred.

Do we need formal policies?

I have suggested earlier that the English LEA developed in a tradition of minimal management, and in a fashion that adjusted pragmatically to that tradition's weaknesses – by appointing advisory staff who became a surrogate for curriculum policy. The advisers developed skills in exploiting what is known in the trade as the professionalism of teachers: their readiness to analyse their own attitudes and actions, their willingness to treat serious work outside the school day and its necessary preparation as part of the normal job, and the seemingly endless disposition of many to seek improved ways of doing their job. The results have included a wide range of notable and influential developments. In some LEAs there have developed widely used certificates of competence in mathematics for school leavers. Graded tests in modern languages have dramatically increased the numbers pursuing a language to the age of 16. In a similarly limited number of authorities, schools have been brought to agree to abandon the traditional separate sciences in favour of a unified or integrated approach to science. The very wide dissemination of a principled approach to language in primary schools, which embraces initial literacy as well as later work in writing and speaking, was initiated by the Bullock Report but has been sustained predominantly by this interaction between teacher professionalism and advisory support. Moreover these developments have not passed without notice at the centres of influence. The examination boards have been obliged to take note of the developments in modern language work, some of them have at long last registered the size of the market for basic competency tests in several curriculum areas, and alternative offerings in the sciences have been available from some boards for some years. The DES Policy Statement on science, issued as this book was being written, had been hammered out in just such LEA developments as I have referred to.

The question must therefore arise whether this combination is not enough. Can the system's needs for curriculum policy and curriculum renewal be met by a combination of relative school autonomy, advisers whose accountability is almost entirely to their sense of profession, and teachers who alone know the needs of their pupils? This is an attractive standpoint to almost everyone concerned. It appeals to the believer in school autonomy; it enhances the influence of advisory staff; it engages teachers in the development work without compulsion; and it enables elected members to feel that crucial curricular decisions are being taken by people better informed than themselves without any one element having a monopoly of influence. There is only one thing at all wrong with it. Because it is a voluntarist approach it discards at the start any wish to compel or coerce the unwilling. But because it relies on the willing to carry forward its developments, it is inherently likely to leave the unwilling behind, and so make their acceptance of the outcomes less likely than ever. Thus, some schools, with numerous less able pupils in dire need of competency certification, regard such tests as beneath their notice. A minority of modern language departments insist that the whole Graded Tests development is a transient fad. There is even now a large scale adherence in primary schools to methods and materials in 'English' totally at variance with the language policies commended by their LEA documents or even professed by the schools involved (Pearce, 1984). And until the DES Policy Statement appeared there were numerous schools bent on preserving three separate sciences for as long as possible, citing in defence the alleged requirements of universities.

The issue of separate versus unitary science is not unlike that of the protection or sacrifice of Latin, or the status of marginal 'subjects' that schools propagate but universities do not want of their entrants (such as economics, psychology, computer studies, business studies). All these issues are alike in needing to be resolved above the level of the individual school. Whether the decision is to sacrifice Latin, or to discourage Advanced Level courses in psychology, or to provide staffing subsidies for uneconomic groups doing A level music, it is one that can properly be made only at the level of the LEA. To the extent that such issues exist, to that extent the combination (or network) of advice, autonomy and teacher professionalism breaks down. That may not signify, however, that the network is an inadequate mechanism in some circumstances or in some parts of the service.

The clearest examples of the benefits of a network system are in special and primary education. The suggestions made in earlier chapters about the number of schools appropriate to an effective primary adviser's workload were based on the belief that the optimum number of teachers for an adviser to relate to in an authority that does not practise much formal inspection is of the order of 350 to 450. A primary adviser limited to such a field can reasonably hope to know two thirds or more of those teachers by name (some would expect to know all of them); to visit between a third and a half of them in their classrooms each year; to engage in more detailed review of the work of one in ten of them; and to see virtually all of them during the year at courses and meetings if not in their schools. The skilful deployment of in-service resources among them, from one-year secondments for a handful down to three after-school sessions for the least eager, coupled with the careful placing of new sample materials, school-based in-service activity, and the other stimulus resources available to an adviser can bring about a remarkable degree of improvement in the quality of children's learning. The genius of English primary education is a distinctive mix of planning, method, classroom organization, firmness, skill, intuition and a personal responsiveness to children. It is a blend that defies delineation in policy documents. It cannot be created in teachers who do not trust their head teachers or their maintaining LEA as sharing their values and endorsing their child-centred convictions. It can be fostered, and senior posts can be filled with people in whom it is recognized. But the trust and the capacity for trust are of direct educational relevance, and how curriculum policy is built from it without damaging the trust is not at all easy to perceive.

The adviser in this kind of situation is clearly exercising power, although the typical adviser would be reluctant to see the matter in that way. In political theory terms the power is exercised in a fashion designed to avoid conflict, and the result is a nice example of what has been called the 'mobilization of bias' (Walsh *et al.*, 1984). The test of this kind of arrangement is a dual one: there is a test of consensus and a test of adjustment. In the first, what happens if the bias is mobilized in directions that the adviser's superiors (be they officers or members) do not endorse? In a climate that minimizes a formal policy, the problem is likely to surface first as a tension over personalities or as a dispute over a minor but symbolic issue such as non-Christian acts of worship, sex or peace education. There is little opportunity for such symbolic dissent between adviser and officer, member or layman to be aired in the wider context of curriculum policy and influence: keeping to the specific issue that surfaces may actually make the problem worse. The arrangement fails the test of consensus.

The test of adjustment concerns the compromises made between the overall thrust of the curriculum policy network and the resistance offered by an individual school or head. There are plenty of heads and schools that make accepting noises about practice they privately dismiss as 'new fangled' or even 'airy-fairy' – charges that advisers are careful to try to avoid attracting to themselves. Where both parties become aware of the real attitudes several compromises are available. The simplest one is to wait: such heads are apt to be older than the proponents of the innovations they reject, and the latter simply have to wait for retirement to take its toll. But such objectors expose the nature of the problem: the bias-mobilization sought by advisory staff in the absence of formal member-level endorsement does not pass the test of adjustment. Rather, such objectors, by refusing to adjust, transpose upwards the issue of who makes curriculum policy. In effect, they challenge the adviser to show the political colour of his curricular money.

Advisers know these realities only too well. They are long practised at establishing what they can count on support for without having any machinery for checking out such hunches. They are long used to finding other ways round the obstacles provided by non-adjusting heads and schools.

In the case of individual subject departments in secondary schools they usually have to rely on winning the support of the head teacher for approaches the department can be expected to reject, and if there is a generic weakness among subject advisers in the LEA service it is in their understanding of how to secure that support. Put crudely, the difficulty is that of moving from a generalized self-image as the friend and supporter of subject teachers to a specific role as the equal of the head teacher in identifying a shared problem. This is a problem readily overcome with the help of training, of which advisory staff in general have too little. In the primary sphere there are other ways of circumventing such obstacles, which include exploiting the adviser's role in short-listing and interviewing for senior staff, bargaining over access to major in-service opportunities, and much else. It is now uncommon, however, for the adviser to have direct access to financial assistance that the head teacher may seek.

It is perhaps surprising, against this background, that the broad run of local authority advisers and inspectors have not sought to develop for themselves, individually or collectively, any significant power-base among officers or members that would enable them to exert curricular influence with the assurance of weighty backing. There are exceptions, where strong chief advisers or inspectors have asserted the claims of their service with chief officers or committee chairmen or both, but the great majority have been content with an altogether lower profile. One of the main reasons for this is the professional history of the typical adviser, which brings him from a head of subject post in a single school into LEA advisory work with little or no preparation, and expects him to build his perspectives through sustained encounters with his former peers. It is easily forgotten that only a small minority of advisory staff have had any experience of attending an education committee or one of its sub-committees: they have nothing on which to base any reading of the political probabilities of endorsement that any of their curricular predispositions might secure. This general position is powerfully reinforced by the almost universal assumption among teachers and advisers (not to mention education officers) that curriculum issues are no concern of members and the profound reluctance of members themselves to enter the curriculum arena.

The politics of curriculum policy

The reliance of local education authorities on a network of teachers, heads of schools, advisory staff, professional commitment, and ritual insistences on academic freedom and school autonomy have taken the service a very long way in the matter of curriculum policy, although a reliance on such a network is bound to stop short of explicit formulation of policy. We have already seen several examples in these pages, however, of aspects of curriculum where the network principle either breaks down or has been subverted. If it is to survive, and there are very strong arguments for it, there is a need for it to seek to be more systematic and to secure a greater degree of political endorsement.

The need for LEA curriculum policy to be more systematic is evident in many ways. There are primary schools which even now reject the demand for serious attention to science by citing the fact that the LEA has not said it wants any. There are others that reject suggestions about serious historical and geographical topic work with claims that the children will get plenty of those 'subjects' when they go to secondary school. The equity of secondary curricula remains in doubt and in some respects is even now far from open to analysis or assessment by anyone outside the school. In some respects the lack is not even as elevated as one of coherence or system: there are junior schools where a ritual insistence on weekly tests, monthly form orders and annual subject prizes causes active educational harm to a majority of children (the majority that does not come top), yet no correction or amelioration by officers or advisers can be risked. For head teachers are in principle just as capable of calculating what will secure the endorsement of members as are advisers, and of taking calculated risks accordingly.

The need for some degree of systematic attention to curriculum issues in each local education authority has been clear to some observers for a long time. The reasons why it has not come about are also clear enough. One is that any arrangements for such attention would require the involvement of the teaching associations, but those are geared by their nature to concerns of a union nature rather than to issues of curriculum. Because the large teaching unions do not spend much time discussing curricular issues (by comparison with other very pressing and proper concerns), they are predisposed against responding to initiatives proposing such consultation. In some LEAs this reluctance has taken the form of actual refusal to appoint representatives to curriculum groups of members. The other reasons have to do with the tradition of school autonomy, the prevailing beliefs about the duties of governing bodies, and the understandable and often influential oppostion of the head teachers.

Even without a more systematic articulation of curriculum policies by the LEA there is still a case for ensuring a more explicit degree of endorsement at the political level of the thrust of curriculum change or emphasis adopted by individual advisory staff. In most LEAs this has not happened, in part because members see themselves as lacking the necessary competence to judge; in part because members have not wished to trespass on what they see as the territory of governors or teachers; and in part because overt political endorsement of advisory inclinations is likely to be viewed by education officers as a threat to the delicate balance of relationships by which they preserve their monopoly of access to committee.

This situation could well have continued indefinitely, but the intervention of the Department of Education and Science showed in the early curriculum circulars that it was under threat. The Policy Document on Science goes much further: it embodies a range of curriculum policy decisions that the LEAs, individually and collectively, have shown themselves unable or unwilling to make. So far so good. But it also indicates that LEAs will be held to account for their implementation of these policies. There is no present hint that failure to implement will bring LEAs into sanctions of any kind, any more than the individual school is subject to sanctions imposed by its maintaining LEA. Few would care to suppose, however, that a central government capable of rate-capping would be deflected from enforcing its will in a much less material domain. The policy imperatives thus fall to the ownership of the individual education authority. This fact, as I shall argue in the next chapter, so far from undermining the network principle that has long governed the accountability relations between school and LEA, places a premium on its survival. Local government, that is to say, faces an inescapable function not merely in implementing the curricular policies that local networks have been unable to achieve but also in mediating and domesticating them for its teachers, parents and electors. For local government to evade or take flight from this duty would invite central direction, and the existing reluctance of local government over curriculum policy constitutes just such an invitation.

What then of the specifically *party* politics of curriculum? Is it professionally proper for an LEA, for example, to instruct its inspectorate to pay assiduous attention in all its work to the need to eradicate racist material and attitudes from schools and their book stocks and teaching? At the other extreme is it proper for an authority to adopt a policy opposing the teaching of peace studies and forbidding the use of LEA funds for the purchase of peace-studies literature and materials? There are many inspectors and advisers, not to mention head teachers, for whom these rulings are not proper to an LEA, and the conventional wisdom would have it that one has to keep education out of politics – by which most people really mean that they want to keep party politics out of education. The underlying suppositions here are that children are gullible, which they are not, and that teachers are all by nature without political attitudes and values, which they are not. The truth is that few social practices are as profoundly political as education. The English education service experienced a long period of 'consensus' – and emerged as seriously deficient.

Education in England has been a laggard service throughout most of its history and its episodes of catching up have all been associated with periods of close and widespread political attention, whether these episodes have given rise to legislation such as the Acts of 1870, 1902 and 1944, or have precipitated marked changes not requiring legislation, such as the outcomes of the Robbins, Plowden and Cockcroft inquiries. Indeed, a very plausible case can be made that education in England has suffered from having too little political attention, not too much, and the under-resourcing that now constitutes its greatest single problem is one part of the evidence.

Should teachers not be protected, then, from what they and many others would see as interference by lay authority just because those laymen have been elected? What is at issue is not interference in day-to-day matters but curriculum policy. One of the invariable penalties of democratic life is that elected representatives have to learn the difference between policy and management, and nowhere is this harder to discern than in education. But the learning process is also capable of giving the service informed policy-making. Where elected members fail to learn, or are in the grip of ideological preconceptions, the position becomes strained, but such cases have not been serious or numerous enough to undermine the principle that public education in a democracy needs close and sustained local political endorsement if it is to be protected from well-intentioned but ultimately tyrannical centralism.

9
Professional Accountability

The purpose of this chapter is to return to the distinction between utilitarian and professional modes of accountability and explore the implications of each in the light of the foregoing analysis. It goes on to suggest that the English education service, while unlikely to suffer the worst forms of utilitarian approaches, nevertheless faces an acute need to ensure that the professional mode is made to work and is seen to work.

Utilitarian or professional?

The underlying principle of utilitarian approaches to the accountability problem is that the teacher is held directly responsible for the learning performances of his pupils. It is not accidental that this approach should have been most fully developed in a society where distinctions of race, caste and class are systematically discounted in the national and local rhetoric of political life: race in the United States cannot respectably be used to account for educational attainment, and social class has been available to explain underachievement much less readily than in the United Kingdom. Hence, the injustices of holding teachers accountable for educational differences built into their pupils' cultures, cognitive abilities or long social experience are less obvious in the USA than they would be in England. It is therefore unlikely that teachers in England will face the rigours of utilitarian accountability to the degree found in the USA.

By the same token it is easier to show in the English context that utilitarian approaches to accountability are logically suspect. The most frequently cited instance would seem to be what is often called 'input – output' analysis. This rests on the premise that if you know the measured cognitive abilities of a cohort of students at the age of 11 or 13, you can assemble an index of their examination performances at 16 and relate the one to the other in order to show the 'productivity' of the school. This makes a series of assumptions. The abilities measured at 'input' are assumed to be those relevant to the process of education. That process itself is assumed to be maximally conducted by the school to generate the requisite output (an assumption HMI clearly would not endorse). The examination results in question are assumed to be comparable one with another (i.e. reflecting similar degrees of scope, pacing–over–the–course, pitch, abstraction, etc. in the work). Each assumption is defective and vitiates the proposed process, and we have not even begun to consider variations between the schools it is intended to compare in this way. It is quite possible that the existence of the GCE system is systematically distorting the national perception of what constitutes a good and desirable outcome of education, much as the existence of HMI has distorted our perception of how best to maintain the quality of the service.

In any case most demands for utilitarian evaluation of the service are pretexts offered by interests more concerned to reduce its costs than improve its benefits. The collapse of public confidence in the service has occurred when its measured outcomes have never been higher or more widely diffused. The slow recovery of public trust that the service has gained locally has restricted the attack on it to three sources, the secretly–funded pressure groups that seek to prove the inherent incompetence of maintained schools, the political right, and the national mass–circulation press. It may be that within a relatively short time the latter will discover that rubbishing state schools is no longer a way of getting readers, although it may be a way of pleasing proprietors.

The utilitarian model has been tested in a number of societies and found wanting. The professional model has not, except in the very restricted sense that present arrangements can be said to constitute such a model. This book has outlined the ways in which the professional model of accountability is less than complete, but the basis for asserting the existence of a system of professional accountability in the English service will have emerged from previous chapters. Its principal problems will also be evident: professional accountability has to be more than accountability to other professionals, but the widespread ignorance about its working extends far beyond the lay public to include numerous elected members, not a few education officers, almost all local authority treasurers and chief executives, and much of the teaching profession itself. Sockett's second requirement is thus clearly not met: adequate information to show that quality is being maintained and improved is not being provided. It may help to improve this situation if we try to understand why it has come about.

First, the quality-support arm of most LEAs has grown almost by stealth, both in the creation and filling of additional posts and in the ways of working favoured by advisory staff. The enduring conviction among head teachers that advisers are superfluous, and hence consumers of manpower better put in front of classes, has been less regularly voiced in recent years, but advisers and teachers remain conscious of it, and the liability of advisory establishments to cuts is felt to be acute – acute enough to affect recruitment in some cases. This situation breeds a sustained devotion to the lowest possible advisory profile within each LEA and inhibits the public presentation of advisory work nationally.

Secondly, the fear of being found superfluous by elected members has interlocked with the reality of being found competitive by education officers, to create in many LEAs, probably in most, a profound separation between members and advisers. In some LEAs, for example, advisory staff's involvement in selection for promotion is defined as ceasing at the point where members become involved: dealing with members is work for officers not advisers. Even where this distinction is overcome, it is unusual for advisers and inspectors to have any regular access to members in committee – all but a handful of my own survey sample expressed surprise at being asked whether they had such access. This deprives advisory staffs both of opportunity to provide information about quality and of any means of securing formal sanction for the constructive thrust of their curriculum work.

Thirdly, little or no attempt has ever been made to assess the cost-benefit of advisory services, and advisers themselves have been among the most strenuous opponents of suggestions that this would be worth attempting. Correspondingly, no attempt has been made to assess the cost to the service of an ineffective teacher, or the benefit of rendering him more effective. These omissions are a specific part of the generic absence of system in LEA advisory work, which in other respects contributes directly to the insecurity just referred to. Thus, head teachers rarely know what number or frequency of advisory visits to expect. Governing bodies usually hear of such visiting only if the head teacher chooses to report it, and since doing so may provoke governors to seek the advisers' own view of the school, head teachers are not quick to mention their presence. Many LEAs cannot even set down the number and pattern of advisory visits for their own officers' information, and rarely is such information made known to members. The same failure to inform governs in-service training, which occupies a staggering share of advisory time and offers one of the best cost-benefit bargains in the service. Members are not informed of the number or nature or outcome of disciplinary proceedings. It is too simple to impute all this to prejudice on the part of officers who construct committee agendas: members bear the main weight of responsibility for not trying to find out what they are getting for a group that costs most LEAs upwards of a third of a million pounds each year. Advisory staffs have also accepted the low profile offered them, and some have paid a high price for doing so.

Sockett's second principle that information about quality should be adequate leads inexorably to the policy of making inspection reports public. The majority of advisers and officers will object: publication has done HMI no good, it will be claimed; publication exposes teachers, especially in one-subject departments; and publication invites dissent and criticism. In reality 'publication' means providing copies of the report for the whole teaching staff, the governors, and the handful of parents who will ask; a properly written press release, in printable-copy form, for local newspapers and media, with the full report as back-up; and an LEA officer who will answer questions in concert with the head teacher. All LEAs do this now, or should be doing it, for HMI reports, and the result is almost always healthy. If the reports provoke dissent, so much the better for the inspectors that they cannot play high and mighty and must defend their critique. They will learn very quickly the pitfalls of careless drafting and the local service will be the stronger for it. If there are occasional leaks, they do less harm than gossip, less harm than the head teacher who receives a confidential full inspection report and allows only his senior staff to see it, less harm than the lay suspicion that the professionals are covering-up for each other. If professional accountability is not to be merely accountability to professionals alone, publication must follow. So must much more sheer information about what is done and how it works.

Professional accountability and local politics

The nexus between professional holding other professional to account and the lay political leaders who pay the salaries of both remains the nub of the problem. Political leaders are elected, and all education committees in England are predominantly made up of elected members. They also comprise, however, significant numbers of co-opted members – not only representatives of the churches and local universities, but 'persons knowledgeable in education'. The latter may be nominees of teaching unions, or in addition to those nominees, and recently retired head teachers, primary and secondary, often figure among 'persons knowledgeable'. Such co-opted members are of some consequence because their knowledge and skills can inform the lay membership while remaining detached from officers. Members both elected and co-opted have a duty of curricular oversight. They can delegate it satisfactorily to governing bodies only to the extent that they can hold governing bodies accountable for their discharge of the duty. (That this is an unreal notion is an issue we come to below.) In any case members can no longer hide behind the formalities of statute and regulations: they have concurred in the development of local advisory services and have a duty of oversight to the same degree as with education officers. It is thus no longer acceptable for education committees to make no provision for the exercise of curricular oversight, however minimal, beyond agreeing to take reports on curricular matters because they happen to have financial implications.

The need in a majority of LEAs is for the development of permanent working parties or standing member groups on curriculum. Such a group would be required to develop a picture of the nature of curriculum in action in a variety of schools, whether by planned visiting or by a deeper association between each member and a handful of schools. It would have a specific duty to receive and note major curricular documents such as HMI surveys and DES policy statements. It might well have vested in it the duty of receiving the inspection reports of HMI and LEA inspectors, meeting with governors and head teacher in each case to hear responses, and returning after a due interval to check on follow-up. And in the course of the four-year life of its appointing committee it would have a duty of review of the work and curricular thrust of the authority's advisory staff. The latter function has some importance in enabling inspectors and advisers who seek particular curricular patterns or developments to secure formal endorsement – and hence in converting officer/adviser predisposition into policy. It would often take the form of receiving and discussing papers written by inspectors about their subjects and the state of teaching in the LEA, but in some curriculum areas a paper is not enough: visits to schools and demonstrations are also necessary. The opportunity to enable lay members to understand the priority of learning over teaching and to perceive the values and perceptions of lay governors and professional advisers about the same schools is one part of this process. Another and much more important part is the growth of an informed understanding of the combination of technical expertise, pupil-management skills and planning that goes into classroom teaching in contemporary conditions.

Rightly developed, the work of such a standing group then becomes a regular component in the agenda of its appointing Education Committee. Mostly it will appear there in the form of matters for report and information – 'we have looked at this and this and this . . . ' Some items however will require decision, and many examples have occurred in previous chapters. Instances that have occurred in various LEAs in recent years include these:

(*a*)   An urban LEA appointed an adviser for mathematics who found that the primary head teachers had reached a collective decision some years earlier, unknown to the LEA, to forbid the use of calculators in class. The Cockcroft Report, appearing shortly after the new adviser's arrival, advocated a different view, and some primary heads followed it – but a minority adhered to their decision and asked for an LEA 'ruling'.

(*b*)   A pressure group composed of parents and fundamentalist church people launched a media campaign against some of the practices of a newly reorganized tertiary college, in particular the use of life models in art classes. The critics rejected the governors' insistence that it was normal practice and wrote to the councillors, most of whom wanted the issue thrashed out more fully than the education committee's agenda had time for.

(*c*) A Midlands LEA had adopted a 'ring fence' for staff, whereby vacant posts for teachers were available only to the authority's existing teaching staff. After three years, the secondary head teachers appealed to the LEA for its repeal, on the grounds that it seriously restricted the scope for recruitment in shortage subjects and prevented them from taking on outstanding women teachers who had moved into the area to live. (For a discussion of the issues and evidence, see Walsh *et al.*, 1984.)

Above all, local authorities are charged under the DES curriculum circulars with the duty of promulgating their policies for the curriculum. They can do this by varying degrees of delegation, as we have seen. Deputing the matter entirely to governing bodies is by common consent and all the evidence unworkable (Kogan *et al.*, 1984). Deputing it to head teachers was the established tradition which LEAs adhered to in theory but abandoned in practice by appointing advisory staff. They are left with deputing it to specialist groups of their own members working with officers and advisers and teachers in the evolution of commonly acceptable formulations of curriculum policy. Precisely how this works will vary from one LEA to another. It is most commonly likely to bring teachers, heads and advisory staff into working groups to develop curriculum papers and guidelines of the sort described in earlier chapters, which then require the close study and approval of members – if necessary after amendment.

It will not overcome the need for machinery of this kind to claim that it represents curriculum control or lay interference. The alternative is utilitarian accountability, a form of curriculum control over which professionals have little or no influence. The professionals are not being asked to settle for a compromise: they are being asked to take an opportunity to strengthen their own credibility and standing. The curricular intentions and aspirations of teachers, in short, now need the *protection* of explicit endorsement by education committees. The reluctance of teachers to concede this need, however, is minuscule beside the abhorrence of many, perhaps most, lay councillors, for whom technicality in any form is a regrettable necessity unless and until it can be made interesting. Those LEAs which have implemented the idea of standing curriculum or evaluation groups have found in practice that their members prove very readily engaged by the technicalities of how schools work. Such members become informed supporters of the service with a depth of knowledge and enthusiasm it badly needs in political circles.

Governing bodies are still in some respects anomalous, in part because the other participants in the accountability network have allowed them to remain so. We cannot predict the potential of governing bodies until their needs are more adequately met than at present. Authorities have a duty, if only born of self-interest, to ensure the provision of lucid manuals of guidance for governors. At least the chair of each governing body should be expected to undergo a minimal degree of training, and all governors need a clear briefing as to their powers and duties and where and how to handle complaints. Governors have a proper function in the general oversight of the welfare and conduct of a school, and their natural predisposition to interpret that as full, uncritical, invariable support for the head teacher is in need of correction. There is a clear case for regarding governing bodies as entitled, in cases of anxiety or doubt, to secure an outside assessment of some aspect of a school without such a request being viewed as inherently a criticism of the head teacher. Where the head teacher has supported the fullest development of the governing body as a regular participant in the school's decision making, the governors will know more about how the LEA works and will be able the more readily to explore such possibilities. At present too many opportunities for this kind of development are lost through the natural reluctance of head teachers to foster what might become a constraint upon themselves, or through the shortage of officer manpower to undertake training work.

Professional accountability at officer level

The role of education officers is a particularly difficult one in the development of professional accountability in the LEA. Until the arrival of a unified career and salary structure covering them, head teachers and LEA advisers, education officers have to continue a long-term process of adaptation. In the not very distant past there was a relatively simple structure of line management in the office, with the schools subject to no more than a peripheral style of management by the LEA, the advisory staff operating almost exclusively in the schools and engaging almost entirely with subject and classroom teachers. The structure now evolving and in need (as this book's argument sees it) of a more planned and directed development spells an end to that convenient simplicity. Advisers need to recognize that many education officers, in refusing to accept the size and functions of advisory staffs as necessary, are adopting a perfectly natural and legitimate position. Advisers need to understand, in many LEAs, that their own numbers and presence constitute what officers see as a threat to their freedom of action and in some cases as a threat to the coherence of the office as a whole. The division between the education officer side and the advisory side is almost complete, not only in the virtual absence of movement between them in a large majority of LEAs, but also in the absence of serious dialogue both locally and more generally. From an objective or consultant's point of view the question is whether the two sides are not artificial divisions of what ought to be a common service. There are one or two authorities which have tried to act on this belief, appointing people to posts of Education Officer (Curriculum) and redistributing the work of the office in different ways. Elsewhere, sadly, the debate is impeded by real differences in salary structure and strongly felt differences in perceived status. Such a state of affairs should best be seen as an opportunity to discuss openly how the collegial culture of the advisory staff can best be fitted into the hierarchical one of the officers without merely assuming that one or other is 'wrong' (Handy, 1984). And both parties need to understand that many of the perceived limitations of advisers stem less from the individuals concerned than from omissions in their management and needless restrictions on their work.

Any study of how advisory staff operate in a variety of LEAs will rapidly expose differences which may seem of no importance to anyone else but which have great symbolic significance. In a majority of LEAs, teachers have right of access to the inspector or adviser appropriate to them, just as, technically speaking, all teachers have access to HMI by right. But in a considerable number of LEAs the teacher or even head teacher who wishes to consult an adviser is expected to 'go through' the local education officer. This may be seen in the office as a necessary protection for the adviser, but its effect is to diminish the adviser in the eyes of teachers to an instrument of the administration and so to destroy his integrity and usefulness. In Sockett's terms, the adviser is reduced from professional to technician. There are of course numerous advisers for whom the technician role is preferable: it is less painful not to have to make judgements and to confine oneself to ways and means. Another way in which authorities may signal a technician status in advisers is by giving them no right of entry to schools and making entry conditional on the invitation of the head teacher. How such an LEA can claim an effective approach to accountability is difficult to see.

Some advisory staffs in the past have endorsed the reluctance of teachers about inspection: the passing vogue for self-evaluation by individual teachers was warmly embraced by some advisers. A number of LEAs have nevertheless opted for formal inspection without serious dispute from the advisory staff whose jobs were transformed in this way. This suggests, however, that advisers generally find it helpful to be engaged in a certain amount of inspection. The change is symbolic in a number of ways, most of all in giving the advisory staff an unmistakable public identification with the LEA, with (in trade union terms) management. This is helpful to advisory staff because the ambiguity which invested their work when they lacked such identification was always a complication and could at times be disabling: the teacher could always suppose, though he might rarely say out loud, that the adviser was only pursuing an individual preference.

The identification involved in undertaking inspection, and in some LEAs in changing to the designation of Inspector, also marks a subtle shift in the relationships with education officers, for whom 'adviser' has often been a sugaring of a pill properly called 'inspector', and who have not always understood advisory ambiguities over the lack of political backing. So they have regularly found advisers very reluctant to inspect, unwilling to be firm with wayward or misguided headteachers about curriculum, hesitant to try to define curricular advice in writing. Advisers know too well that such definiteness will be challenged, and that the necessary back-up of political will is rarely forthcoming. Education officers who have not the same scale of field experience with teachers sometimes view these hesitations as mealy-mouthed evasions, without realizing that these aspects of LEA curricular management are not susceptible of advisory control unaided. The sad truth seems to be that education officers and advisers scarcely talk to one another – locally or nationally. The accountability systems of LEAs are not likely to become adequately professional until they do.

The quality of the quality arm

The professional model of accountability has to depend above all on the quality of head teachers, but for its fullest realization on the LEA's advisers and inspectors. In many LEAs, possibly most, their position is in need of a systematic process of up-rating. Put plainly, advisory staffs have become accustomed to headship salaries and have yet to be given the opportunity to develop the skills and the vision to be worthy of them, or the resources, training and equipment that any holding a headship on comparable scales is given as a matter of course. It is grotesque that advisers should in any LEA be graciously permitted to attend a three-day course of training once every two years as a reward for good behaviour or some kind of privilege. It is folly to employ a group of inspectors whose salaries collectively exceed £250,000 p.a. and provide them with no secretarial help or exclusive use of telephone time, yet several LEAs do just this. It is beyond belief that advisers and inspectors who are employed above all else to conduct sensitive and confidential business are in dozens of LEAs expected to work in open-plan offices without access to interview rooms or in ramshackle former mobile classrooms where every conversation is audible to everyone in the building. Social workers are similarly used to being a low form of office life, but that does not ease the day-to-day difficulty. If advisers and inspectors were obliged to undergo the training appropriate to their duties they might feel better equipped for the curious combination of generous responsibilities and mean status that too many LEAs impose.

Even after the 1975 salary award, LEAs neglected the opportunity to recruit at deputy-head level and continued to bring in heads of subject departments (or of ordinary primary schools) with little experience of work with a wide variety of teachers. Many were propelled into the work with little induction, no training, minimal supervision, and the enduring handicap of status uncertainty. The remedies called for are these:

1　Advisory appointments need to draw on teachers with some quasi-advisory experience, such as leading in-service courses or curriculum development, and job-descriptions need to make this requirement explicit.

2　LEAs need to understand and make plain that advisory work places a high premium on writing ability, time-management and the ability to cope with stress.

3　Advisory staff have to oversee careful arrangements for the induction of newcomers to the teaching profession, and ought at least to be offered some induction to their own work – in specific initiatory tasks, observing experienced colleagues, information about LEA structures, practices and finances, and a designated mentor for the first year.

4　Advisers and inspectors require training (in almost the same proportions as they deny the need): in counselling skills, team-building skills, the dynamics of curriculum change, analysing organizational cultures, curriculum analysis and timetable construction, and awareness of their own impact on others. In practice such support for in-service training as most advisers can secure is limited to further reinforcement of a subject role already too narrow in scope for the needs of the LEA. The enlightened authority will insist that its advisory staff should rank with its heads and senior managers for full-scale management development training.

5　LEA managements need to ensure that advisory staff's accumulated knowledge of the service is used. The usual claim is that since every school is known by someone in the team, all is well. That is, precisely, the minimalist tradition in operation. The claim often will not stand serious investigation; the knowledge referred to is usually knowledge-in-the-head, uncertain of date and of dubious availability. The point is in any case not merely to have coverage, but to be seen to have it and to make use of it. The principle that accountability has to be seen to be in place points to some audiences. There is a potent audience among teachers for formally disseminated good practice, and skilfully presented material will find a large audience among parents, governors and members. *Education in Cheshire* was a well-produced annual glossy, but it did wonders for the confidence of its readers in the service it described for many years.

6   The deployment of advisory staff requires to be managed. Most advisers 'roam the range', their priorities untested and their choices of where to call unexamined, or dictated by others without serious review. Roaming the range might corral every school in a year, but very few LEAs would know, since few take the trouble to record or analyse advisory visiting. This position makes advisers themselves unaccountable, and is indefensible.

In some LEAs, but at present probably only a minority, the deployment of the local inspectorate is planned in relation to the needs of the service. The commonest patterns are the List and the Parish. In the one, every school in the LEA is assigned to one of the advisers, who has to visit his 'list' at stipulated frequencies. The visiting is in good practice given a set of concrete purposes: to check material or professional needs that can be met; to review the health and progress of the school with the head teacher in relation to previous such reviews and other advisory comment and in the light of the adviser's visit to every classroom; to ensure a positive alignment between the needs of the staff and the opportunities for professional improvement open to them; and to identify aspects of the life of the school on which the support or advice of a specialist colleague is called for. The parish principle assigns a group of advisers, including a primary specialist, a secondary general adviser and a number of subject specialists, to a cluster of secondary schools and their feeder primaries. Here the same requirements operate, but the parish team provides for a majority of the needs of the schools in the parish, and the responsibility for ensuring adequate cover (and frequent enough cover) is lodged with the team leader in the parish. There is evidence of a clear movement towards the parish principle in those larger LEAs where deployment of advisory staff has been given systematic thought. Once again, the surface motive of reducing travelling time overlays a more important aim, of increasing the visibility of the team in the schools.

Any deployment of an advisory staff faces a wide range of tests of its effectiveness, and below certain levels of manning will fail all of them. Certainly it is not a professional test that asks how many ineffective teachers the service got rid of in a given year: the aim is not to get rid of weak teachers but to turn them into strong ones. It is not a professional test that counts ticks on a list of schools and gives the team marks according as it scores high for visits. It is not a professional test that sets up some kind of norm of time to be spent in classrooms and measures the team's performance accordingly. Above all is it not professional to assess the effectiveness of an advisory staff by the 'performance measure' of its perceived influence in the schools as the teachers or heads judge that: the digits on a clock-face cannot judge the timekeeping of the clock. The test of effectiveness that an advisory service would look to be judged by is in four parts. The first is the degree of change over time in the quality of children's learning. The second is the rate at which objectionable classroom practice disappears. The third is the depth and quality of teachers' own engagement in the evolution of LEA policy. The fourth, and by far the most important, is the level of awareness among teachers that the LEA is an agency with a positive interest in educational quality – the sort of interest that wishes to establish not that a handful of teachers are bad and have to be 'weeded out' but that most schools are good and can become much better.

The response of the school

Teachers have every possible interest in the choice of a professional model of accountability. That preference has some implications. First, professional accountability can only work in some degree of trust between school and LEA: the notion that the LEA has no proper interest in accountability is an academic fantasy. The absence of trust is very difficult to remedy, but the quickest builder of trust among teachers is candour. The weak teacher or head knows there is weakness: the adviser who glosses over or skirts round gains no trust. Likewise, the adviser who falls short of expectation will want to be told. The vice of utilitarian models of accountability is that they are quite without reciprocity: pupils take the test, pupils score badly, teacher is dismissed – no interaction, no access to recovery, no means of grace. In a professional model, reciprocity is of the essence.

It is through reciprocity and trust that schools, with a frequency that would astound the layman, *ask* for inspection or review. Such a request reflects a practised acceptance of advisory candour by the school, and an experienced skill in speaking as one finds without throwing the school's teachers on the defensive. Professional accountability has to rely on enlisting the inspected in the search for remedy, and whether that is done by formal inspection, or less formal review, or school self-evaluation is a matter for local choice endorsed (once again) as LEA policy. The opportunity and the obligation of the LEA is critical here. Teachers feel accountable to people they know, and need the maximum reduction of the uncertainties besetting them. The need is particularly acute in times of limited resources and sharp contraction of numbers: falling rolls in the secondary sector will continue to make LEAs preoccupied and teachers insecure for many years. The national incoherence over curriculum policy stems in part from the total omission of even the mention of curriculum from the 1944 Act and the consequences of that (*cf.* Aldrich and Leighton, 1984), but also from structural developments such as those in the post-16 sector which have outdated the legislative foundations of the service. One of the consequences is that central government is able to bring about not only a major change in the ideology of its relationship with local authorities and the joint bodies it sustains with them (Salter and Tapper, 1981), but also a change in the distribution of powers between centre and locality which could well be permanent. One aspect of that is likely to be an insistence on the LEA's duties to ensure quality as well as delivery in the curriculum.

This devolution to the LEAs is likely to be echoed by a local devolution to the schools in matters of finance. The belief that schemes like ILEA's Alternative Use of Resources or Cambridgeshire's experimental Local Financial Management must save office costs for the LEA dies hard but is open to doubt: in the long term they probably transfer some costs from the office, where they are visible, to the school, where they may not be. The notion that the same devolution can be effected in matters of educational quality is fallacious as long as it accepts permanent appointment to headship and separation between the corps of head teachers and that of officers and inspectors. In any case the Department of Education and Science is demanding a codification of curriculum policy that feels novel and centralist but is historically only a duty the LEAs have long neglected through being too ill-equipped to perform it, an argument few of them could properly advance today.

One hesitates to assume that the Department of Education and Science is aware that it faces a problem of defining curriculum policy just enough to be effective without defining it so precisely and in such detail as to leave the LEAs nothing to do. That is, nevertheless, the preliminary impression of its publications to date. In other words, the Department is providing the LEAs with an opportunity – one not as daunting as that enshrined in the post-1944 consensus, but one which would allow the LEA to become a real force in the curriculum and its evaluation. The price of failing to grasp that opportunity must be a further decline in public confidence in the service or a further extension of central control. It is vital to test and mark out the proper limits of that control, to develop and implement the accountability of schools on a professional model, and to put central government out of the business of defining or determining the quality of education in detail.

The accountable school

We can now identify more precisely the characteristics of the properly accountable school. We must presume that the tradition of autonomy will continue to inform the reactions of most organized associations of teachers and heads to most attempts to impose order and coherence on the educational system. We must also presume, however, that teachers and heads in general will be less content than their organizations with the minimal management of the LEAs or with being left alone to satisfy society and parents and central government as best they can. The old automatic association between good quality in schools and headmasterly autonomy and academic 'freedom' has broken down. What features will replace it?

First, schools and teachers have been very attached to talking about networks of accountability but much less ready to behave accordingly. The participant in a network looks for and offers reciprocity to the other participants, most particularly to the other professionals. Each participant looks for a clear definition of who is responsible for what, and this has positive as well as negative consequences. Thus, there is a need for clear assignment of responsibility for curriculum policy decisions – some to classroom teachers, some to schools, some to governing bodies, some to LEAs and some to central government. There is also a need for the participants to recognize what the other participants can and cannot be expected to achieve: teachers have become accustomed to blaming their LEAs for financial stringencies that are in reality to be laid at the door of central government, and they and head teachers fail to see the connection (for example) between severe cutbacks in spending on books and the maintenance of grossly excessive surplus places in under-occupied schools. The same holds for central government: the 1985 policy document on science lays out a programme that is manifestly unattainable in the existing conditions of recruitment and training of primary teachers (let alone of secondary science specialists). To suggest that some of the participants in the accountability network have unrealistic expectations of each other does not argue against such an approach to accountability, but it does mean that a network of professional accountability will operate successfully only if its participants show a professional realism.

Secondly, the accountable school will be prepared to talk with its clients, parents and pupils and governors and others, about standards and its approach to them. It will talk with rather than at them, and it will do so regularly and often. Pupils will be shown their objectives for each subject each term. Parents will be the active participants in the network that they usually want to be – and the school will refuse to be deflected by the child's skill and resource in keeping it and parents apart. Head teachers will drive their governing bodies into recognizing and discharging their proper duties, so that those individual governors who cannot sustain them give place to those who will. The head's annual report to governors will also be a report to the LEA, capable of the local inspector's endorsement as well as the perceptive governor's approval.

Thirdly, the accountable school will have a substance behind its giving of information that standards are being pursued. The other part of Sockett's notion of professional accountability is that besides giving information about the search for quality, the school (and the LEA) is actively seeking it. This is the most searching demand of all, because it implies that each and every head teacher has a duty to be pursuing the quality of each and every teacher on his staff. In nothing is the head teacher so plainly required to be a manager as in managing the quality of teaching. What might that mean?

It means a regular reviewing of each department scheme of work, with the technical help of the adviser where necessary. It certainly means a regular examination of the quality, condition, date and mode of use of staple teaching materials. It can hardly exclude serious attention to the differentiation of materials according to different levels of aptitude among the pupils. The nub of all this, however, lies in the classroom, in the way the teacher operates as a creator not of teaching but of learning, and the head teacher who is serious about managing the quality of teaching is observing lessons, and many of them, all the time. There are heads who greatly prize the disposition to 'walk school' in their deputy heads. Those who prize even more highly the disposition to 'see class' usually find they have better schools, because the heart of a school is in its pedagogy. Head teachers have in all but the smallest schools the opportunity that inspectors prize most, to see lessons taking place. If they were to take it, they would come in time, as most advisers and HMI have done, to see for themselves the priorities as they should be, with teaching seen as instructional performances carrying little weight, and teaching as the designing of learning by pupils carrying the only weight that matters.

These emphases in the proper work of the accountable head of an accountable school are not uniformly present in schools in England today. It is doubtful whether a school can ever be professionally accountable until they become normal, because without them the teacher who faces his head for an appraisal interview once a year is facing one sham with another: what the head teacher can ask about or judge is limited by the scope of his observation of the teacher in the workplace, while the teacher can present the outward picture, and even manipulate it, in the knowledge that the pedagogic realities cannot be searchingly questioned. It is this conversion of appraisal into a paper exercise, an empty form, that every serious discussion has pointed out as the main danger in making appraisal obligatory. Its danger lies less in the effect on teachers and schools than in the damage it would do to the public acceptance that accountability is working. Such damage would bring much closer the recourse to utilitarian forms of accountability that all professionals rightly fear. It is too early to tell whether the service can in the event afford the cost of professional appraisal for all teachers, but we can tell already that it will never be able to afford an appraisal system in the absence of that care for the quality of teaching that the appraisal will properly seek to support and consolidate.

None of this means that schools that are accountable will in the English system be more standardized or uniform than they are now. The development and maintenance of a quality of teaching that will sustain and thrive on appraisal cannot be brought about by head teachers on their own: they will need the active support both of their teaching staffs and of LEA advisers and inspectors, who are far too diverse and individualistic to be instruments of uniformity. In any case there are many schools where that level of quality is already in place: the message of every HMI publication from the Primary Survey to the present, and of the 1985 White Paper *Better Schools,* is that if the average were to reach the quality of the best, the difference in public esteem would be very marked.

The accounting LEA

I have contended throughout this book that the accountability of a school must rest on a professional model, not only in order to be acceptable to its teachers, but primarily to be effective in improving the standards of schooling. It suits the electoral convenience of both ends of the political spectrum to vest the school's accountability in parents. The left chooses to rest this claim on political and individual rights that, on the evidence available so far, only an activist minority of parents have ever wished to exercise. The far right makes a facile equation between being in the market for parents' payment of fees and being educationally accountable to them. It is not difficult to see that both positions point to utilitarian models of accountability. It must lie with the local education authority to mediate to its schools a professional model of accountability that is visible enough to be acceptable to all the pertinent lay interests.

Such an obligation is very far from being discharged today: we return once again to the diversity of LEAs. Oxfordshire is only the most public case of those authorities which have accepted the obligation: it seeks to run an accountability system that engages elected members without alienating its teachers, while also dealing with those whose accounts end in the red. There are other authorities which seek a similar effect by less public means – and the lack of public knowledge could become a fatal omission. The officers of such authorities have developed this positive role mainly by stealth, by imperceptible shifts in the climate and with a minimum of overt declaration. But many LEAs, almost certainly a majority and quite possibly a large majority, would view such a posture as improper. They would feel ill-equipped to undertake the work and deeply uncertain of the necessary political will to stiffen its conduct. The central contention of this book has been that so minimalist a stance will no longer serve. It will not do to cling to a theory of partnership which has long been more rhetoric that reality and claim that holding schools accountable will disturb a delicate balance between partners. The collapse of confidence signifies that parents and electors are no longer content with such arguments, and the curriculum circulars that embody central government's response to that profound change of attitude are evidence that they do not persuade Whitehall either. If the careful relationship between local and central government is regarded as part of that balance between partners, central government has now demonstrated that the balance must change. Indeed, it may be that the principal source of disturbance to that balance is not so much any alleged centralism on the part of the Department of Education and Science, but rather the failure of political and governmental will on the part of local education authorities. Too many of them, for too long, have been content to see local government in education as the best kind of administration.

So the issue of how we hold schools accountable, and to whom, is ultimately the issue of what sort of entity the local education authority is to be. The point emerges ever more clearly as the service comes to terms with its post-1976 realities – for example in the review of teacher appraisal conducted for the DES by a team from the Suffolk LEA (Suffolk LEA, 1985). Its opening summary defines the role of the LEA in unambiguously positive terms. Many an education officer will have read that definition and blenched: so aggressive a posture is altogether too forceful and alien to the local authority tradition as many of its practitioners have come to know it. But the officers, advisers and (hence) the elected members of LEAs are in a dilemma. Either they must accept the implications of governing a complex service so that its units and their managers are held properly accountable, or that management will ineluctibly pass to others. For the English LEA as it has developed since 1902 the message is stark: if the local education authority system is itself to survive, the accountability of schools must become effective.

Appendix A A model for assessing the advisory manpower needs of a Local Education Authority requiring routine monitoring of schools and colleges.

	Method	*Example*			
		Primary	Special	Secondary	Further
Step 1	Identify the number of establishments in each category to be reckoned in for this purpose.	250	15	45	6
Step 2	Determine the visit-entitlement of each category for monitoring purposes (i.e. excluding staffing, trouble-shooting, in-service, secondments, etc.) per annum.	4	12	Gen'l 12 Subj. 24	10
Step 3	Multiply product of Step 1 with that of Step 2 (in each category).	1000	180	1620	60
Step 4	Sum the product of Step 3 and apportion the resulting total of visits between full-day and 'other' to yield total Adviser-days-equivalent (ADE).	2860 = 1430 ADE + 1430 'other'			
Step 5	Assume that the routine administrative and organizing tasks of advisers are fitted round the 'other' visits, so that in practice 'other' visits cannot normally be made at a rate of more than one a day. Sum the ADE required.	1430 + 1430 = 2860			
Step 6	Using known personnel data, assess the level of advisory visiting for purposes other than those in Step 5 (i.e. for staffing, interviewing, re-deployment, etc.).	Vacancies for posts requiring adviser participation occur approx 100 p.a. primary and special, 120 p.a. secondary. Each requires 1.3 ADE for shortlisting, interview, etc. (average). ADE required: 286.			
Step 7	Determine the maximum of in-school-hours time that advisers may devote to in-service courses for teachers.	20 ADE per adviser.			
Step 8	Assess the number of term-time ADE required for other tasks, deriving data from actual diaries.				

Tasks etc	(ADE)	
	Term-time	Non-term
Conferences, etc.	6	6
Ctees, Govng Bodies	5	–
Full inspections	20	–
Meetings (officers, HE staff, wardens, HMI)	15	5
Personal, medical etc	3	–

Step 9 The statutory school year being 190 days, deduct from 190 the sum of Step 7 and Step 8 (term-time).

$$190 - (20 + 49) = 121 \text{ ADE}$$

Step 10 Divide the product of Step 5 (total ADEs required by the decisions in Steps 1–5) by the product of Step 9 (the term-time ADEs available per adviser for routine visits).

$$2860 \div 121 = 23.6$$

Step 11 Where the product of Step 10 exceeds 8, add one post (chief adviser/inspector).

$$23.6 + 1 = 24.6$$

Step 12 For every six posts after the first six (or part thereof) add one senior post for phase/area duties.

$$24.6 - 6 = 18.6 \div 6 = 3.1$$
$$24.6 + 3.1 = 27.7$$

Step 13 Establish average distance between advisory base and schools, etc. to be visited. To allow for visiting loss by travelling time, add one post for every four miles by which this average exceeds 10 miles.

Average school–office distance: 18m.

$$18 - 10 = 8 \div 4 = 2.0 \quad 27.7 + 2.0 = 29.7$$

Notes

1 The product of Step 13 is the notional required advisory manpower for an LEA of the size and number of establishments specified in the example, on the basis of the assumptions and decisions made, and no other.

2 The calculations given in the example relate to a mythical county LEA some 65 miles long and 20 miles wide with its base office rather to one end of it. Larger LEAs experience an exponential effect of travelling time on non-visiting duties, for which allowance should be made.

3 The model offers a theoretical scheme, but its practical use requires close study of actual diaries if the critical assumptions in Steps 1 to 6 are to be realistic. Similarly, in an authority using full inspection regularly allowance should be made for writing-up and reporting but also for follow-up (omitted above since full inspections are assumed in the example to be infrequent).

References

ALDRICH, R. and LEIGHTON, P. (1984). *Education: Time for a New Act. Bedford Way Papers 23.* London: Heinemann.

BALL, S.J. (Ed) (1984). *Comprehensive Schooling: a Reader.* Lewes: The Falmer Press.

BARR, N. (1984). 'Week by Week'. *Education,* **163**,13, March 30.

BARTON, L. and WALKER, S. (1981). *Schools, Teachers and Teaching.* Lewes: The Falmer Press.

BECHER, T., ERAUT, M. and KNIGHT, J. (1981). *Policies for Educational Accountability.* London: Heinemann.

BECHER, T. and MACLURE, S. (1978). *Accountability in Education.* Windsor: NFER Publishing Company.

BERNSTEIN, B. (1971). 'On the Classification and Framing of Educational Knowledge'. In: YOUNG, M.F.D. (Ed) *Knowledge and Control.* London: Collier Macmillan.

BOARD OF EDUCATION (1924). *Report of the Board of Education for the Year 1922–23* (Cmd. 2179). London: HMSO.

BOLAM, R., SMITH, G. and CANTER, H. (1978). *L.E.A. Advisers and the Mechanisms of Innovation.* Windsor: NFER Publishing Company.

BRIGHOUSE, T.R.P. (1984). *School Self-Evaluation in Oxfordshire.* Oxford: Oxfordshire Education Department (mimeographed).

BROOKSBANK, K. (Ed) (1980). *Educational Administration.* London: Councils and Education Press.

BULLOCK REPORT. DEPARTMENT OF EDUCATION AND SCIENCE. COMMITTEE OF INQUIRY UNDER THE CHAIRMANSHIP OF SIR ALAN BULLOCK (1975). *A Language for Life.* London: HMSO.

BURGESS, T. and ADAMS, E. (Eds) (1980). *Outcomes of Education.* London: Macmillan.

COCKCROFT REPORT. REPORT OF THE COMMITTEE OF INQUIRY INTO THE TEACHING OF MATHEMATICS IN SCHOOLS UNDER THE CHAIRMANSHIP OF DR. W.H. COCKCROFT (1982). *Mathematics Counts.* London: HMSO.

DEAN, A.J. (1975a). 'The Advisory Team and the Professional

Development of Teachers'. *NAIEA Journal*, **2**,1.

DEAN, A.J. (1975b). 'The Advisory Team: Introduction'. *NAIEA Journal*, **3**, 1.

DELAMONT, S. (1983). *Interaction in the Classroom*, 2nd edn. London: Methuen.

DELAMONT, S. (Ed) (1984). *Readings on Interaction in the Classroom*. London: Methuen.

DEPARTMENT OF EDUCATION AND SCIENCE (1977). *Curriculum 11 – 16: Working Papers by HM Inspectorate*. Stanmore: DES Publications Centre.

DEPARTMENT OF EDUCATION AND SCIENCE (1978). *Primary Education in England: A Survey by HM Inspectors of Schools*. London: HMSO. (The 'Primary Survey'.)

DEPARTMENT OF EDUCATION AND SCIENCE (1979a). *Local Authority Arrangements for the School Curriculum: Report on the Circular 14/77 Review*. London: HMSO.

DEPARTMENT OF EDUCATION AND SCIENCE (1979b). *Aspects of Secondary Education in England: a survey by HM Inspectors of Schools*. London: HMSO. (The 'Secondary Survey'.)

DEPARTMENT OF EDUCATION AND SCIENCE (1980a). *Report by Her Majesty's Inspectors on Educational Provision by the Inner London Education Authority*. Stanmore: DES Publications Centre.

DEPARTMENT OF EDUCATION AND SCIENCE (1980b). *Girls in Science*. London: HMSO.

DEPARTMENT OF EDUCATION AND SCIENCE (1981). *Curriculum 11–16: A Review of Progress*. London: HMSO.

DEPARTMENT OF EDUCATION AND SCIENCE (1982a). *Ten Good Schools: Studies by HM Inspectors*. London: HMSO.

DEPARTMENT OF EDUCATION AND SCIENCE (1982b). *Education 5 to 9: an illustrative survey of 80 first schools in England*. London: HMSO.

DEPARTMENT OF EDUCATION AND SCIENCE (1983a). *Music in Primary Schools*. London: HMSO.

DEPARTMENT OF EDUCATION AND SCIENCE (1983b). *9 – 13 Middle Schools: an Illustrative Survey*. London: HMSO.

DEPARTMENT OF EDUCATION AND SCIENCE (1983c). *Teaching Quality: White Paper from the Secretary of State* (Cmd. 8836). London: HMSO.

DEPARTMENT OF EDUCATION AND SCIENCE (1983d). *A Study of Her Majesty's Inspectorate*. London: HMSO. (The 'Rayner Scrutiny'.)

DEPARTMENT OF EDUCATION AND SCIENCE (1983e). *The Work of Her Majesty's Inspectorate in England and Wales: a Policy Statement*. Stanmore: DES Publications Centre.

DEPARTMENT OF EDUCATION AND SCIENCE (1983f). *HM Inspectors Today: Standards in Education*. Stanmore: DES Publications Centre.

DEPARTMENT OF EDUCATION AND SCIENCE (1983g). *Curriculum 11 – 16: Towards a Statement of Entitlement*. Stanmore: DES Publications Centre.

DEPARTMENT OF EDUCATION AND SCIENCE (1984a). *Slow Learning and Less Successful Pupils in Secondary Schools – evidence from some HMI visits.* Stanmore: DES Publications Centre.

DEPARTMENT OF EDUCATION AND SCIENCE (1984b). *Education Observed: a review of the first six months of published reports by HM Inspectors.* Stanmore: DES Publications Centre.

DEPARTMENT OF EDUCATION AND SCIENCE (1984c). *English 5 to 16. Curriculum Matters 1.* London: HMSO.

DEPARTMENT OF EDUCATION AND SCIENCE (1984d). *Education Observed 2: a review of published reports by HM Inspectors.* Stanmore: DES Publications Centre.

DEPARTMENT OF EDUCATION AND SCIENCE (1985a). *Science 5–16: a statement of policy.* London: HMSO.

DEPARTMENT OF EDUCATION AND SCIENCE (1985b). *Better Schools: A White Paper.* (Cmd. 9469). London: HMSO.

DEPARTMENT OF EDUCATION AND SCIENCE (1985c). *The Curriculum from 5 to 16. Curriculum Matters 2.* London: HMSO.

DEPARTMENT OF EDUCATION AND SCIENCE (1985d). *Mathematics 5 to 16. Curriculum Matters 3.* London: HMSO.

DEPARTMENT OF EDUCATION AND SCIENCE (1985e). *Quality in Schools: Evaluation and Appraisal.* London: HMSO.

EDMONDS, E.L. (1962). *The School Inspector.* London: Routledge.

ELLIOTT, G. (n.d.). *Self-Evaluation and the Teacher: an annotated bibliography and report on current practice.* Parts 1 to 3, 1980. Part 4, 1981. University of Hull (mimeographed).

ELLIOTT, J. *et al.* (1981a). *Case Studies in School Accountability.* I, II and III. Cambridge: Institute of Education.

ELLIOTT, J. *et al.* (1981b). *School Accountability.* London: Grant McIntyre.

FINCH, A. and SCRIMSHAW, P. (1980). *Standards, Schooling and Education.* London: Hodder and Stoughton.

FLETCHER, C. *et al.* (1985). *Schools on Trial.* Milton Keynes: Open University Press.

FISKE, D. (1979). 'The Adviser's Skills'. *NAIEA Journal,* No. 11.

FOUCAULT, M. (1975). *Surveiller et Punir: Naissance de la Prison.* Paris: Gallimard. (Tr., Sheridan 1979, Penguin.)

GIBSON, R. (1984). *Structuralism and Education.* London: Hodder and Stoughton.

GIPPS, C. and GOLDSTEIN, H. (1983). *Monitoring Children: an Evaluation of the Assessment of Performance Unit.* London: Heinemann.

GIPPS, C. *et al.* (1983). *Testing Children: Standardised Testing in Local Education Authorities and Schools.* London: Heinemann.

GOODSON, I.F. (1983). *School Subjects and Curriculum Change.* London: Croom Helm.

GOODSON, I.F. and BALL, S.J. (1984). *Defining the Curriculum: Histories and Ethnographies.* Lewes: The Falmer Press.

GORDON, P. and LAWTON, D. (1978). *Curriculum Change in the Nineteenth and Twentieth Centuries.* London: Hodder and Stoughton.

GOULDING, S., BELL, J., BUSH, T., FOX, A. and GOODEY, J. (Eds) (1984). *Case Studies in Educational Management*. London: Harper and Row.

GRAY, H.L. (Ed) (1982). *The Management of Educational Institutions*. Lewes: The Falmer Press.

HADOW REPORT. BOARD OF EDUCATION. REPORT OF THE CONSULTATIVE COMMITTEE (1926). *The Education of the Adolescent*. London: HMSO.

HAMMERSLEY, M. and HARGREAVES. A. (1983). *Curriculum Practice: some sociological case studies*. Lewes: The Falmer Press.

HANDY, C. (1984). *Taken For Granted? Understanding Schools as Organizations*. York: Longman for Schools Curriculum Development Committee.

HARGREAVES, D. (1972). *Interpersonal Relations and Education*. London: Routledge and Kegan Paul.

HARGREAVES, D. *et al.* (1975). *Deviance in Classrooms*. London: Routledge and Kegan Paul.

HARGREAVES, D. (1982). *The Challenge for the Comprehensive School*. London: Routledge and Kegan Paul.

HARLING, P. (Ed) (1984). *New Directions in Educational Leadership*. Lewes: Falmer Press.

HARRIS, A. *et al.* (Eds) (1975). *Curriculum Innovation*. London: Croom Helm.

HOYLE, E. (1975). 'The creativity of the school'. In: HARRIS, A. *et al.*, *op. cit. sup.*

HOYLE, E. (1976). *Strategies of Curriculum Change, E.203, Curriculum Design and Development*, Unit 23. Milton Keynes: Open University Press.

HOUSE OF COMMONS (1968). *Report from the Select Committee On Education and Science: Part I, Her Majesty's Inspectorate (England and Wales)*. London: HMSO.

HULL, R. (1985). *The Language Gap: How Classroom Dialogue Fails*. London: Methuen.

INGOLDSBY, A. (1976). 'Looking at Secondary Schools'. *NAIEA Journal*, **1**, 4.

INNER LONDON EDUCATION AUTHORITY (1976). *Report of Public Inquiry into William Tyndale Junior and Infant Schools held by R. Auld Q.C..* London: ILEA, County Hall.

INNER LONDON EDUCATION AUTHORITY (1977). *Keeping the School Under Review*. (Revised and enlarged, 1982.) London: ILEA, County Hall.

INNER LONDON EDUCATION AUTHORITY (1984). *Improving Secondary Schools*. (The Hargreaves Report.) London: ILEA, County Hall.

JACKSON, B. and MARSDEN, D. (1962). *Education and the Working Class*. London: Routledge and Kegan Paul.

JONES, G. and STEWART, J. (1983). *The Case for Local Government*. London: Allen and Unwin.

KOGAN, M. (Ed) *et al.* (1984). *School Governing Bodies.* London: Heinemann.

LACEY, R. (1968). *Hightown Grammar.* Manchester: University Press.

LAMBERT, K. (1984). 'The Changing Nature of Headship Skills and Public Confidence'. *Aspects of Education,* 33, University of Hull.

LAWTON, D. (1980). *The Politics of the School Curriculum.* London: Routledge and Kegan Paul.

LEGRAND, L. (1982). *Pour un collège démocratique.* Paris: Ministère de l'Education Nationale.

LELLO, J. (Ed) (1979). *Accountability in Education.* London: Ward Lock.

LEVY, P. and GOLDSTEIN, H. (1984). *Tests in Education.* London: Academic Press.

LOWNDES, G.A.N. (1937). *The Silent Social Revolution,* 2nd edn, 1969. Oxford: University Press.

MARLAND, M. (1978). *The Craft of the Classroom.* London: Heinemann.

MCCORMICK, R. *et al.* (Eds) (1982). *Calling Education to Account.* London: Heinemann.

MCCORMICK, R. and JAMES, M. (1983). *Curriculum Evaluation in Schools.* London: Croom Helm.

MACLURE, J.S. (Ed) (1969). *Educational Documents, England & Wales 1816–1968.* London: Methuen.

MCMAHON, A. *et al.* (1984). *Guidelines for Internal Review and Development in Schools: Primary School Handbook; Secondary School Handbook.* York: Longman for Schools Curriculum Development Committee.

MORGAN, C. *et al.* (1983). *The Selection of Secondary School Headteachers.* Milton Keynes: Open University Press.

NASH, R. (1973). *Classrooms Observed.* London: Routledge and Kegan Paul.

NATIONAL ASSOCIATION OF INSPECTORS AND EDUCATIONAL ADVISERS (1974ff) *Journal* **1–15,** *Inspection and Advice: Journal of NAIEA* **16**–*date.* Driffield: Studies in Education Ltd.

NATIONAL ASSOCIATION OF INSPECTORS AND EDUCATIONAL ADVISERS (1983). *Policy Paper No 1: A Summary of the Functions of an L.E.A. Educational Inspection/Advisory Service.* Hitchin: NAIEA Office.

NATIONAL ASSOCIATION OF INSPECTORS OF SCHOOLS AND EDUCATIONAL ORGANISERS (1959). *A History of the National Association 1919–1959.*

NEWSOM REPORT. DEPARTMENT OF EDUCATION AND SCIENCE. CENTRAL ADVISORY COUNCIL ON EDUCATION (CHAIRMAN, SIR JOHN NEWSOM) (1963). *Half our Future.* London: HMSO.

NUTTALL, D.L. (1981). *School Self-Evaluation: Accountability with a Human Face?* London: Longman for Schools Council.

OXFORDSHIRE EDUCATION DEPARTMENT (1979). *Starting Points in Self-Evaluation.* Oxford: County Education Offices.

PEARCE, J. (1984). 'Some travels with a donkey'. *Education,* **164,** 16.

PEARCE, J. *et al.* (1985a). *Assessment in West-German Schools*. Huntingdon: Cambridgeshire Education Department (mimeographed).
PEARCE, J. (1985b). *Heart of English: 9 to 14*. Oxford: University Press.
PILE, W. (1979). *The Department of Education and Science*. London: Allen and Unwin.
PLOWDEN REPORT. GREAT BRITAIN. DEPARTMENT OF EDUCATION AND SCIENCE. CENTRAL ADVISORY COUNCIL FOR EDUCATION (ENGLAND) (1967). *Children and their Primary Schools*. London: HMSO.
RANSON, S. (1980). 'Changing Relations between Centre and Locality in Education'. *Local Government Studies,* **6,** 6, 25–38.
REE, H. (1973). *Educator Extraordinary. The Life and Achievement of Henry Morris 1889–1961*. London: Longman.
REGAN, D.E. (1977). *Local Government and Education*. London: Allen and Unwin.
REYNOLDS, D. (Ed) (1985). *Studying School Effectiveness*. Lewes: Falmer Press.
RHODES, G. (1981). *Inspectorates in British Government: law enforcement and standards of efficiency*. London: Allen and Unwin.
SALTER, B. and TAPPER, T. (1982). *Education, Politics and the State*. London: Grant McIntyre.
SEABORNE, M. (1971). *The English School, its Architecture and Organization, Vol. I 1370–1870*. London: Routledge.
SEABORNE, M. and LOWE, R. (1977). *The English School, its Architecture and Organization, Vol. II 1870–1970*. London: Routledge.
SHIPMAN, M. (1979). *In-School Evaluation*. London: Heinemann.
SHIPMAN, M. (1983). *Assessment in Primary and Middle Schools*. London: Croom Helm.
SHIPMAN, M. (1984). *Education as a Public Service*. London: Harper and Row.
SKILBECK, M. (1984). *Evaluating the Curriculum in the Eighties*. London: Hodder and Stoughton.
SMALL, N. (1984). 'Evaluating the Evaluators: the Role of Local Education Authority Inspectors'. In: GOULDING *et al.* (Eds) *op. cit. supra.*
SOCKETT, H. (1976). 'Teacher Accountability'. *Proceedings of the Philosophy of Education Society of Great Britain,* **X,** 34–55. Also in FINCH and SCRIMSHAW, *op. cit. supra.*
SOCKETT, H. (Ed) (1980). *Accountability in the English Educational System*. London: Hodder and Stoughton.
SOLIHULL L.E.A. (1979). *Evaluating the School: guides for primary and secondary schools in the Metropolitan Borough of Solihull*. Solihull: Education Department.
STOCKPORT L.E.A. (1983). *Guides to Self-Evaluation*. Stockport: Education Department (mimeographed).
SUFFOLK L.E.A. (1985). *Those having torches . . .* Ipswich: County Education Department.

TAYLOR REPORT. DEPARTMENT OF EDUCATION AND SCIENCE. COMMITTEE OF ENQUIRY UNDER CHAIRMANSHIP OF MR. T. TAYLOR. (1977). *A New Partnership for our Schools*. London: HMSO.

TOOGOOD, P. (1984). *The Head's Tale*. Telford: Dialogue.

WALKER, R. (1981). 'Classroom Practice: the observation of LEA Advisers, Headteachers and others.' Report to Social Science Research Council. Norwich: University of East Anglia (mimeographed).

WALSH, K. *et al.* (1984). *Falling School Rolls and the Management of the Teaching Profession*. Windsor: NFER-Nelson Publishing Company.

WILLIAMS, V. (1981). *West Midlands Metropolitan Boroughs: Survey of Duties and Responsibilities of LEA Inspectors and Advisers, 1979–80*. University of Oxford Department of Education Studies (mimeographed).

WILSON, M. (1984). *Epoch in English Education: Administrator's Challenge*. Sheffield: Sheffield City Polytechnic.

WINKLEY. D. (1982). 'LEA Inspectors and advisers: a developmental analysis', *Oxford Review of Education*, 8, 2, pp. 121–137.

WORSWICK, G.D.N. (Ed) (1984). *Education and Economic Performance*. London: Gower Press.

Index